THE TRANSFORMERS
IRONHIDE

THE TRANSFORMERS
IRONHIDE

Written by
MIKE COSTA

Art by
CASEY COLLER

Colors by
JOANA LAFUENTE

Lettering by
CHRIS MOWRY & NEIL UYETAKE

Original Edits by
**ANDY SCHMIDT, DENTON J. TIPTON,
& CARLOS GUZMAN**

Collection Edits by
JUSTIN EISINGER

Collection Design by
CHRIS MOWRY

Licensed By:

Special thanks to Hasbro's Aaron Archer, Michael Kelly, Amie Lozanski, Ed Lane, Michael Provost, Val Roca, Erin Hillman, Jos Huxley, Samantha Lomow, and Michael Verrecchia for their invaluable assistance.

www.IDWPUBLISHING.com   ISBN: 978-1-60010-806-8   13 12 11 10   1 2 3 4

IDW Publishing is: Operations: Ted Adams, CEO & Publisher • Greg Goldstein, Chief Operating Officer • Matthew Ruzicka, CPA, Chief Financial Officer • Alan Payne, VP of Sales • Lorelei Bunjes, Director of Digital Services • Jeff Webber, Director of ePublishing • AnnaMaria White, Dir. Marketing and Public Relations • Dirk Wood, Dir. Retail Marketing • Marci Hubbard, Executive Assistant • Alonzo Simon, Shipping Manager • Angela Loggins, Staff Accountant • Cherrie Go, Assistant Web Designer • Editorial: Chris Ryall, Chief Creative Officer, Editor-In-Chief • Scott Dunbier, Senior Editor, Special Projects • Andy Schmidt, Senior Editor • Bob Schreck, Senior Editor • Justin Eisinger, Senior Editor, Books • Kris Oprisko, Editor/Foreign Lic. • Denton J. Tipton, Editor • Tom Waltz, Editor • Mariah Huehner, Editor • Carlos Guzman, Assistant Editor • Bobby Curnow, Assistant Editor • Design: Robbie Robbins, EVP/Sr. Graphic Artist • Neil Uyetake, Senior Art Director • Chris Mowry, Senior Graphic Artist • Amauri Osorio, Graphic Artist • Gilberto Lazcano, Production Assistant • Shawn Lee, Graphic Artist

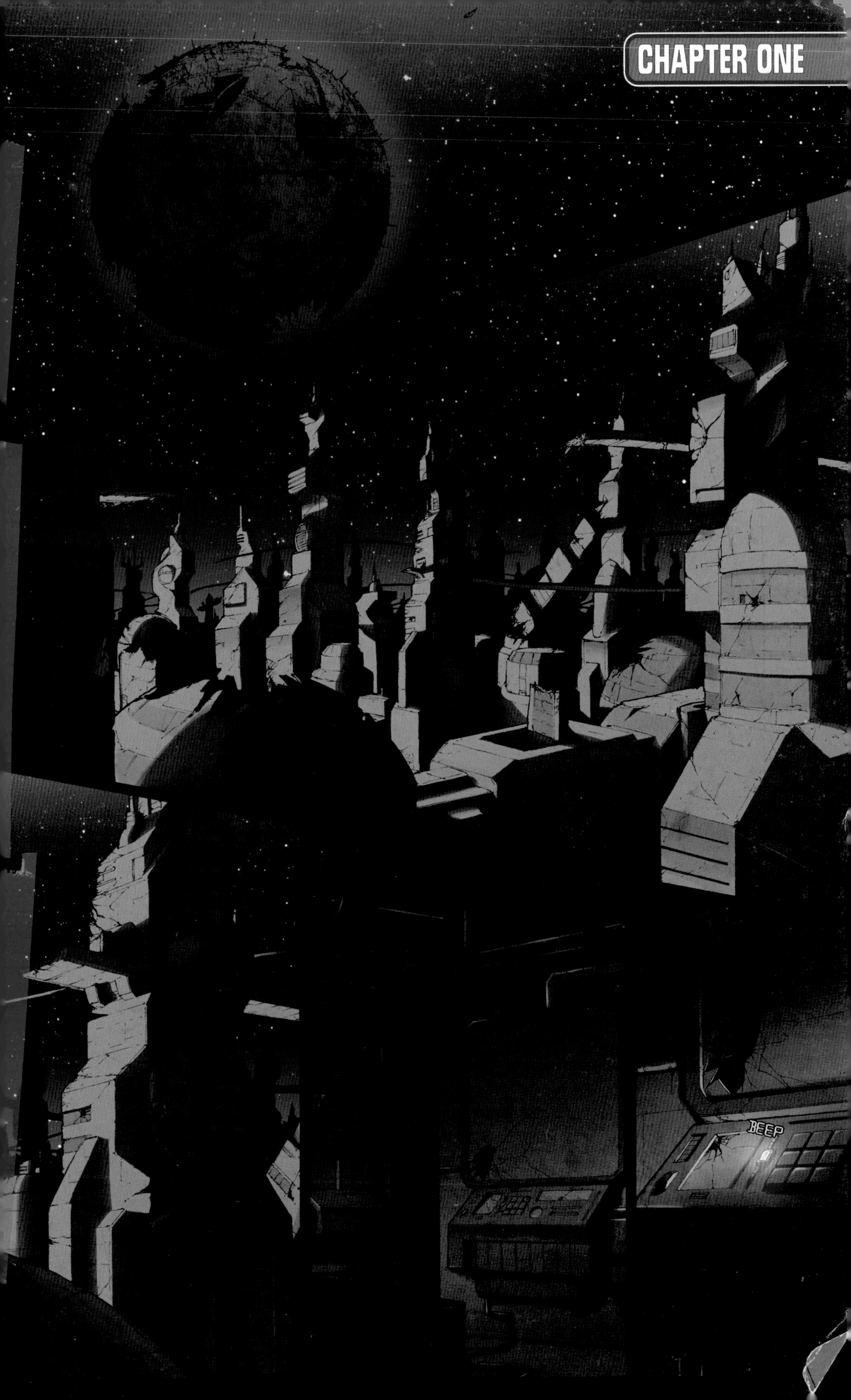
CHAPTER ONE
BEEP

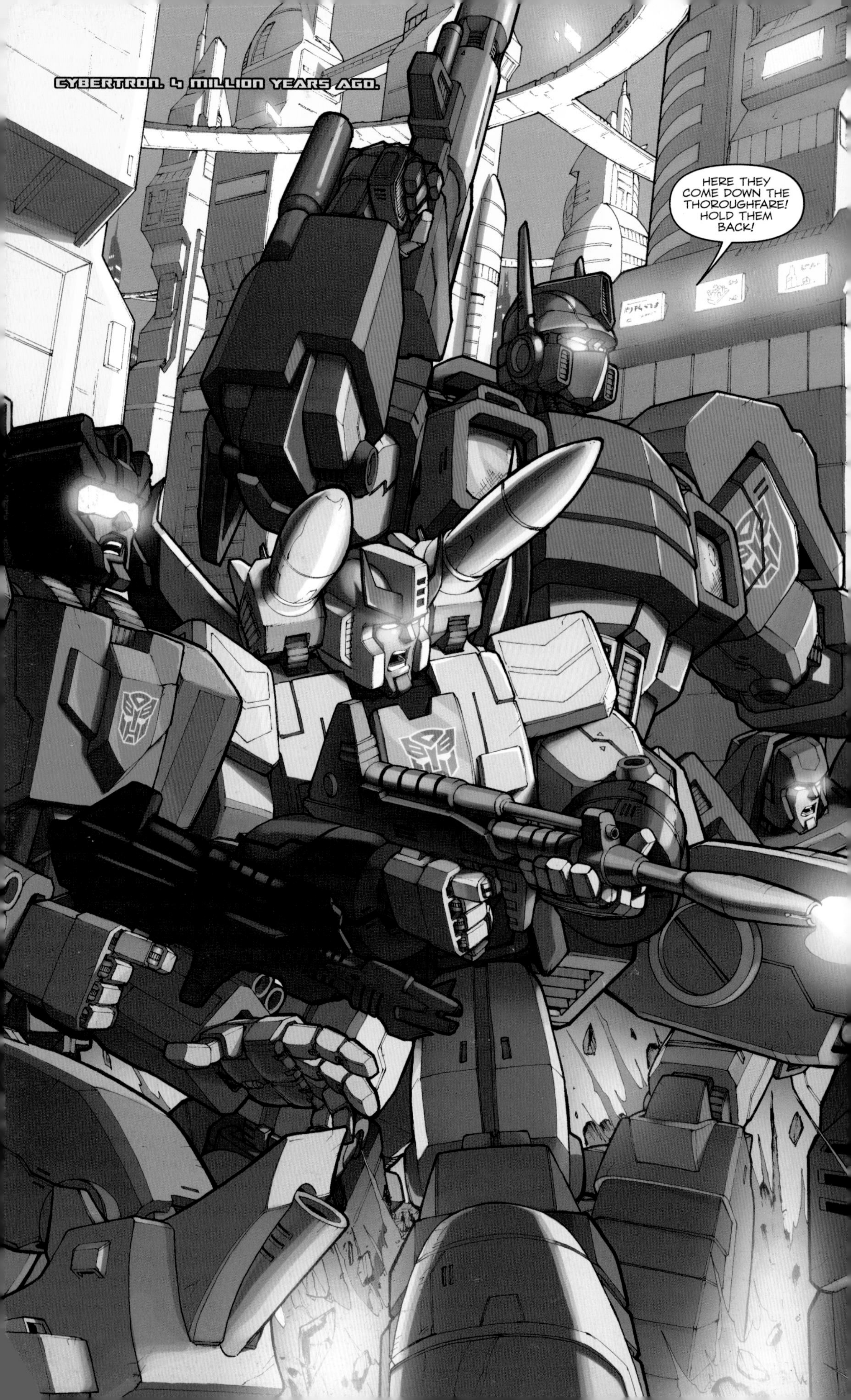
CYBERTRON. 4 MILLION YEARS AGO.
HERE THEY COME DOWN THE THOROUGHFARE! HOLD THEM BACK!

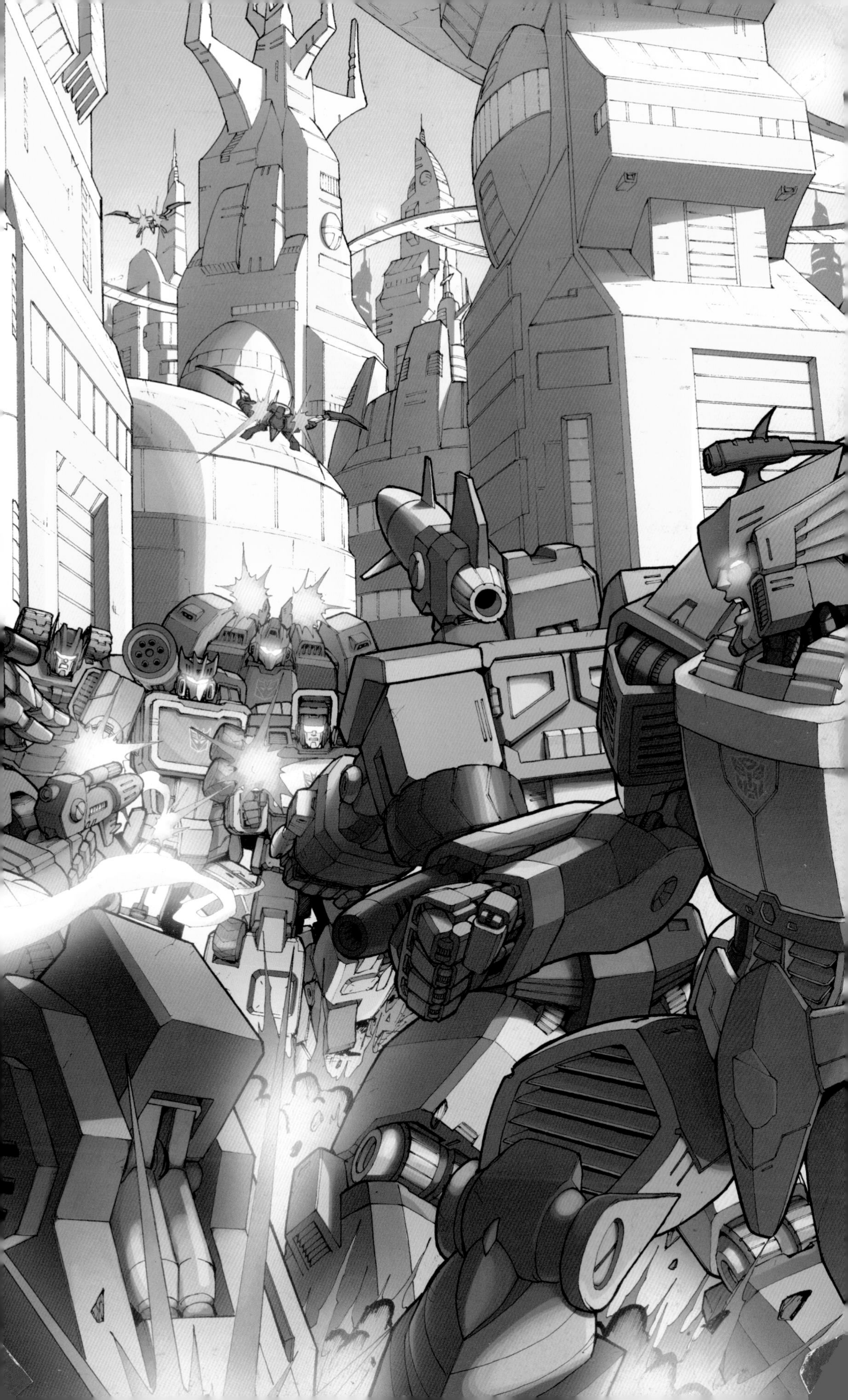

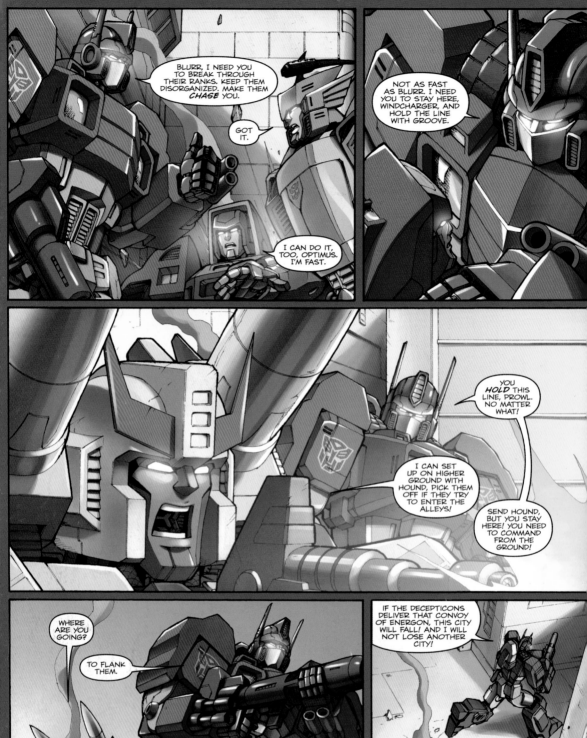

BLURR, I NEED YOU TO BREAK THROUGH THEIR RANKS. KEEP THEM DISORGANIZED. MAKE THEM *CHASE* YOU.

GOT IT.

I CAN DO IT, TOO, OPTIMUS. I'M FAST.

NOT AS FAST AS BLURR. I NEED YOU TO STAY HERE, WINDCHARGER, AND HOLD THE LINE WITH GROOVE.

YOU *HOLD* THIS LINE, PROWL. NO MATTER WHAT!

I CAN SET UP ON HIGHER GROUND WITH HOUND, PICK THEM OFF IF THEY TRY TO ENTER THE ALLEYS!

SEND HOUND, BUT YOU STAY HERE! YOU NEED TO COMMAND FROM THE GROUND!

WHERE ARE YOU GOING?

TO FLANK THEM.

ALONE? THAT'S SUICIDE!

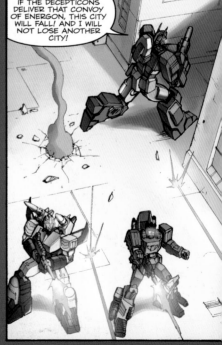

IF THE DECEPTICONS DELIVER THAT CONVOY OF ENERGON, THIS CITY WILL FALL! AND I WILL NOT LOSE ANOTHER CITY!

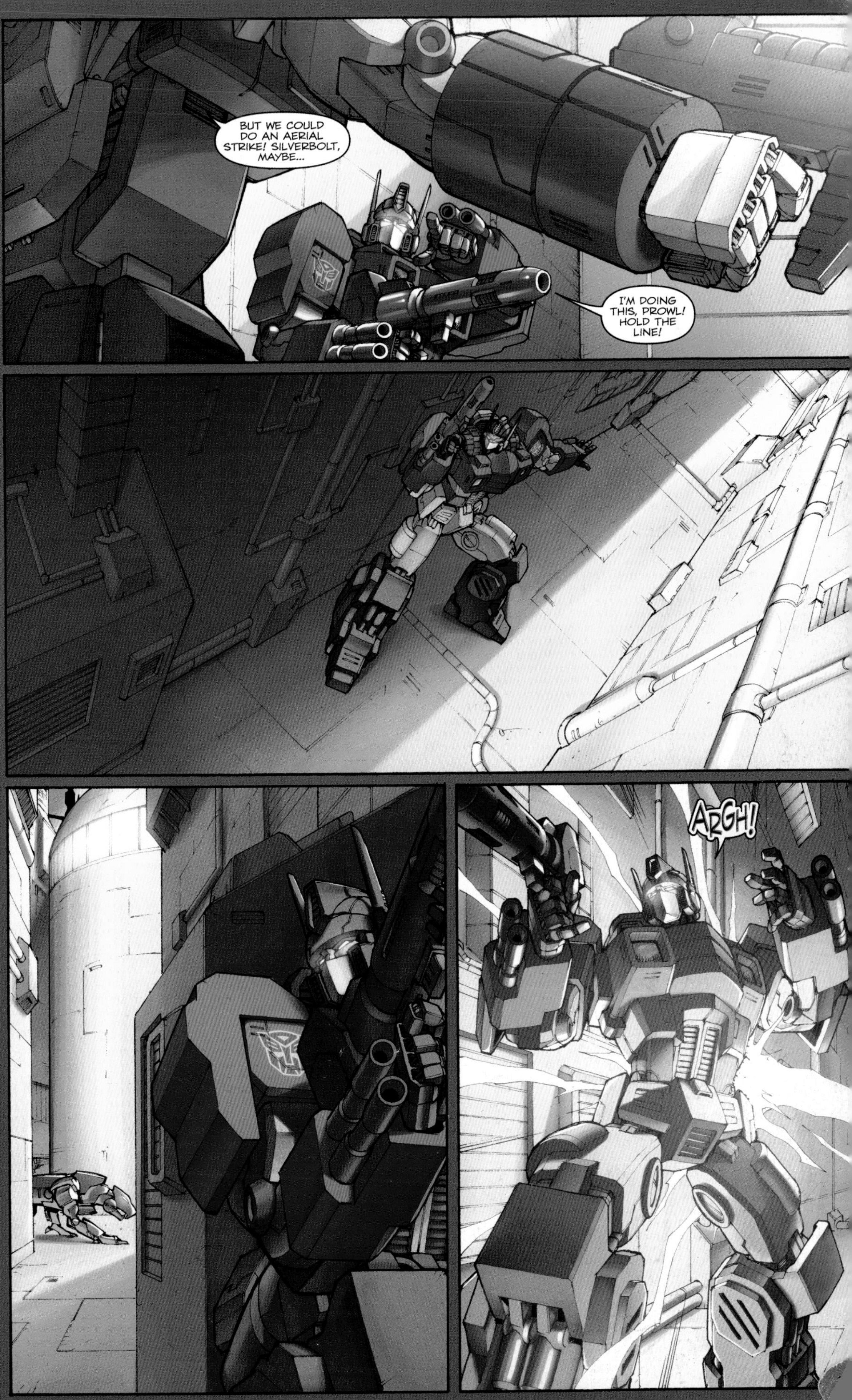
BUT WE COULD DO AN AERIAL STRIKE! SILVERBOLT, MAYBE...
I'M DOING THIS, PROWL! HOLD THE LINE!
ARGH!

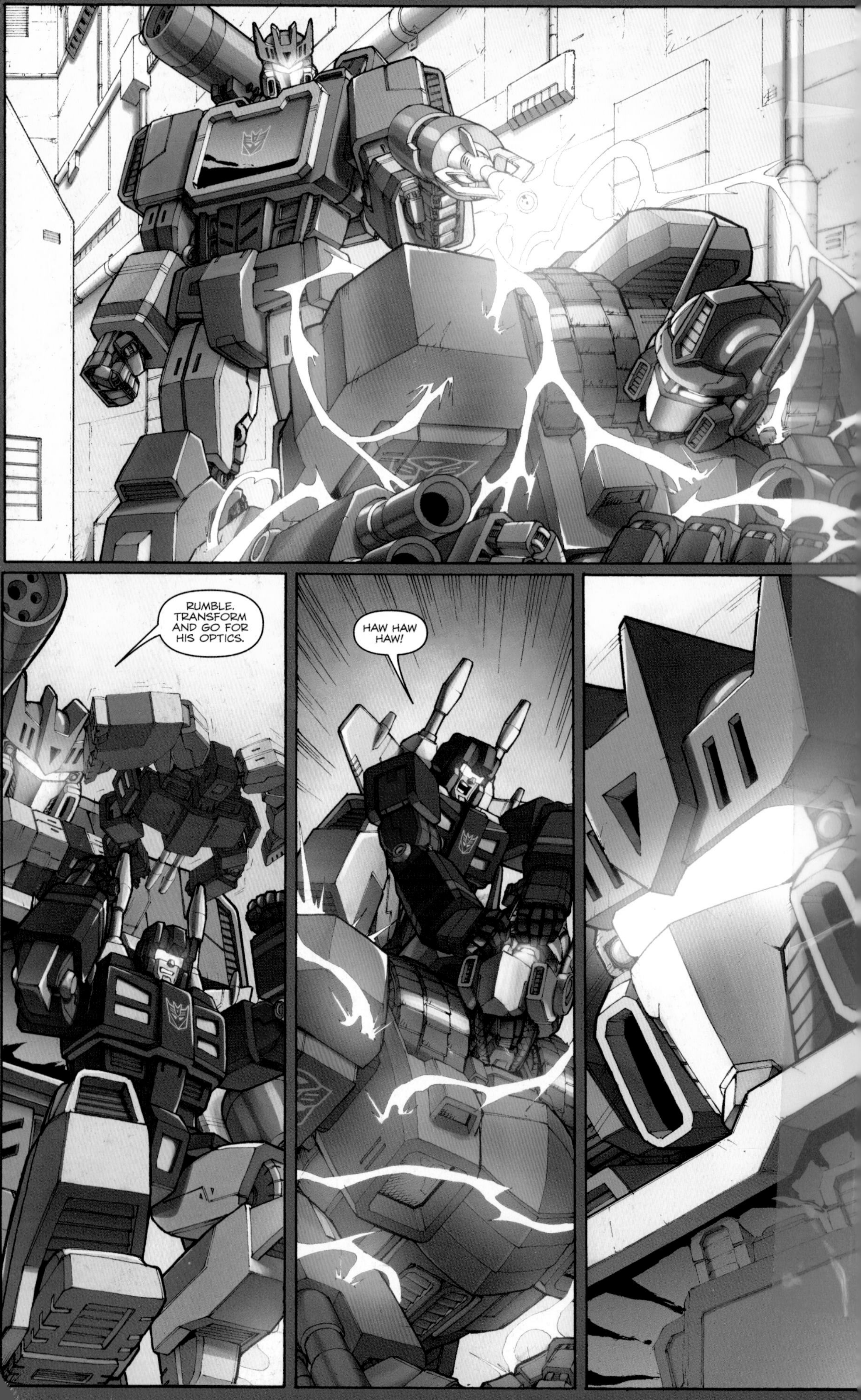
RUMBLE. TRANSFORM AND GO FOR HIS OPTICS.
HAW HAW HAW!

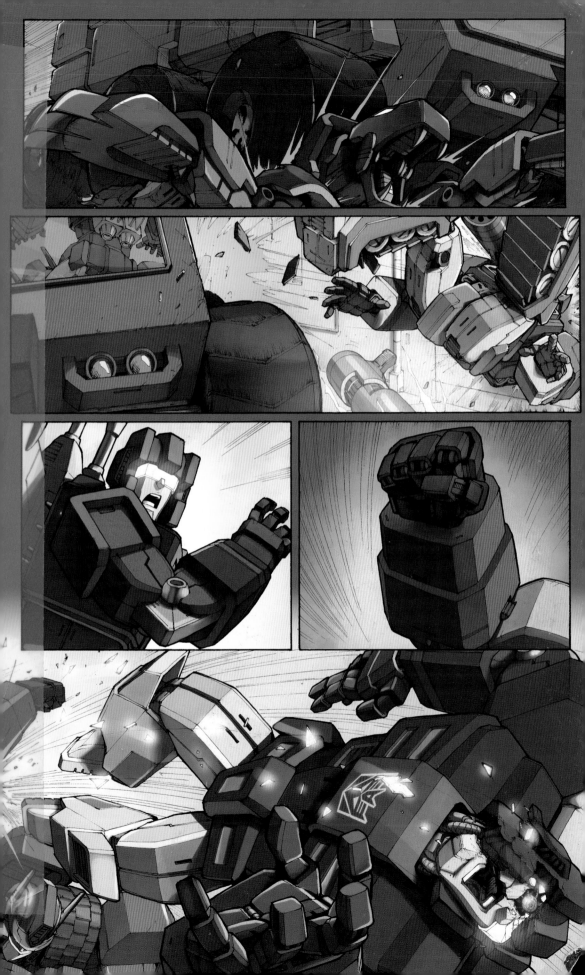

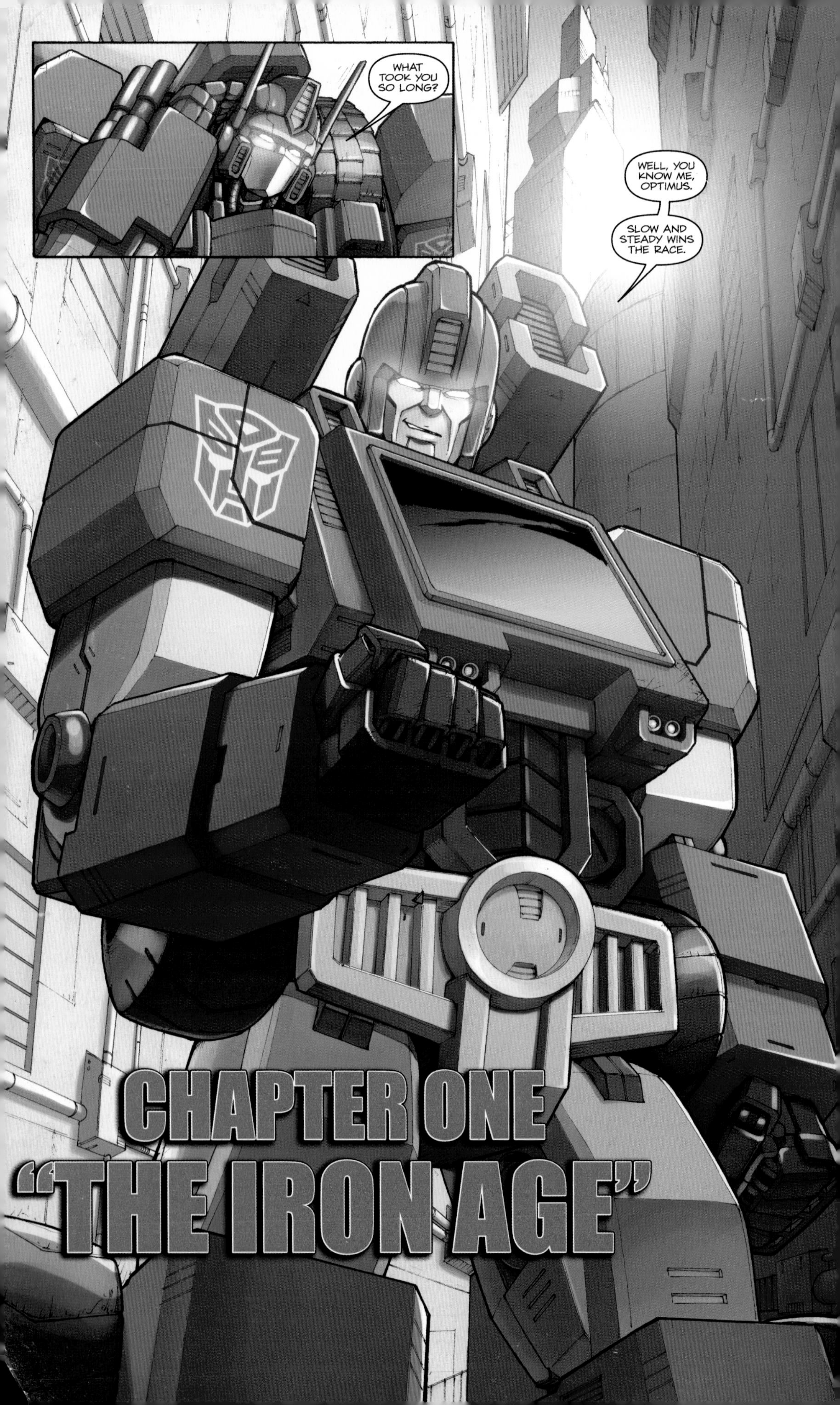
WHAT TOOK YOU SO LONG?
WELL, YOU KNOW ME, OPTIMUS.
SLOW AND STEADY WINS THE RACE.
CHAPTER ONE
"THE IRON AGE"

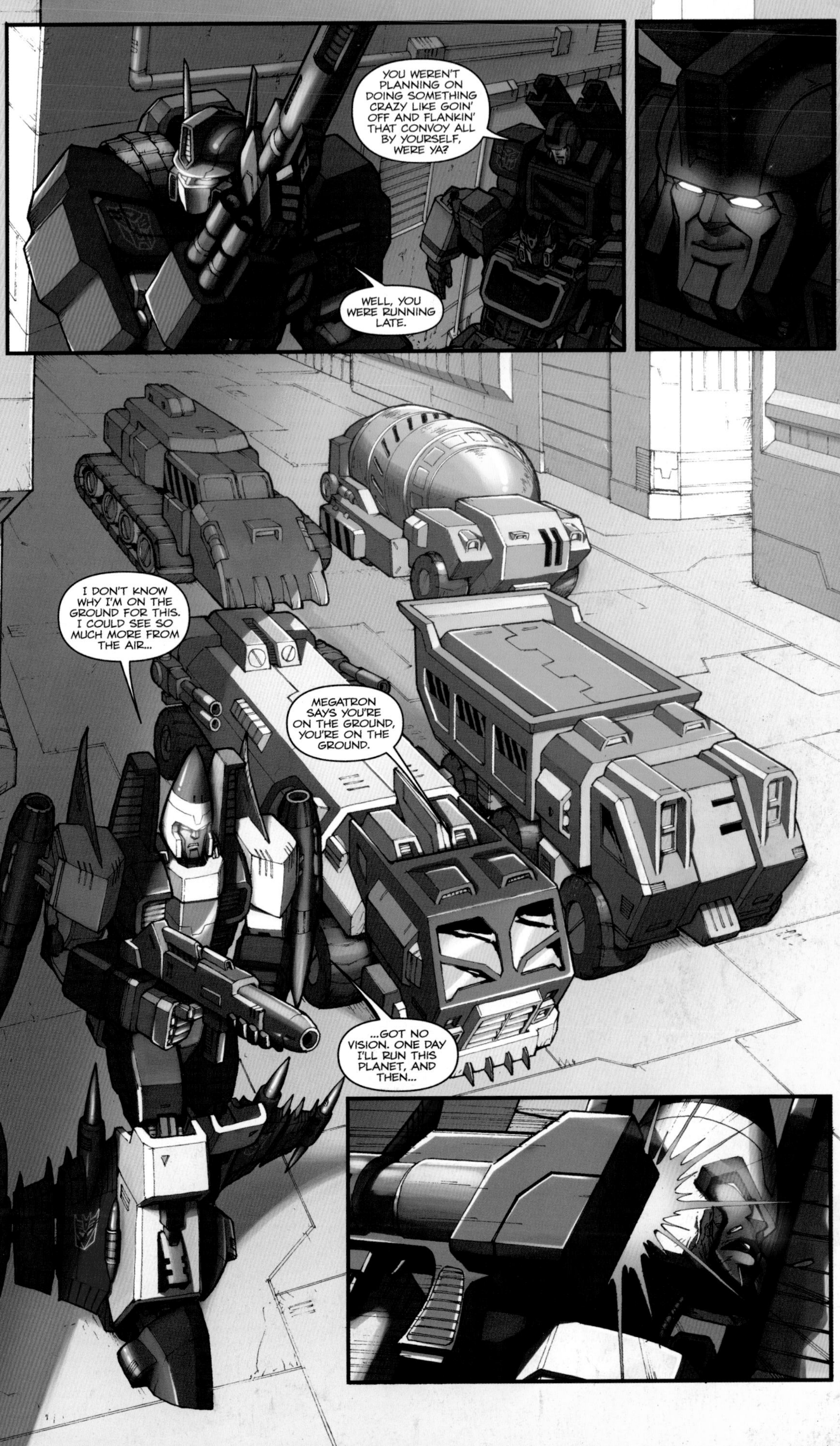
YOU WEREN'T PLANNING ON DOING SOMETHING CRAZY LIKE GOIN' OFF AND FLANKIN' THAT CONVOY ALL BY YOURSELF, WERE YA?
WELL, YOU WERE RUNNING LATE.
I DON'T KNOW WHY I'M ON THE GROUND FOR THIS. I COULD SEE SO MUCH MORE FROM THE AIR...
MEGATRON SAYS YOU'RE ON THE GROUND, YOU'RE ON THE GROUND.
...GOT NO VISION. ONE DAY I'LL RUN THIS PLANET, AND THEN...

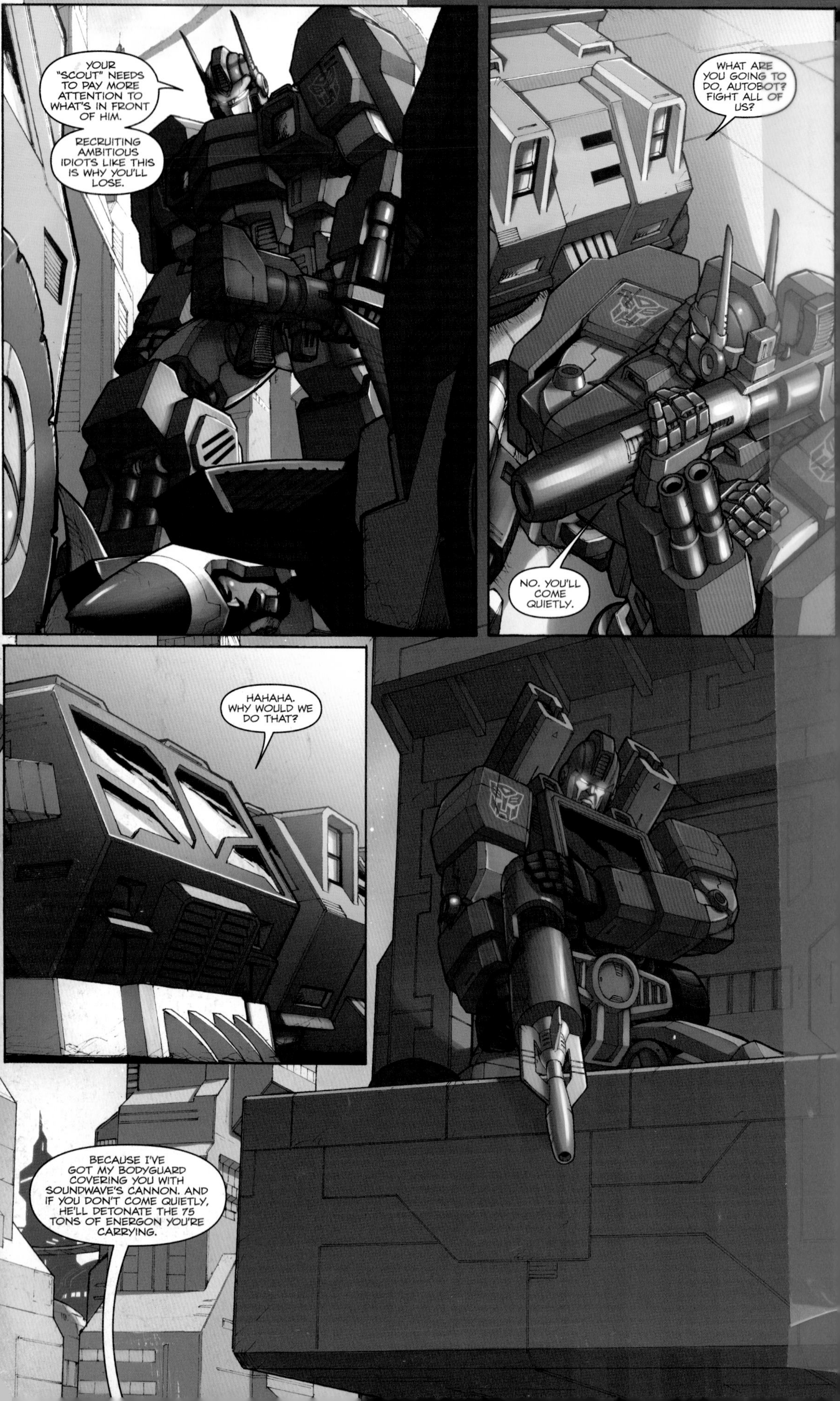

YOUR "SCOUT" NEEDS TO PAY MORE ATTENTION TO WHAT'S IN FRONT OF HIM.
RECRUITING AMBITIOUS IDIOTS LIKE THIS IS WHY YOU'LL LOSE.
WHAT ARE YOU GOING TO DO, AUTOBOT? FIGHT ALL OF US?
NO. YOU'LL COME QUIETLY.
HAHAHA. WHY WOULD WE DO THAT?
BECAUSE I'VE GOT MY BODYGUARD COVERING YOU WITH SOUNDWAVE'S CANNON. AND IF YOU DON'T COME QUIETLY, HE'LL DETONATE THE 75 TONS OF ENERGON YOU'RE CARRYING.

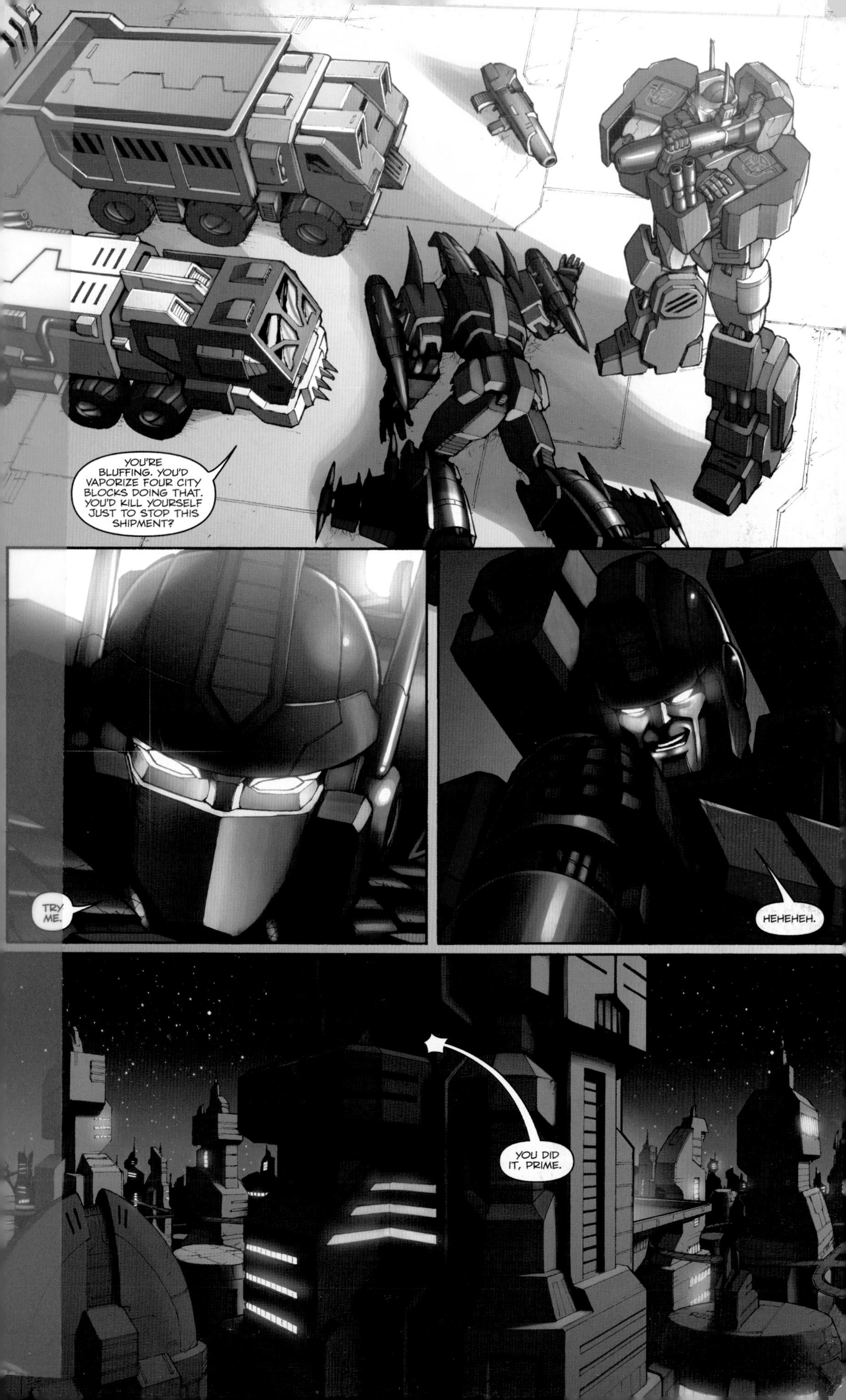
YOU'RE BLUFFING. YOU'D VAPORIZE FOUR CITY BLOCKS DOING THAT. YOU'D KILL YOURSELF JUST TO STOP THIS SHIPMENT?
TRY ME.
HEHEHEH.
YOU DID IT, PRIME.

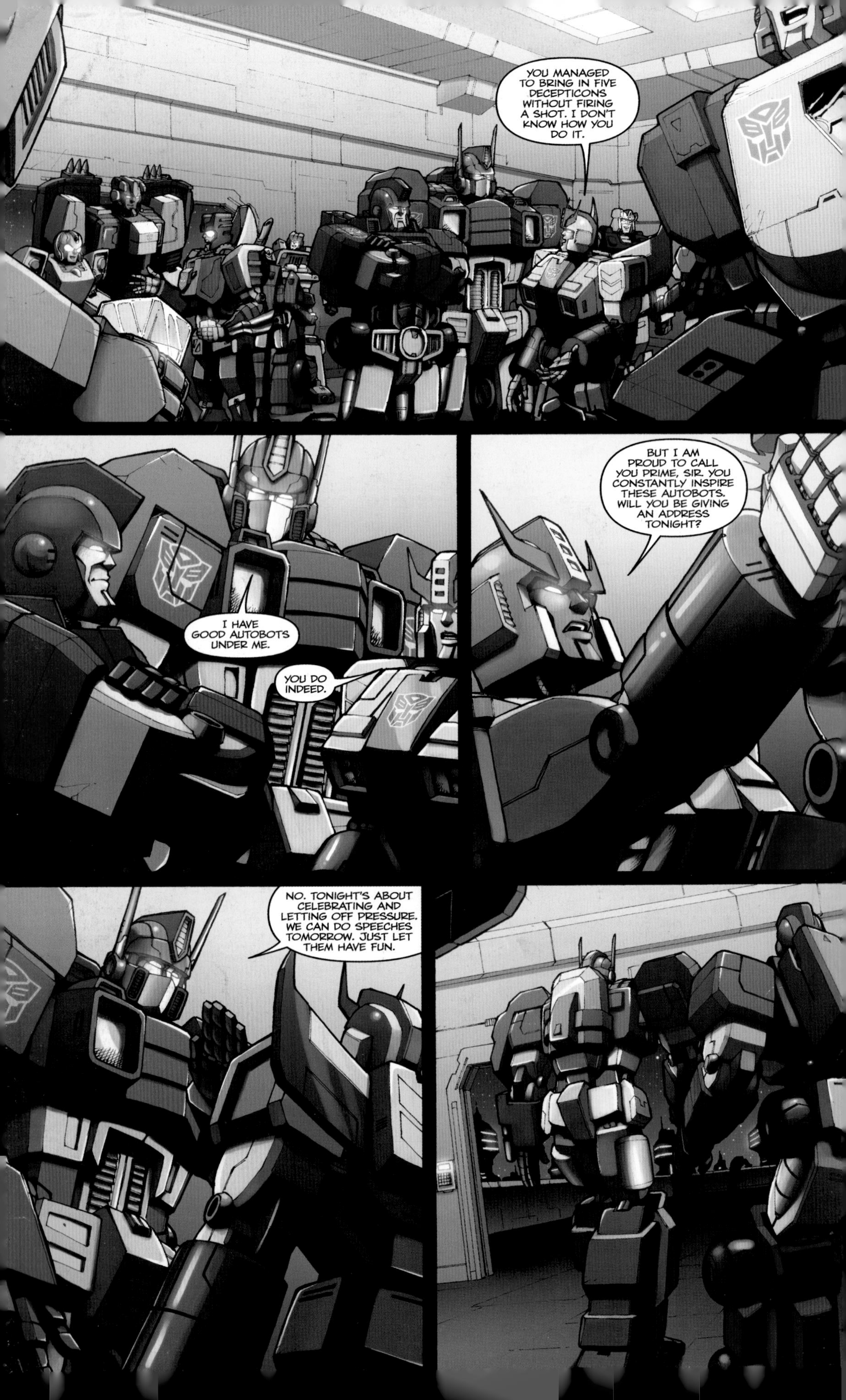
YOU MANAGED TO BRING IN FIVE DECEPTICONS WITHOUT FIRING A SHOT. I DON'T KNOW HOW YOU DO IT.
I HAVE GOOD AUTOBOTS UNDER ME.
YOU DO INDEED.
BUT I AM PROUD TO CALL YOU PRIME, SIR. YOU CONSTANTLY INSPIRE THESE AUTOBOTS. WILL YOU BE GIVING AN ADDRESS TONIGHT?
NO. TONIGHT'S ABOUT CELEBRATING AND LETTING OFF PRESSURE. WE CAN DO SPEECHES TOMORROW. JUST LET THEM HAVE FUN.

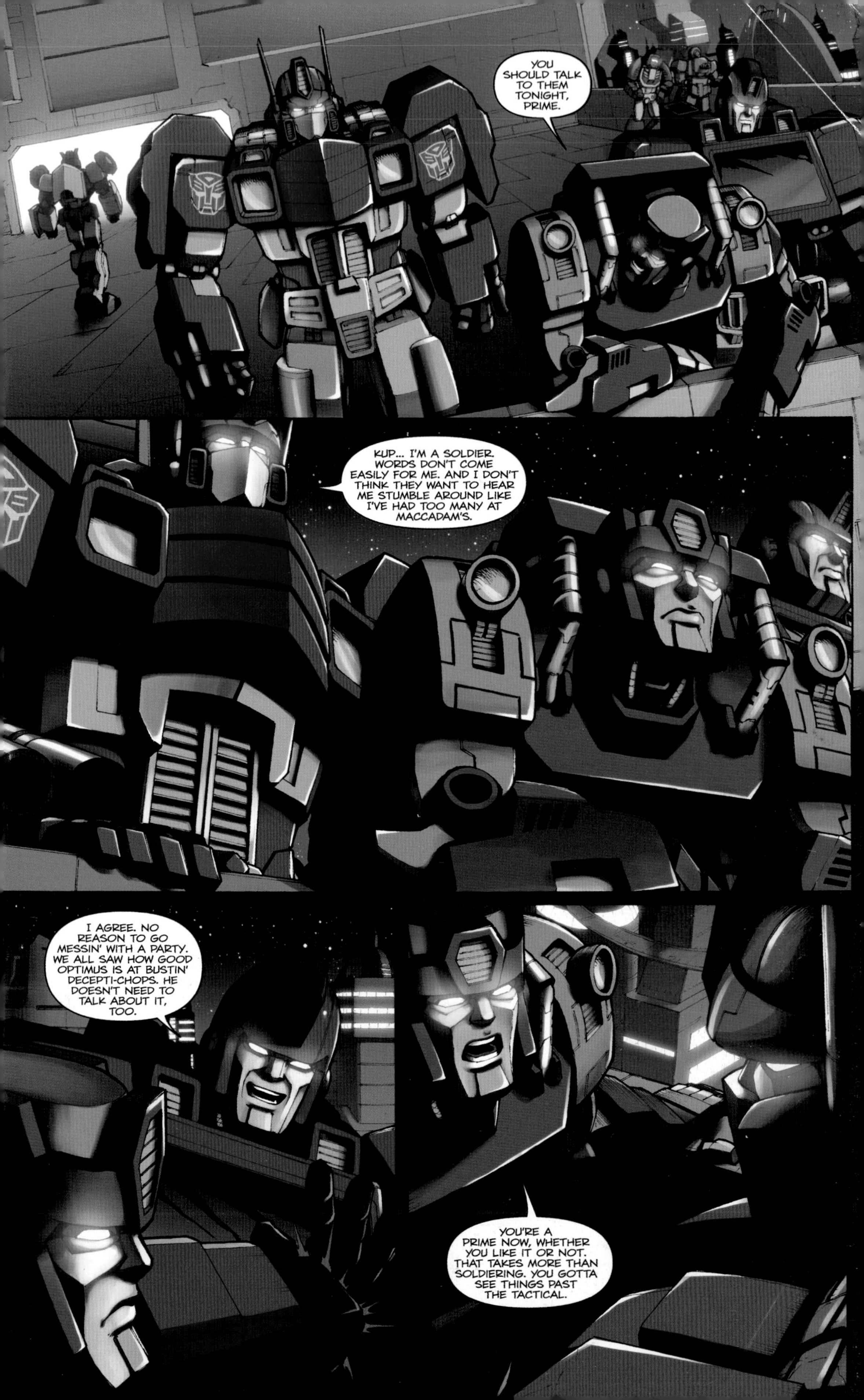
YOU SHOULD TALK TO THEM TONIGHT, PRIME.
KUP... I'M A SOLDIER. WORDS DON'T COME EASILY FOR ME. AND I DON'T THINK THEY WANT TO HEAR ME STUMBLE AROUND LIKE I'VE HAD TOO MANY AT MACCADAM'S.
I AGREE. NO REASON TO GO MESSIN' WITH A PARTY. WE ALL SAW HOW GOOD OPTIMUS IS AT BUSTIN' DECEPTI-CHOPS. HE DOESN'T NEED TO TALK ABOUT IT, TOO.
YOU'RE A PRIME NOW, WHETHER YOU LIKE IT OR NOT. THAT TAKES MORE THAN SOLDIERING. YOU GOTTA SEE THINGS PAST THE TACTICAL.

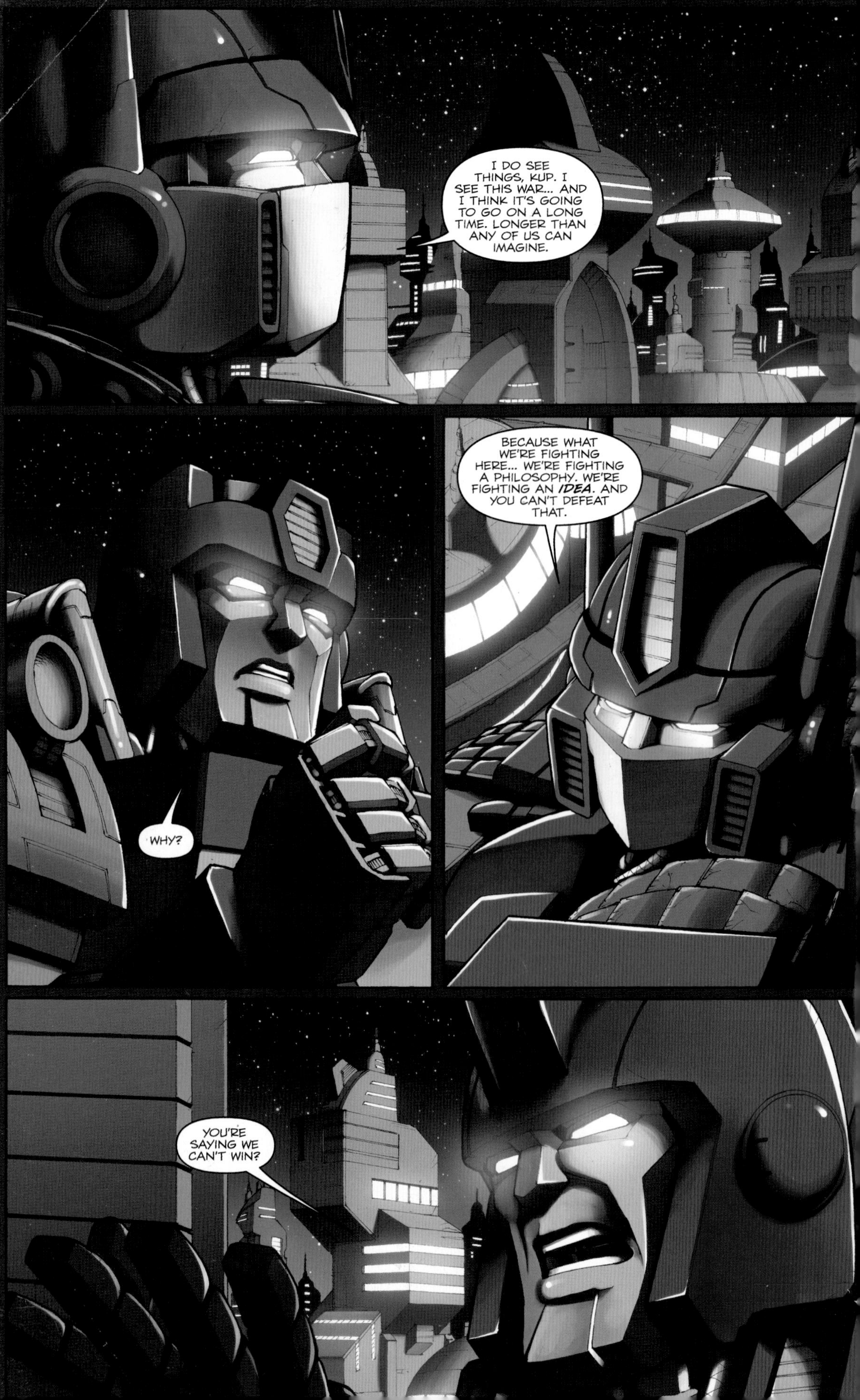
I DO SEE THINGS, KUP. I SEE THIS WAR... AND I THINK IT'S GOING TO GO ON A LONG TIME. LONGER THAN ANY OF US CAN IMAGINE.
WHY?
BECAUSE WHAT WE'RE FIGHTING HERE... WE'RE FIGHTING A PHILOSOPHY. WE'RE FIGHTING AN *IDEA*. AND YOU CAN'T DEFEAT THAT.
YOU'RE SAYING WE CAN'T WIN?

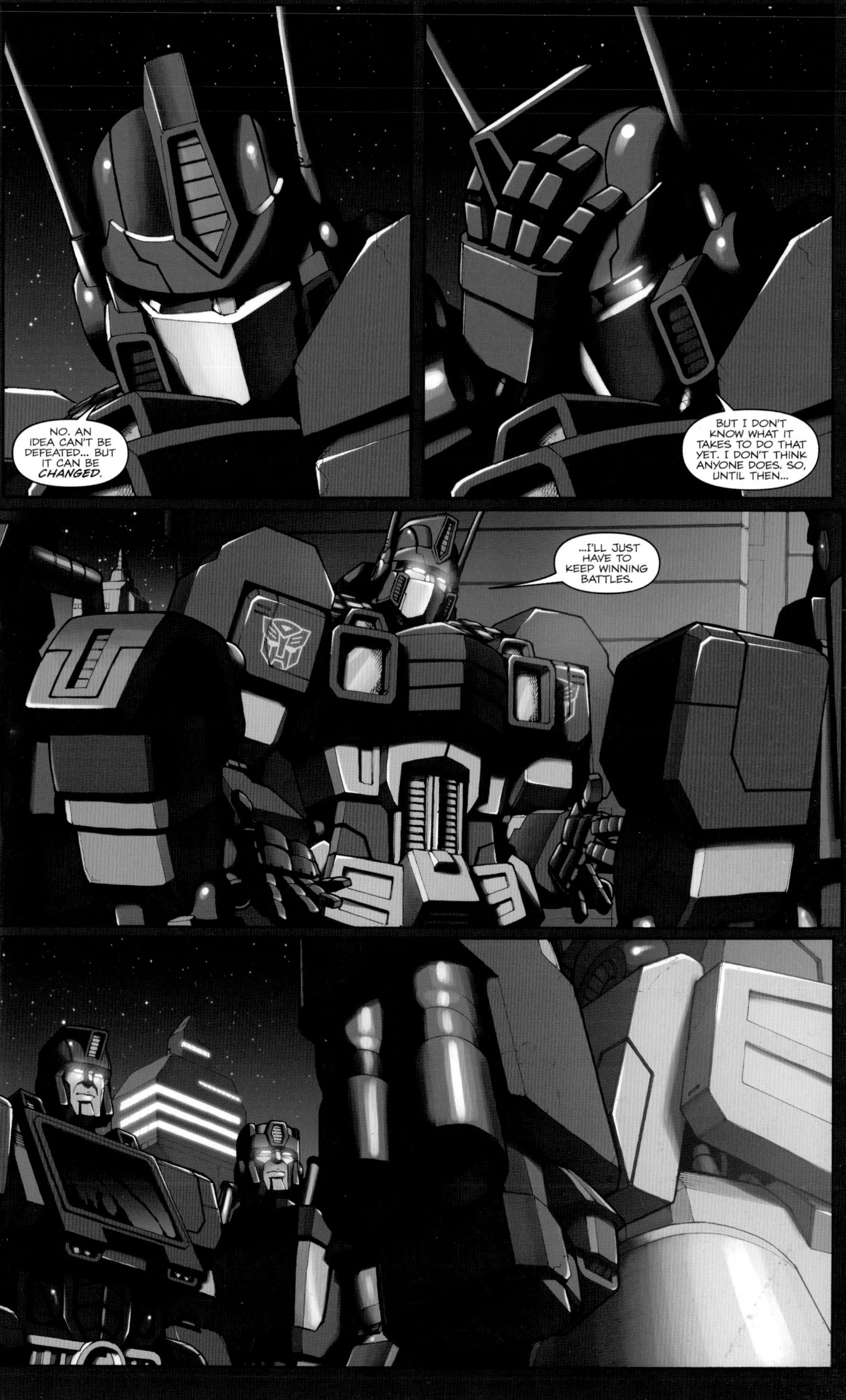
NO. AN IDEA CAN'T BE DEFEATED... BUT IT CAN BE *CHANGED*.
BUT I DON'T KNOW WHAT IT TAKES TO DO THAT YET. I DON'T THINK ANYONE DOES. SO, UNTIL THEN...
...I'LL JUST HAVE TO KEEP WINNING BATTLES.

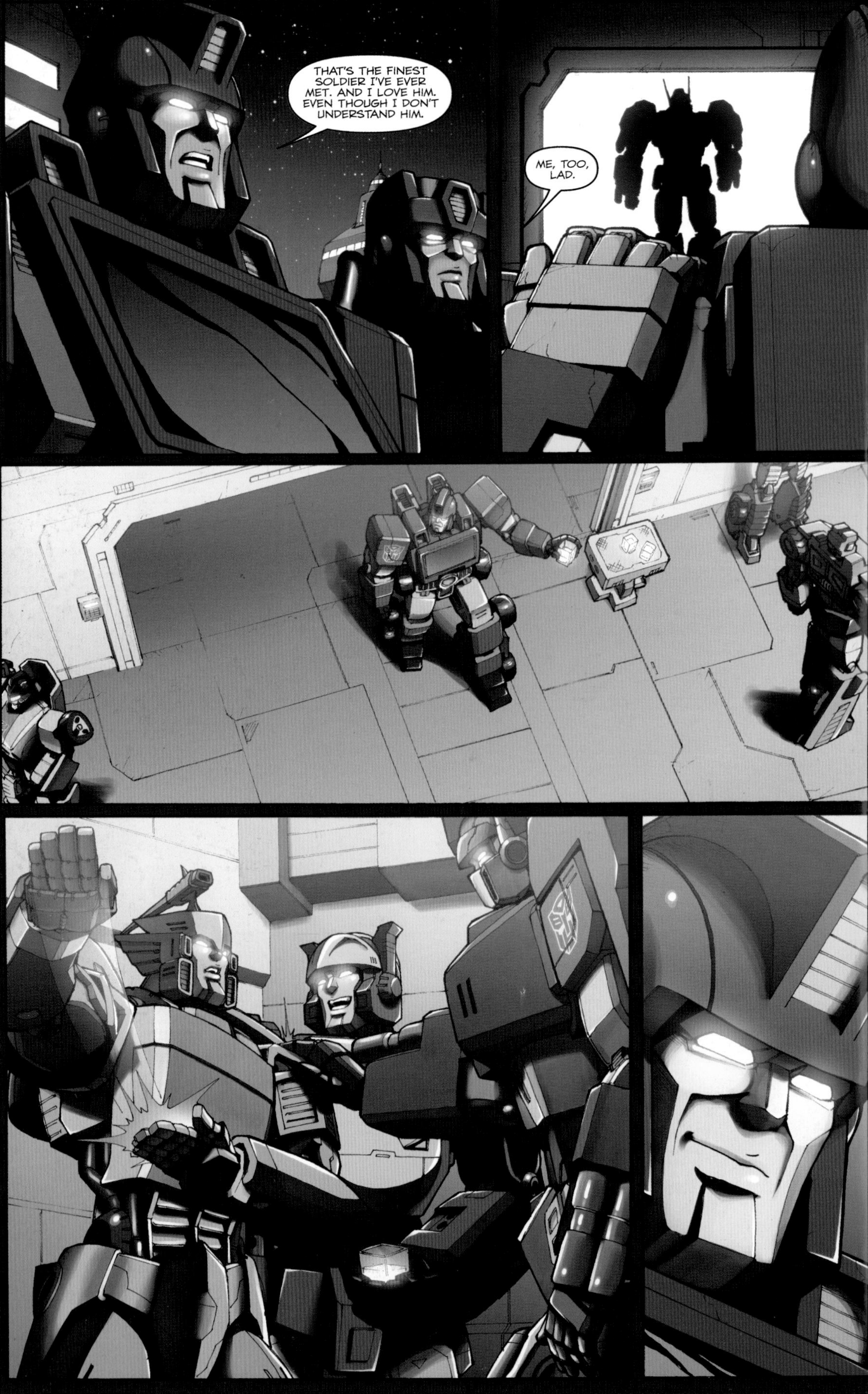
THAT'S THE FINEST SOLDIER I'VE EVER MET. AND I LOVE HIM. EVEN THOUGH I DON'T UNDERSTAND HIM.
ME, TOO, LAD.

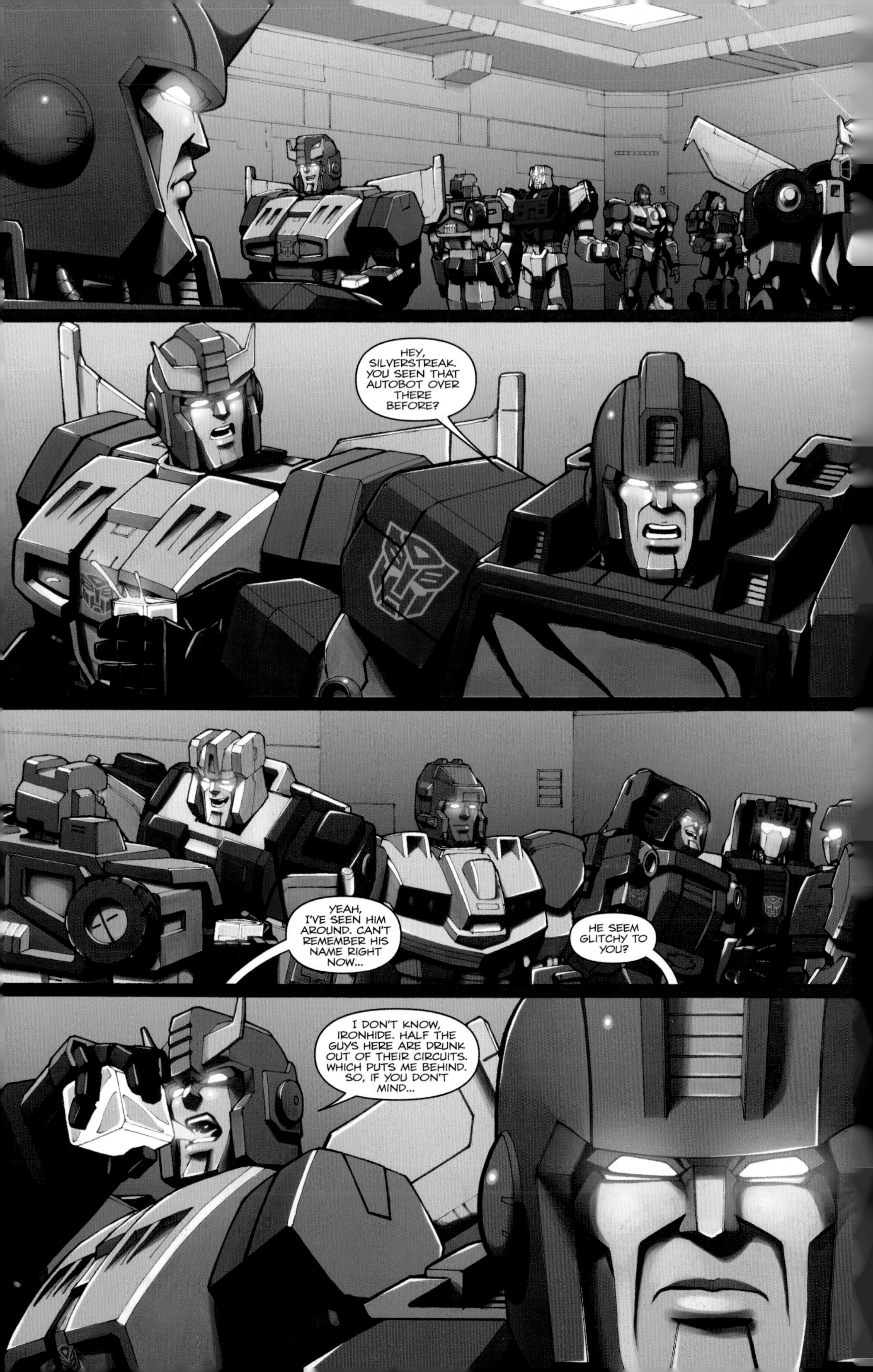
HEY, SILVERSTREAK. YOU SEEN THAT AUTOBOT OVER THERE BEFORE?
YEAH, I'VE SEEN HIM AROUND. CAN'T REMEMBER HIS NAME RIGHT NOW...
HE SEEM GLITCHY TO YOU?
I DON'T KNOW, IRONHIDE. HALF THE GUYS HERE ARE DRUNK OUT OF THEIR CIRCUITS. WHICH PUTS ME BEHIND. SO, IF YOU DON'T MIND...

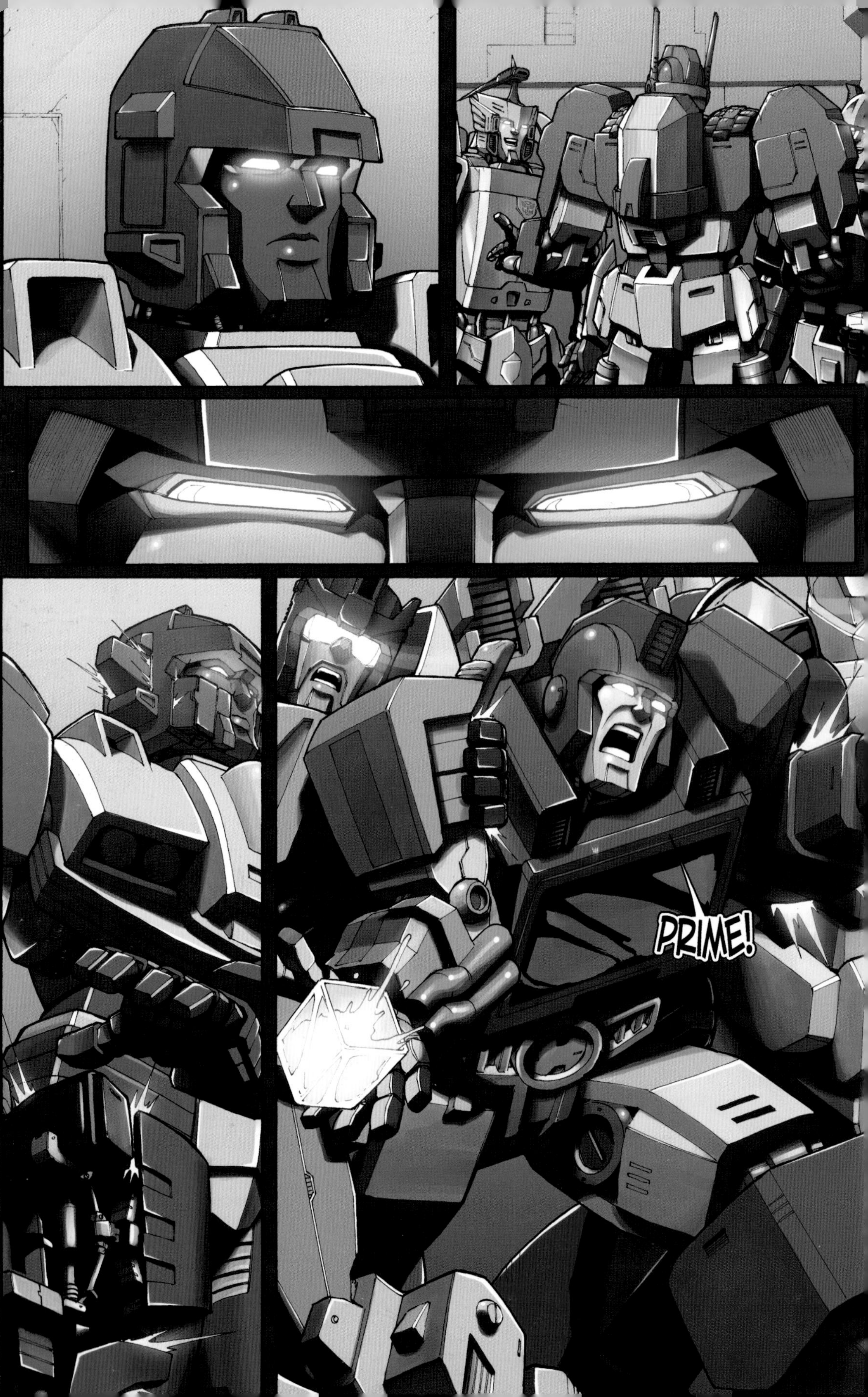

PRIME!

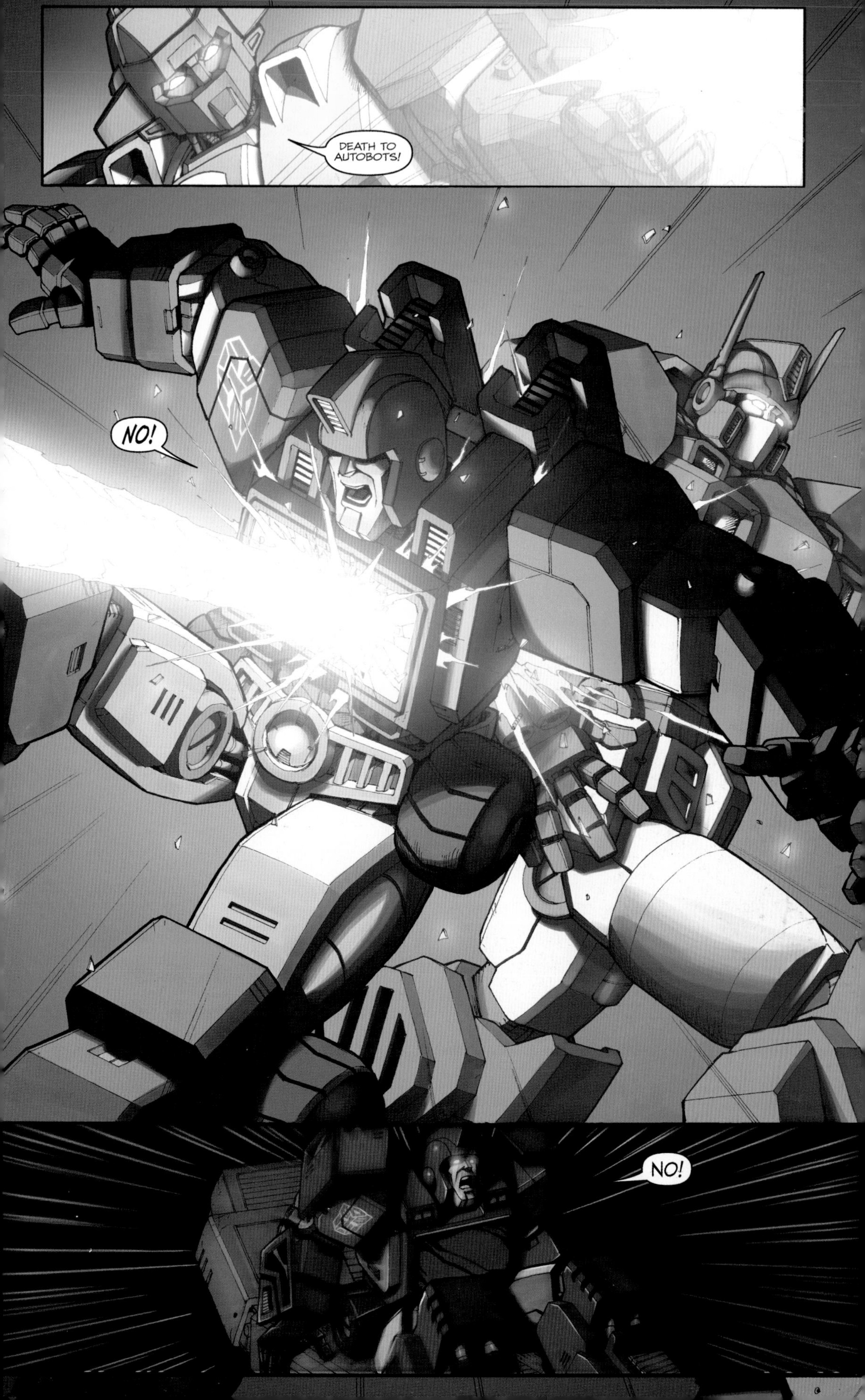
DEATH TO AUTOBOTS!
NO!
NO!

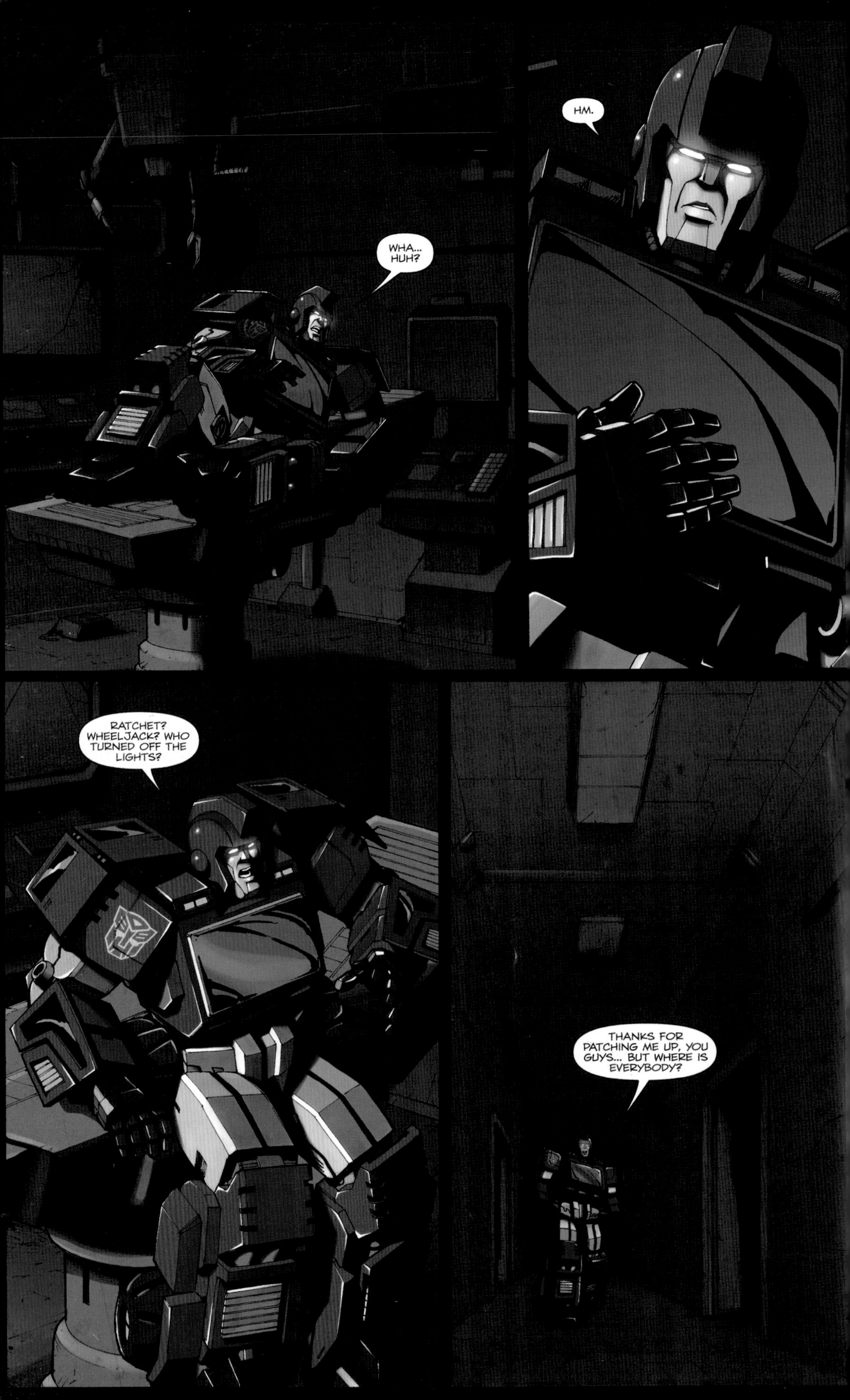
WHA... HUH?
HM.
RATCHET? WHEELJACK? WHO TURNED OFF THE LIGHTS?
THANKS FOR PATCHING ME UP, YOU GUYS... BUT WHERE IS EVERYBODY?

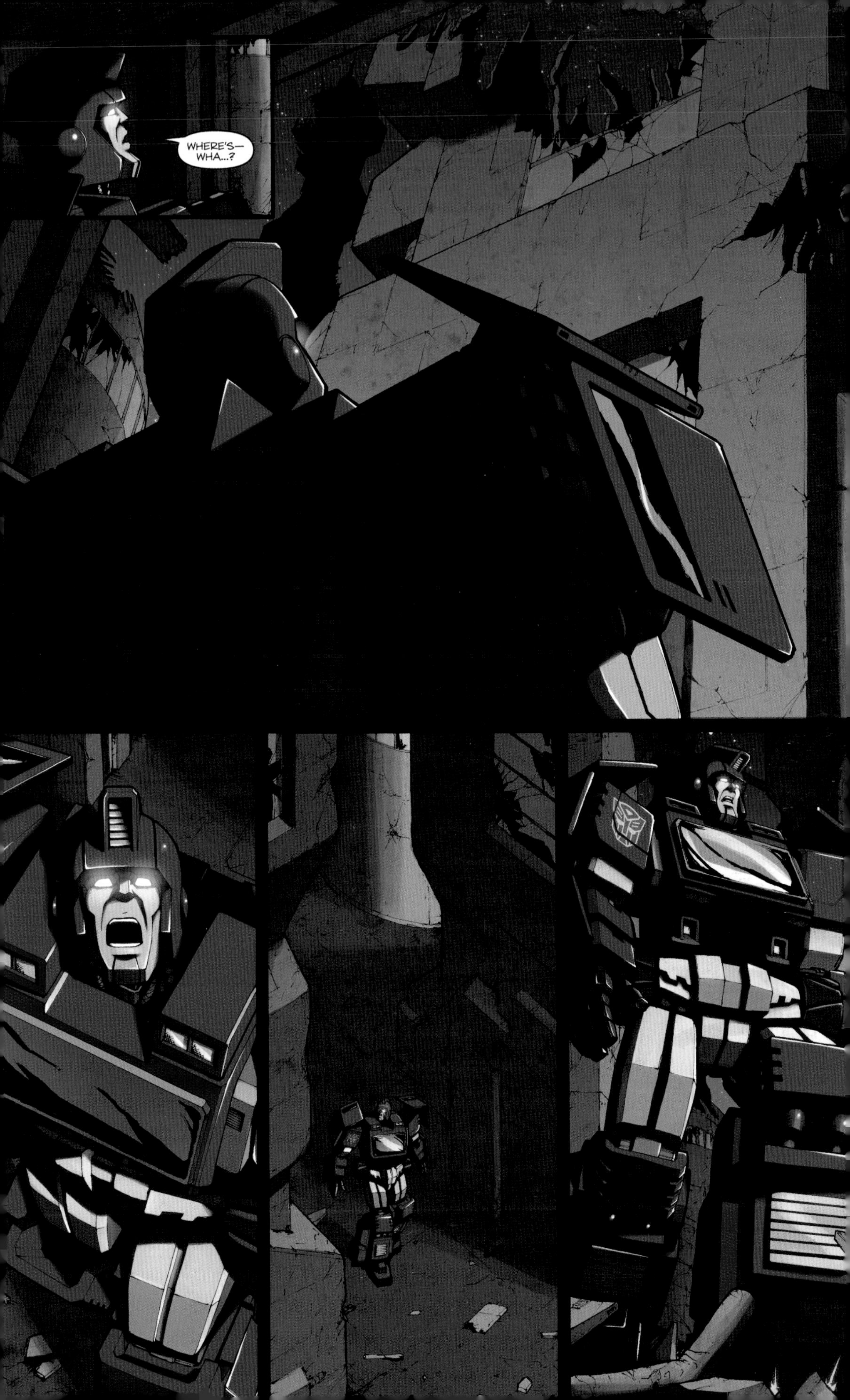
WHERE'S—
WHA...?

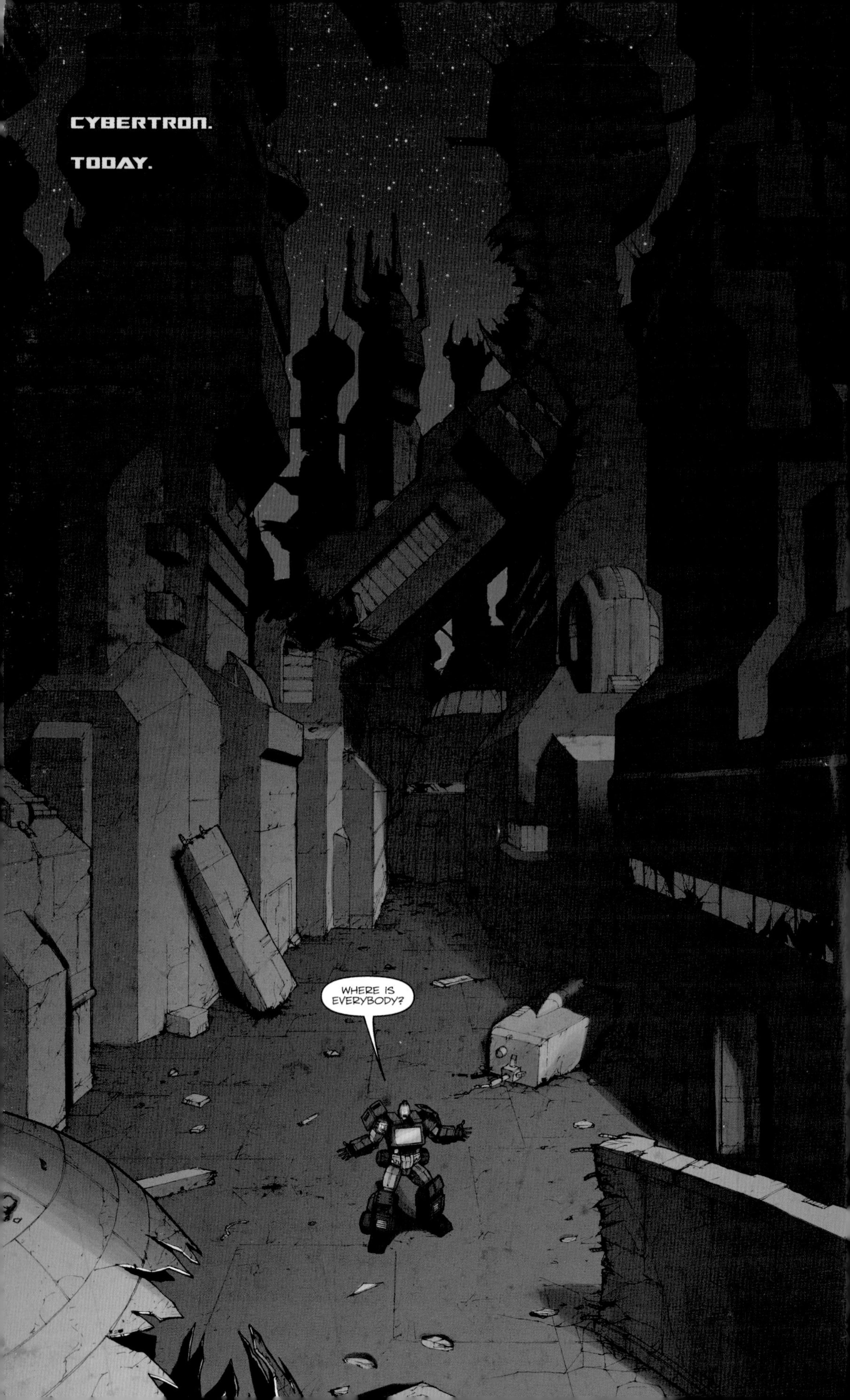
CYBERTRON.
TODAY.
WHERE IS EVERYBODY?

CYBERTRON!

GLITTERING LIKE AN AMETHYST IN THE EMPTY, UNFORGIVING VOID! THERE ARE NO PROMISES IN THE VACUUM OF SPACE, SAVE ONE...

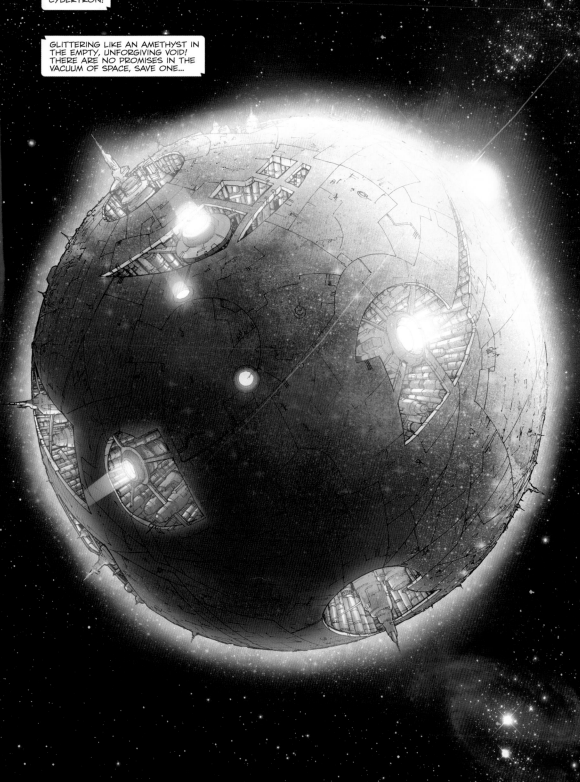

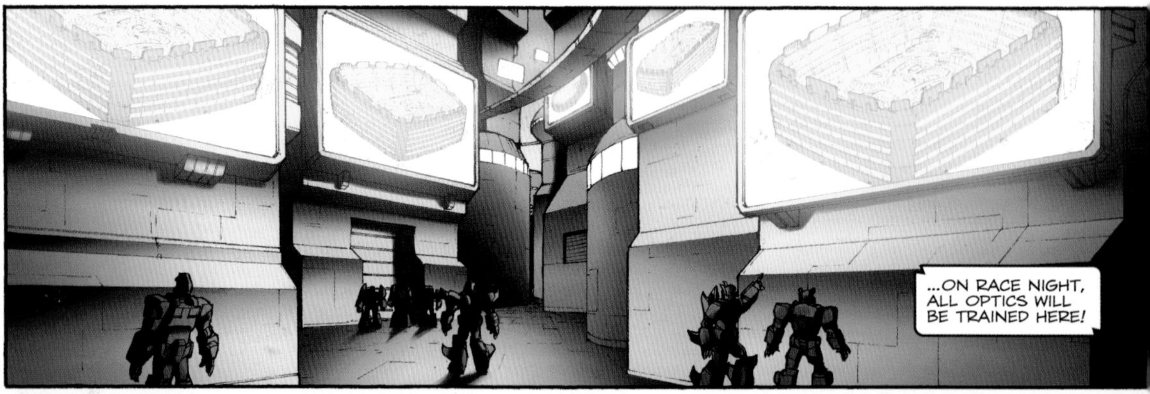
...ON RACE NIGHT, ALL OPTICS WILL BE TRAINED HERE!

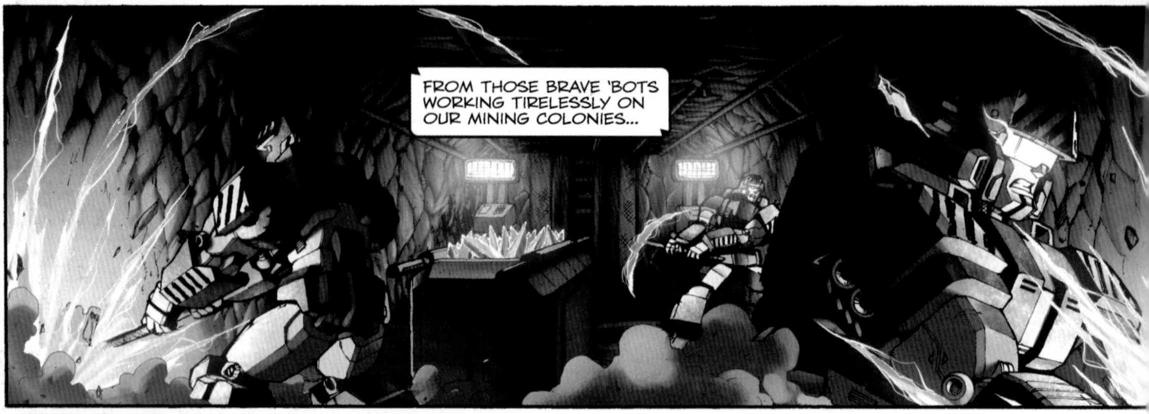
FROM THOSE BRAVE 'BOTS WORKING TIRELESSLY ON OUR MINING COLONIES...

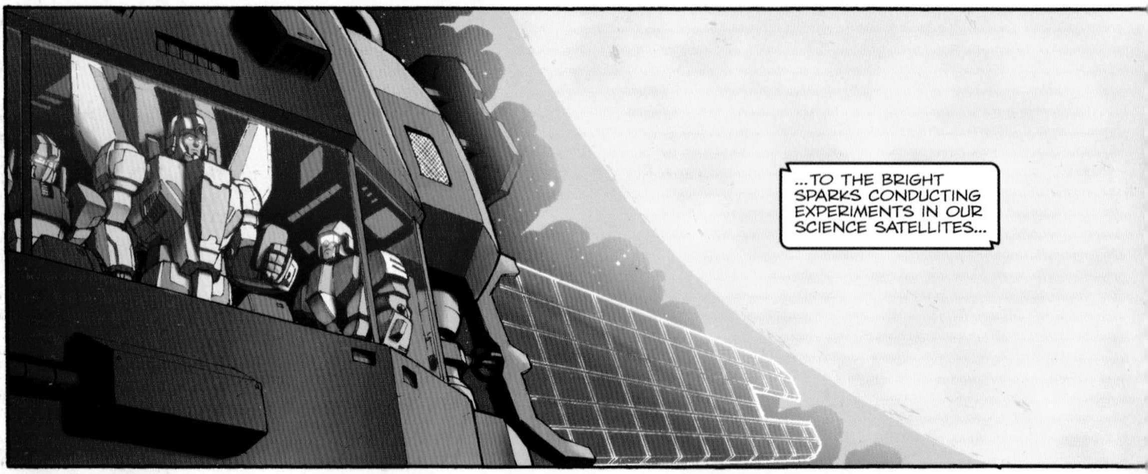
...TO THE BRIGHT SPARKS CONDUCTING EXPERIMENTS IN OUR SCIENCE SATELLITES...

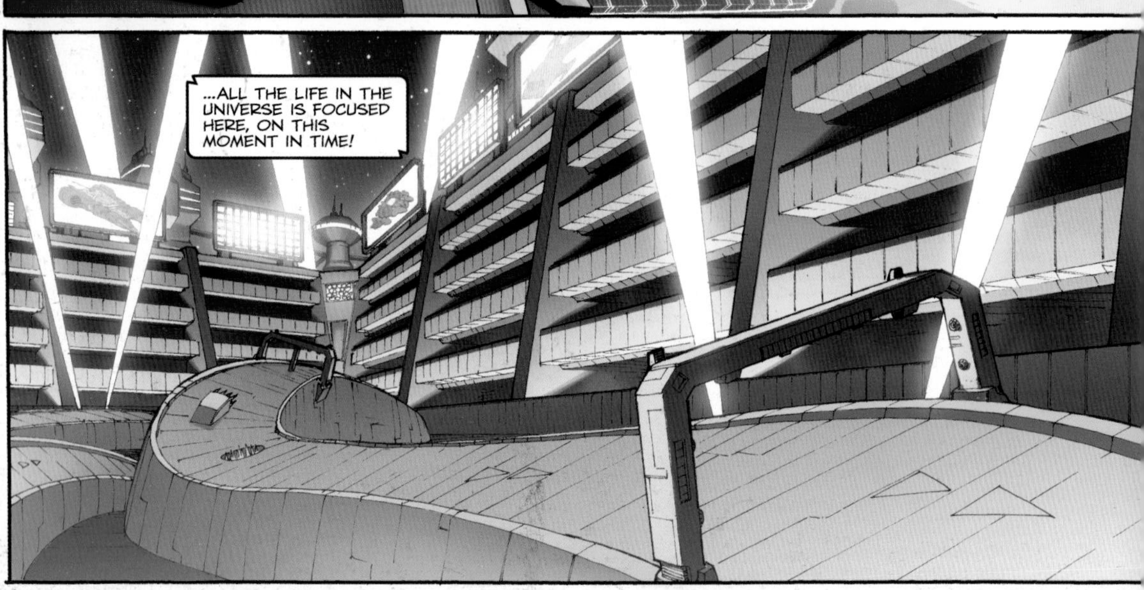
...ALL THE LIFE IN THE UNIVERSE IS FOCUSED HERE, ON THIS MOMENT IN TIME!

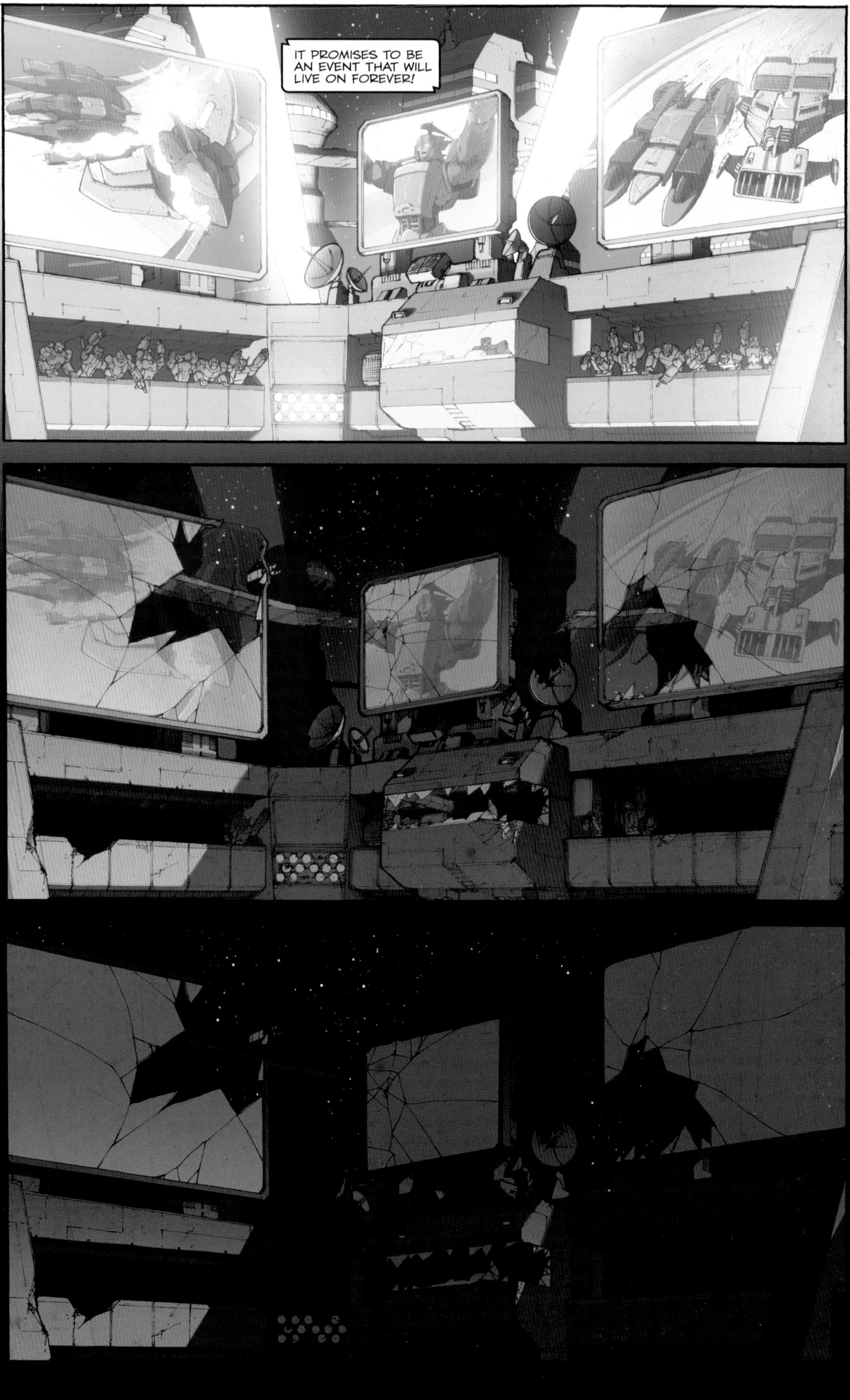
IT PROMISES TO BE AN EVENT THAT WILL LIVE ON FOREVER!

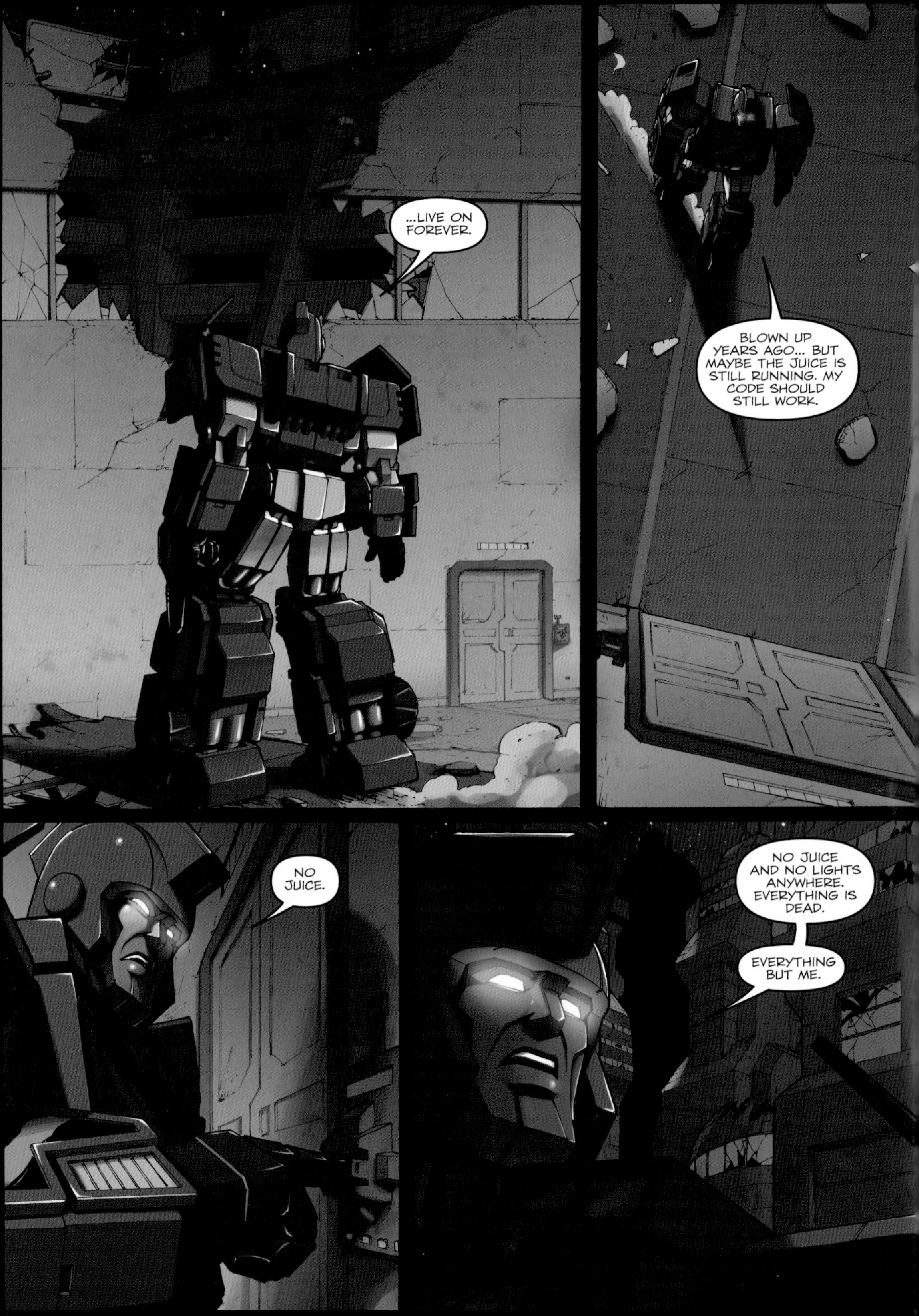
...LIVE ON FOREVER.
BLOWN UP YEARS AGO... BUT MAYBE THE JUICE IS STILL RUNNING. MY CODE SHOULD STILL WORK.
NO JUICE.
NO JUICE AND NO LIGHTS ANYWHERE. EVERYTHING IS DEAD.
EVERYTHING BUT ME.

CHAPTER TWO: "IRON IN THE BLOOD"

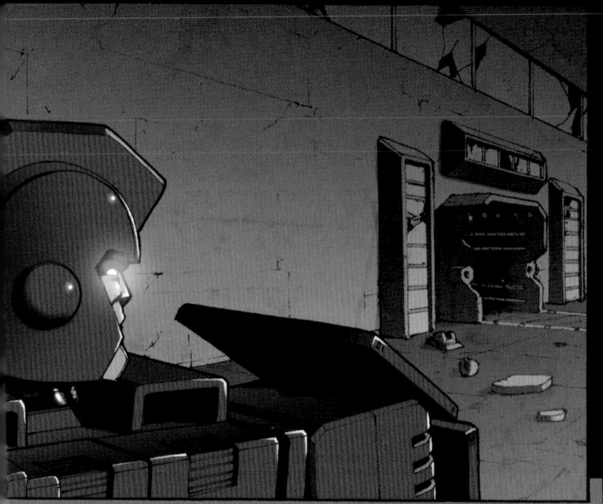

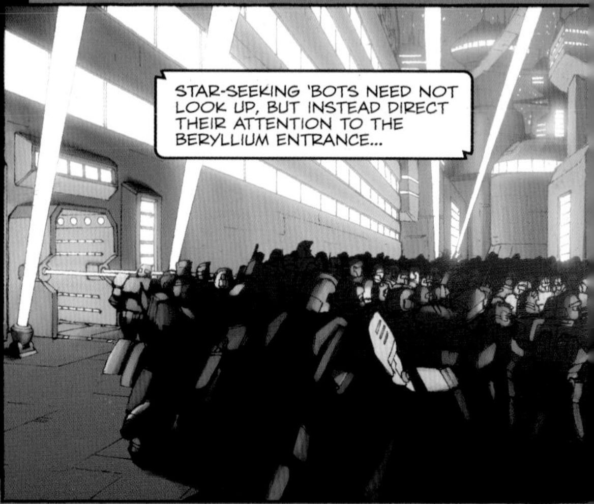
STAR-SEEKING 'BOTS NEED NOT LOOK UP, BUT INSTEAD DIRECT THEIR ATTENTION TO THE BERYLLIUM ENTRANCE...

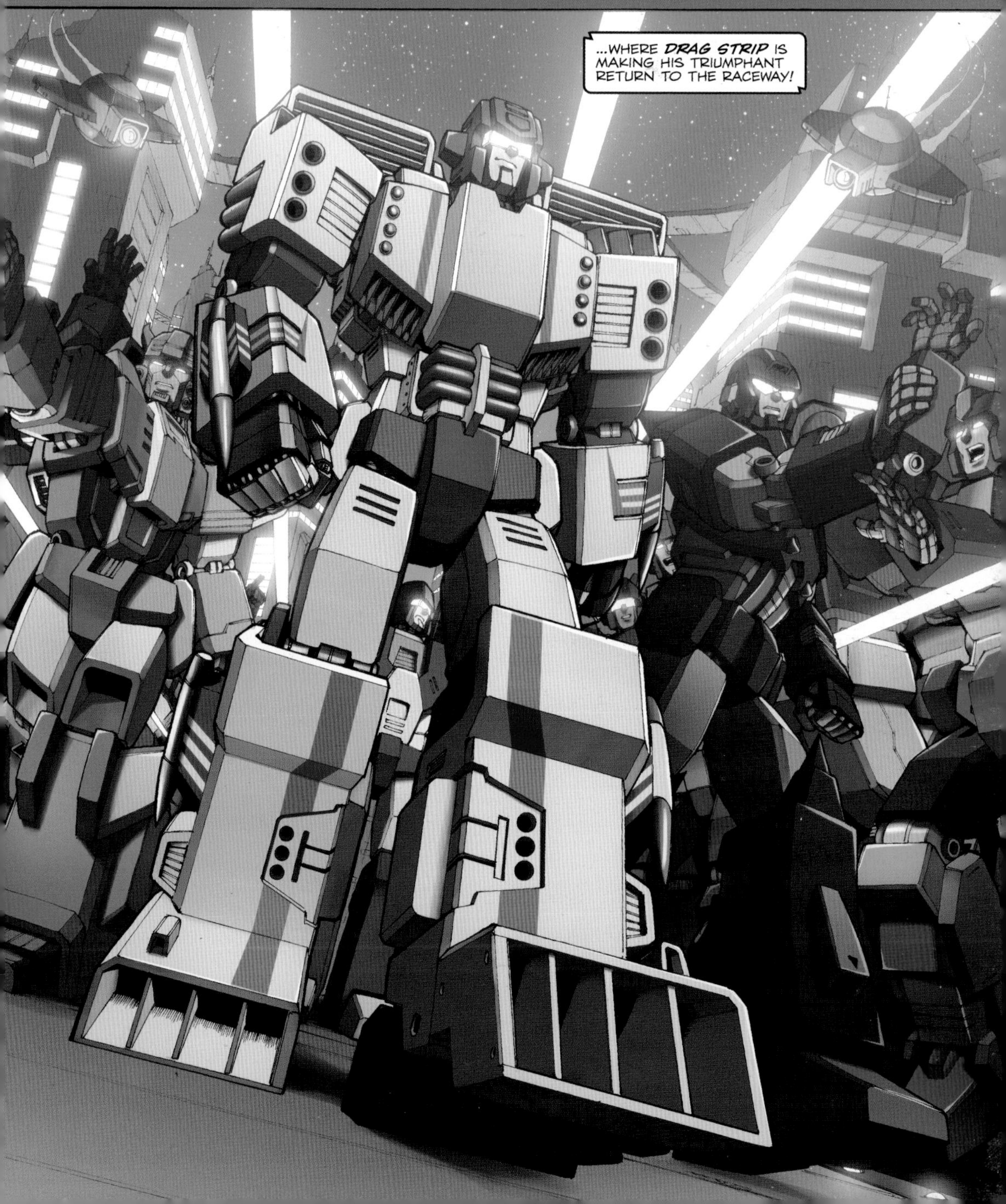
...WHERE DRAG STRIP IS MAKING HIS TRIUMPHANT RETURN TO THE RACEWAY!

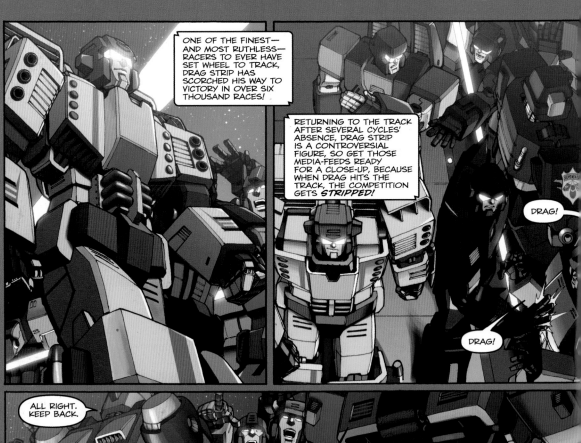

ONE OF THE FINEST— AND MOST RUTHLESS— RACERS TO EVER HAVE SET WHEEL TO TRACK, DRAG STRIP HAS SCORCHED HIS WAY TO VICTORY IN OVER SIX THOUSAND RACES!

RETURNING TO THE TRACK AFTER SEVERAL CYCLES' ABSENCE, DRAG STRIP IS A CONTROVERSIAL FIGURE, SO GET THOSE MEDIA-FEEDS READY FOR A CLOSE-UP, BECAUSE WHEN DRAG HITS THE TRACK, THE COMPETITION GETS *STRIPPED!*

DRAG!

DRAG!

ALL RIGHT. KEEP BACK.

DRAG! OVER HERE!

NO AUTOGRAPHS.

HEY, STOP—UNGH!

GUN!

HEY!

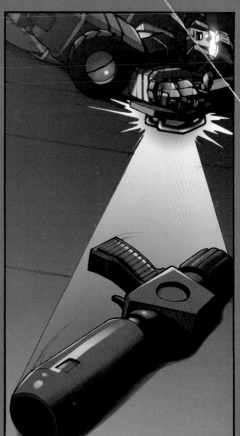

WE SAID NO AUTOGRAPHS.

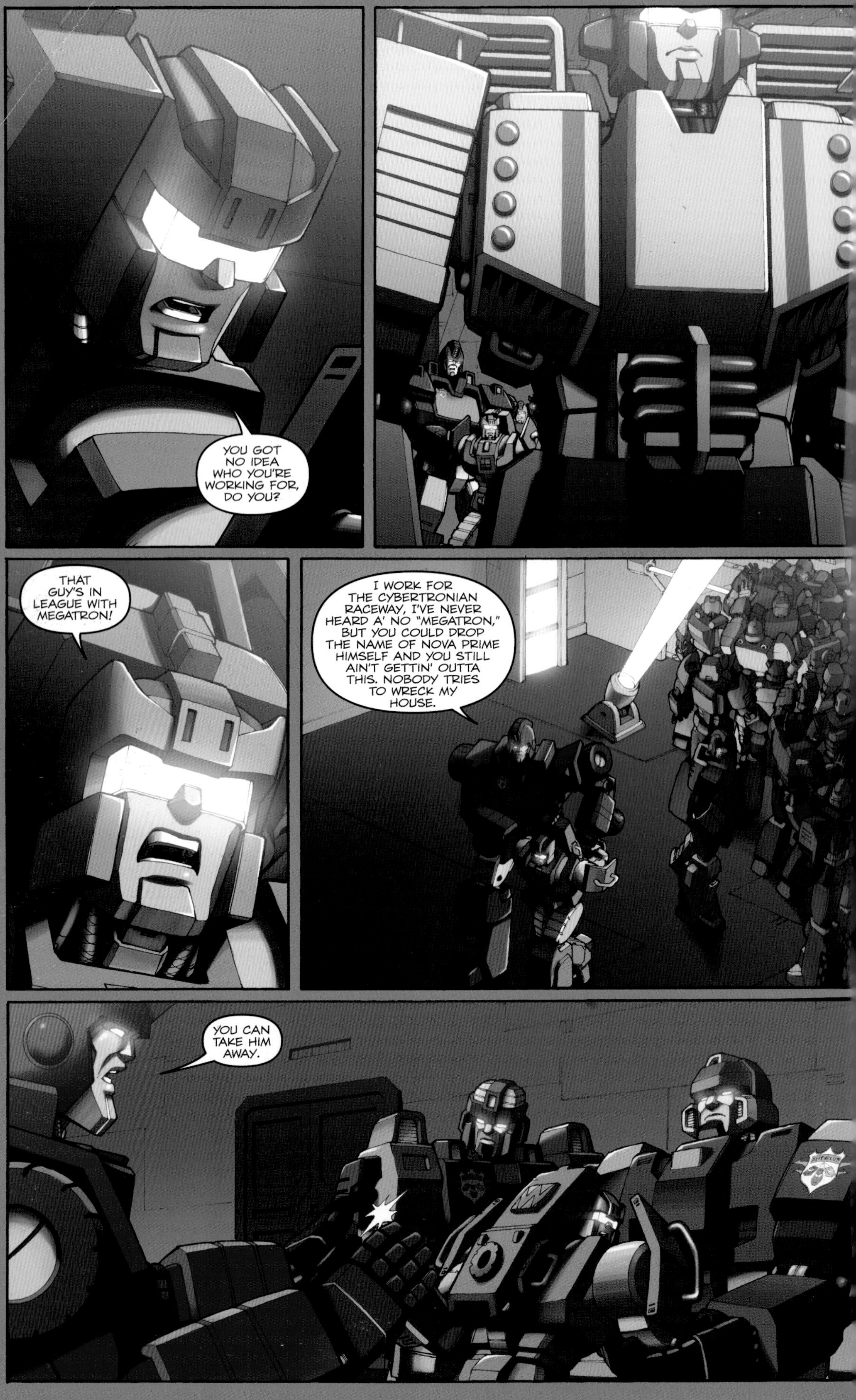
YOU GOT NO IDEA WHO YOU'RE WORKING FOR, DO YOU?
THAT GUY'S IN LEAGUE WITH MEGATRON!
I WORK FOR THE CYBERTRONIAN RACEWAY, I'VE NEVER HEARD A' NO "MEGATRON," BUT YOU COULD DROP THE NAME OF NOVA PRIME HIMSELF AND YOU STILL AIN'T GETTIN' OUTTA THIS. NOBODY TRIES TO WRECK MY HOUSE.
YOU CAN TAKE HIM AWAY.

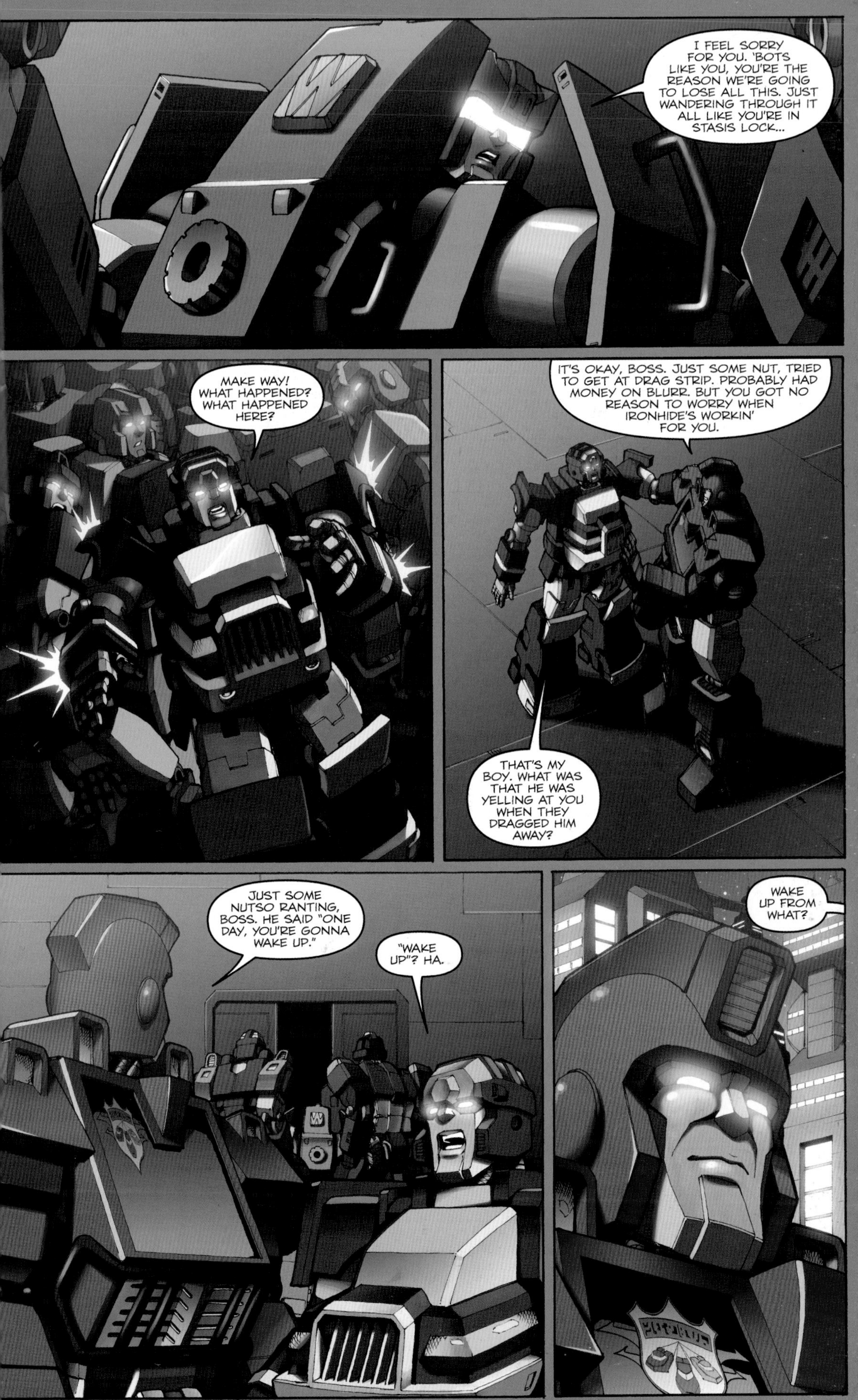
I FEEL SORRY FOR YOU. 'BOTS LIKE YOU, YOU'RE THE REASON WE'RE GOING TO LOSE ALL THIS. JUST WANDERING THROUGH IT ALL LIKE YOU'RE IN STASIS LOCK...
MAKE WAY! WHAT HAPPENED? WHAT HAPPENED HERE?
IT'S OKAY, BOSS. JUST SOME NUT, TRIED TO GET AT DRAG STRIP. PROBABLY HAD MONEY ON BLURR. BUT YOU GOT NO REASON TO WORRY WHEN IRONHIDE'S WORKIN' FOR YOU.
THAT'S MY BOY. WHAT WAS THAT HE WAS YELLING AT YOU WHEN THEY DRAGGED HIM AWAY?
JUST SOME NUTSO RANTING, BOSS. HE SAID "ONE DAY, YOU'RE GONNA WAKE UP."
"WAKE UP"? HA.
WAKE UP FROM WHAT?

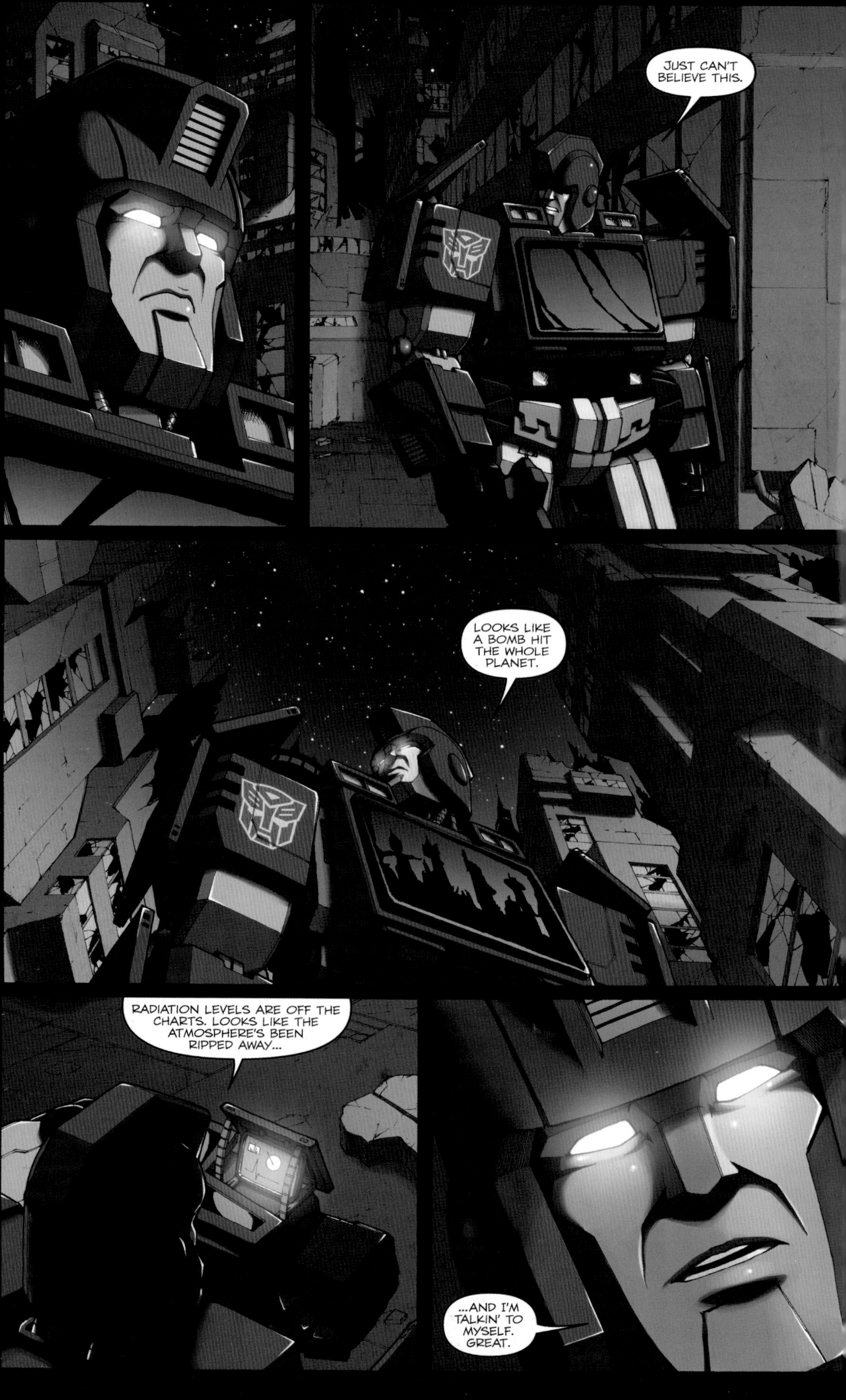
JUST CAN'T BELIEVE THIS.
LOOKS LIKE A BOMB HIT THE WHOLE PLANET.
RADIATION LEVELS ARE OFF THE CHARTS. LOOKS LIKE THE ATMOSPHERE'S BEEN RIPPED AWAY...
...AND I'M TALKIN' TO MYSELF. GREAT.

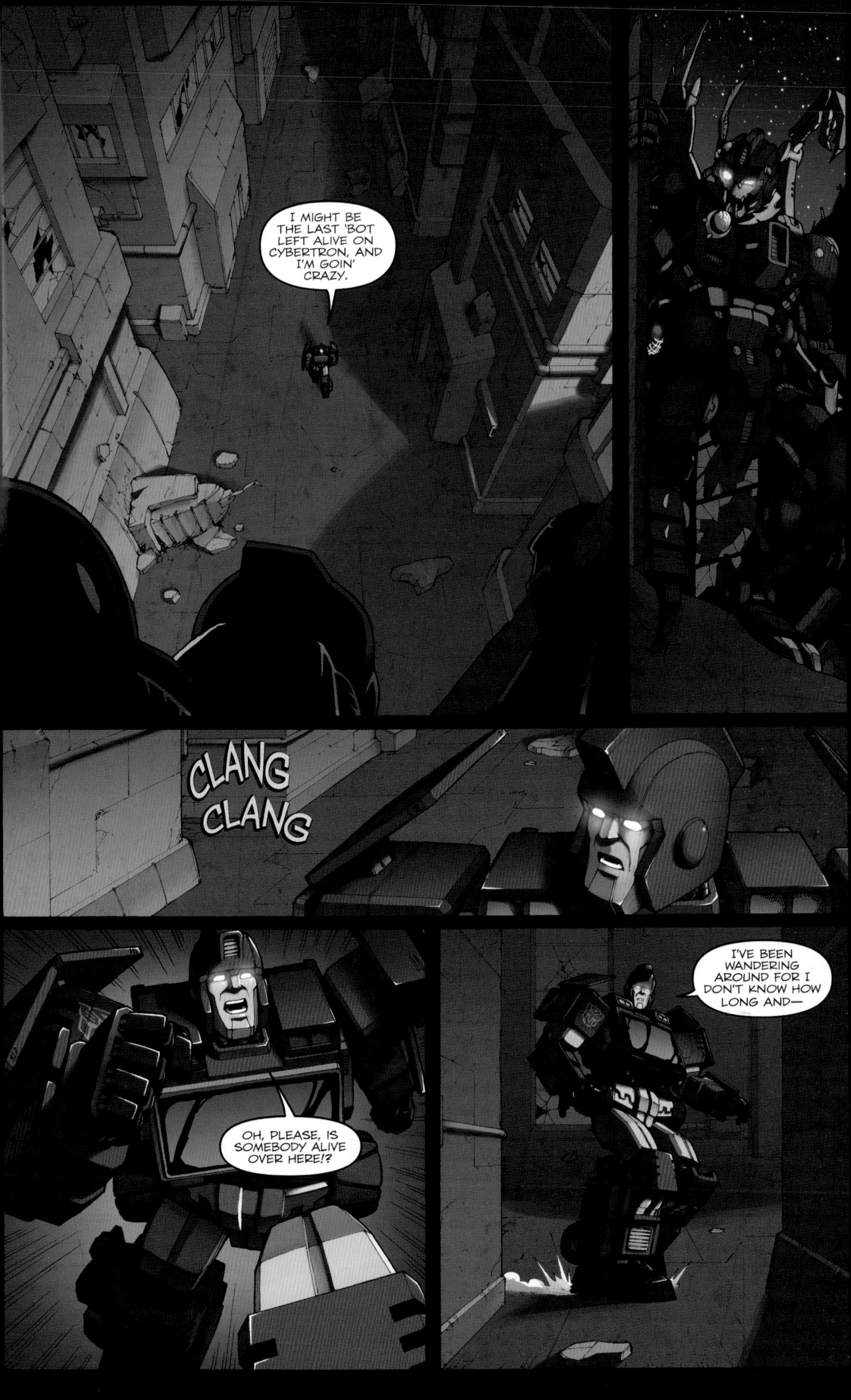

I MIGHT BE THE LAST 'BOT LEFT ALIVE ON CYBERTRON, AND I'M GOIN' CRAZY.
CLANG
CLANG
OH, PLEASE, IS SOMEBODY ALIVE OVER HERE!?
I'VE BEEN WANDERING AROUND FOR I DON'T KNOW HOW LONG AND—

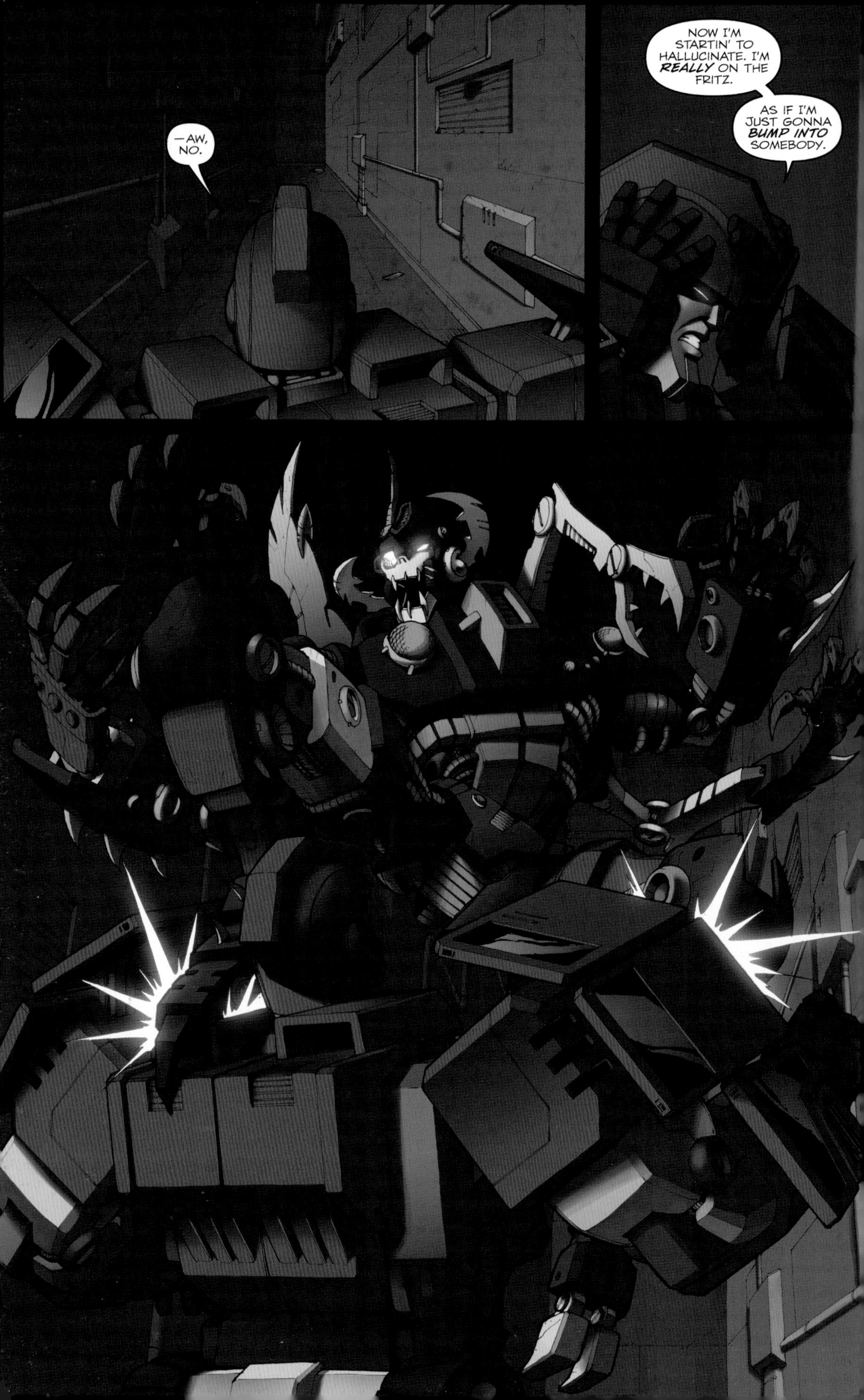
—AW, NO.
NOW I'M STARTIN' TO HALLUCINATE. I'M REALLY ON THE FRITZ.
AS IF I'M JUST GONNA BUMP INTO SOMEBODY.

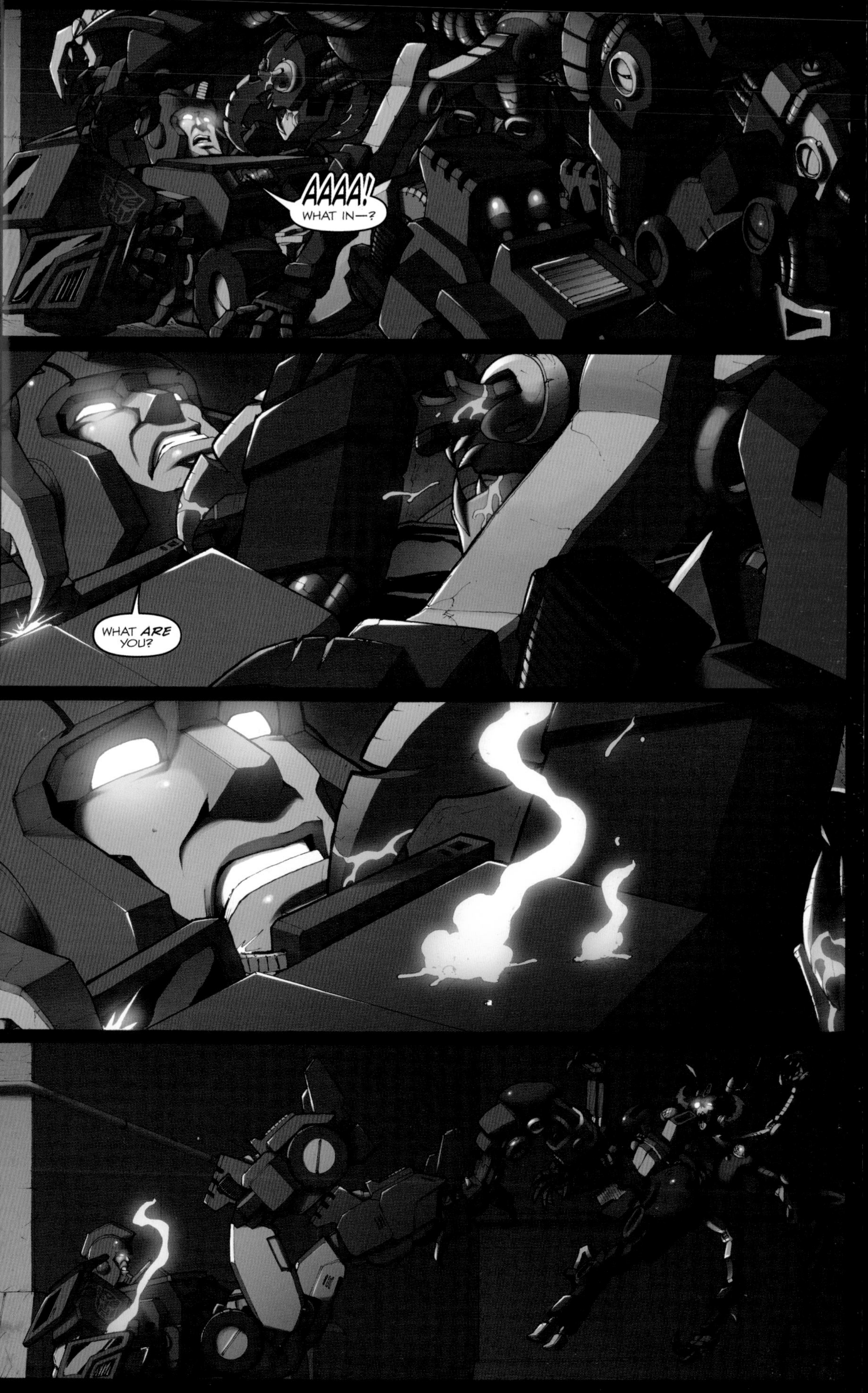
AAAA! WHAT IN—?
WHAT ARE YOU?

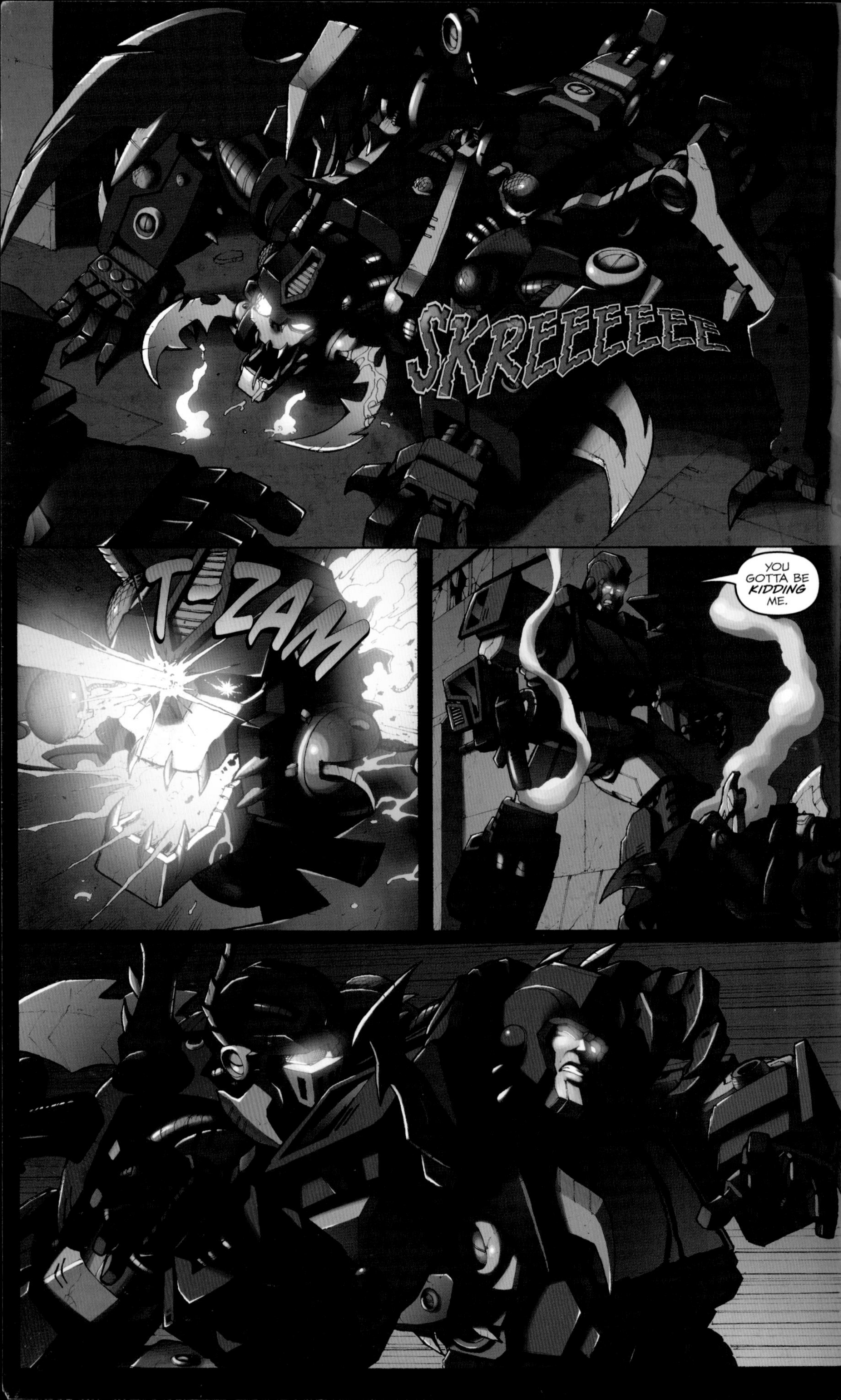
SKREEEEEE
T-ZAM
YOU GOTTA BE KIDDING ME.

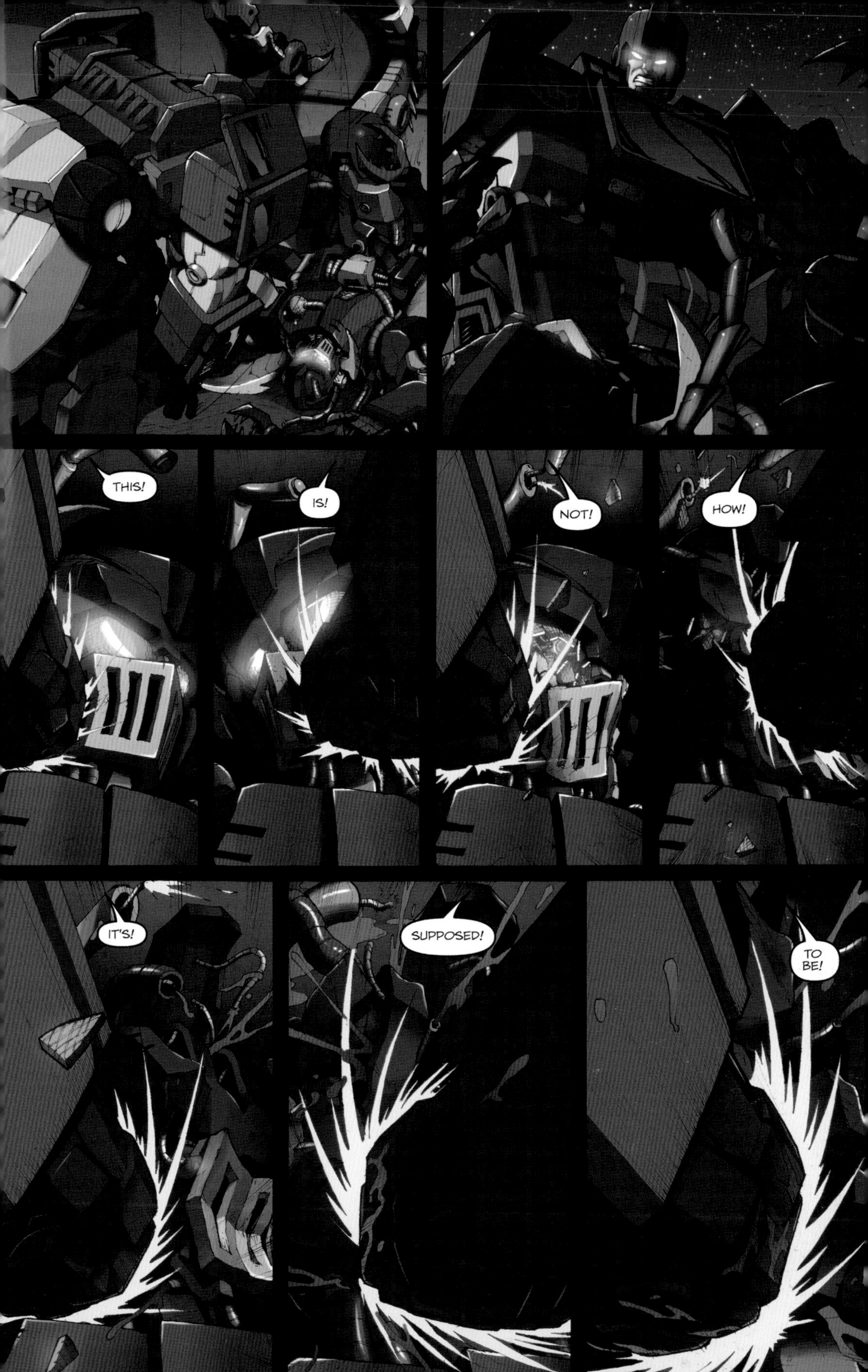
THIS!
IS!
NOT!
HOW!
IT'S!
SUPPOSED!
TO BE!

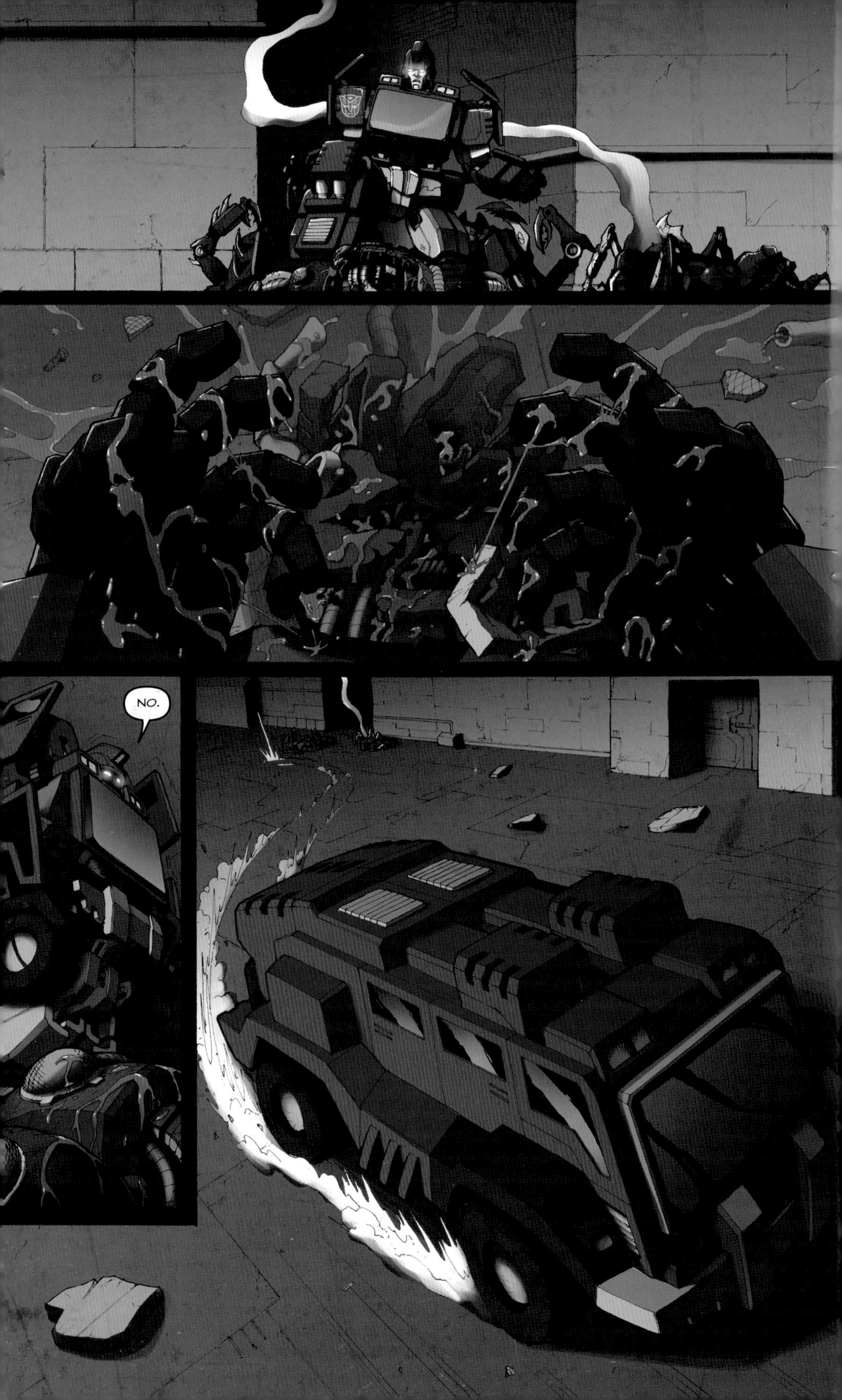
NO.

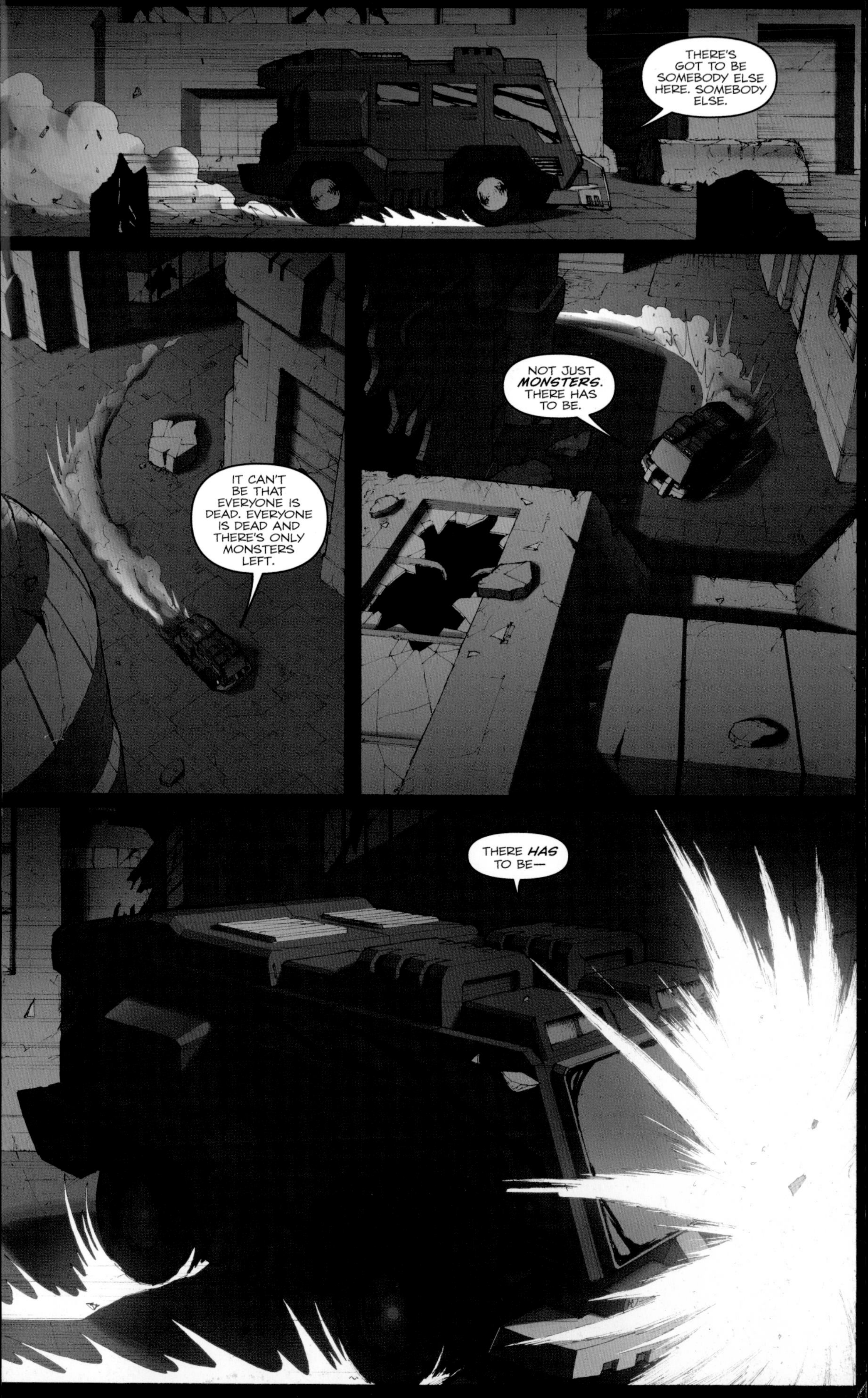
THERE'S GOT TO BE SOMEBODY ELSE HERE. SOMEBODY ELSE.
IT CAN'T BE THAT EVERYONE IS DEAD. EVERYONE IS DEAD AND THERE'S ONLY MONSTERS LEFT.
NOT JUST MONSTERS. THERE HAS TO BE.
THERE HAS TO BE—

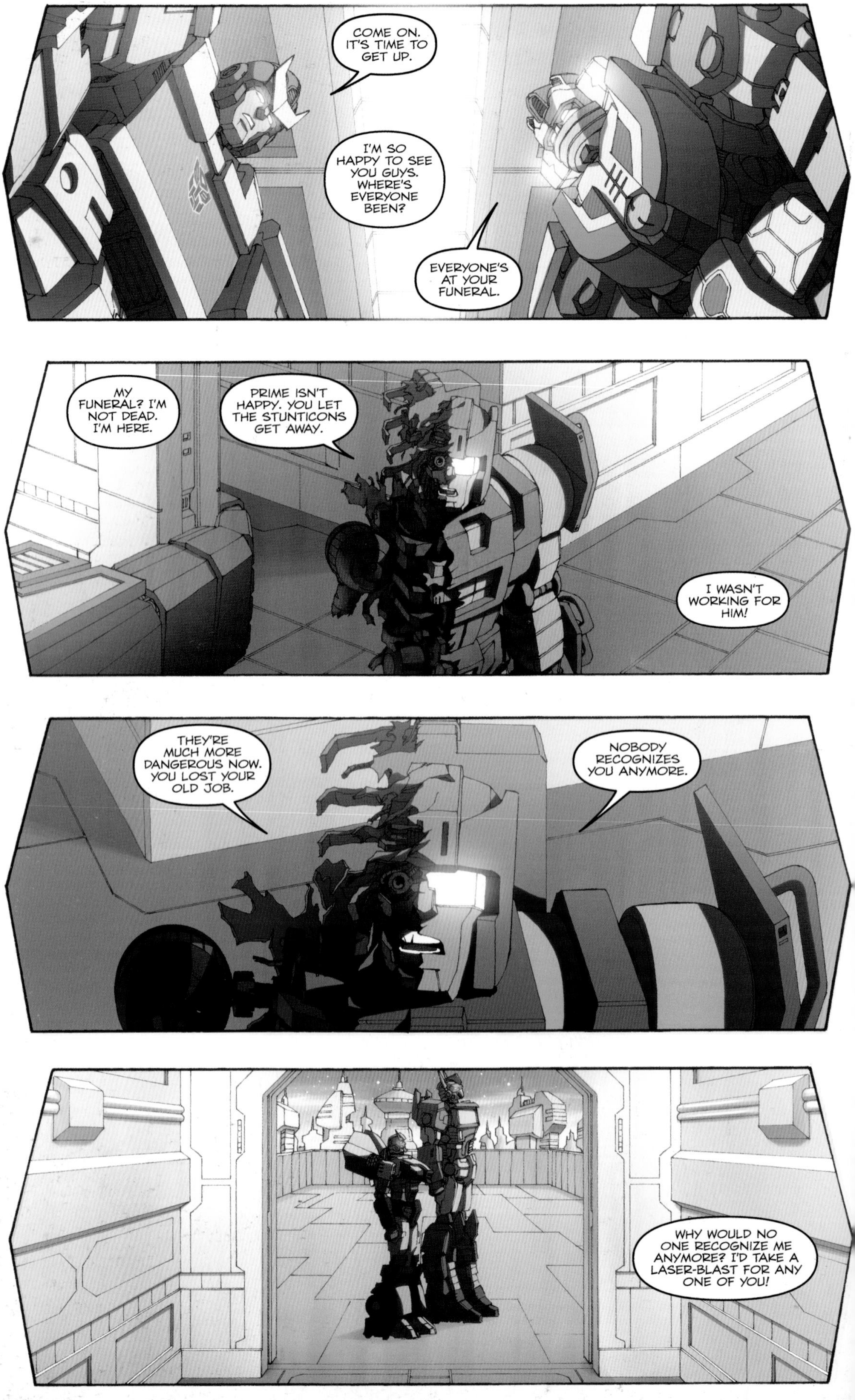
COME ON. IT'S TIME TO GET UP.
I'M SO HAPPY TO SEE YOU GUYS. WHERE'S EVERYONE BEEN?
EVERYONE'S AT YOUR FUNERAL.
MY FUNERAL? I'M NOT DEAD. I'M HERE.
PRIME ISN'T HAPPY. YOU LET THE STUNTICONS GET AWAY.
I WASN'T WORKING FOR HIM!
THEY'RE MUCH MORE DANGEROUS NOW. YOU LOST YOUR OLD JOB.
NOBODY RECOGNIZES YOU ANYMORE.
WHY WOULD NO ONE RECOGNIZE ME ANYMORE? I'D TAKE A LASER-BLAST FOR ANY ONE OF YOU!

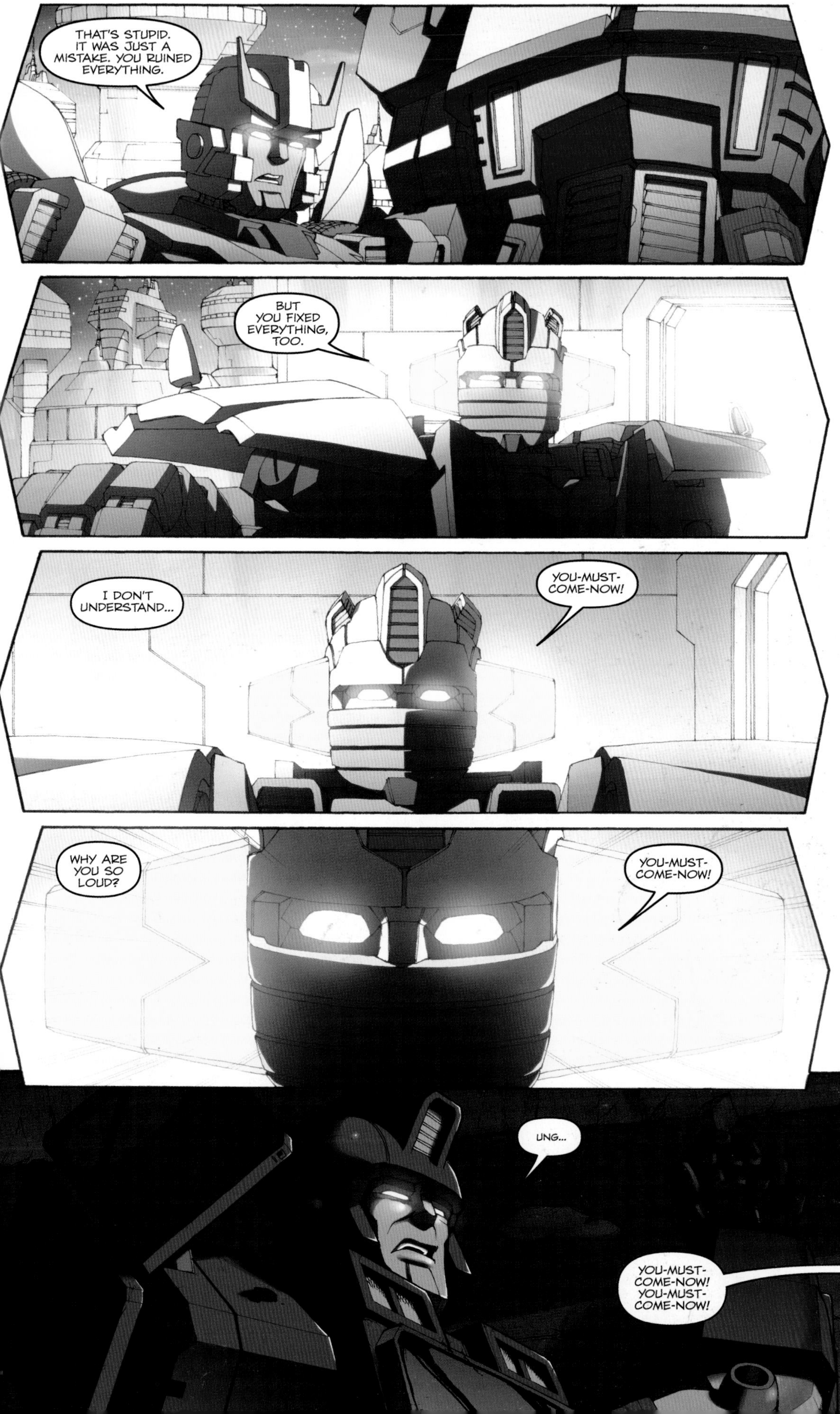
THAT'S STUPID. IT WAS JUST A MISTAKE. YOU RUINED EVERYTHING.
BUT YOU FIXED EVERYTHING, TOO.
I DON'T UNDERSTAND...
YOU-MUST-COME-NOW!
WHY ARE YOU SO LOUD?
YOU-MUST-COME-NOW!
UNG...
YOU-MUST-COME-NOW! YOU-MUST-COME-NOW!

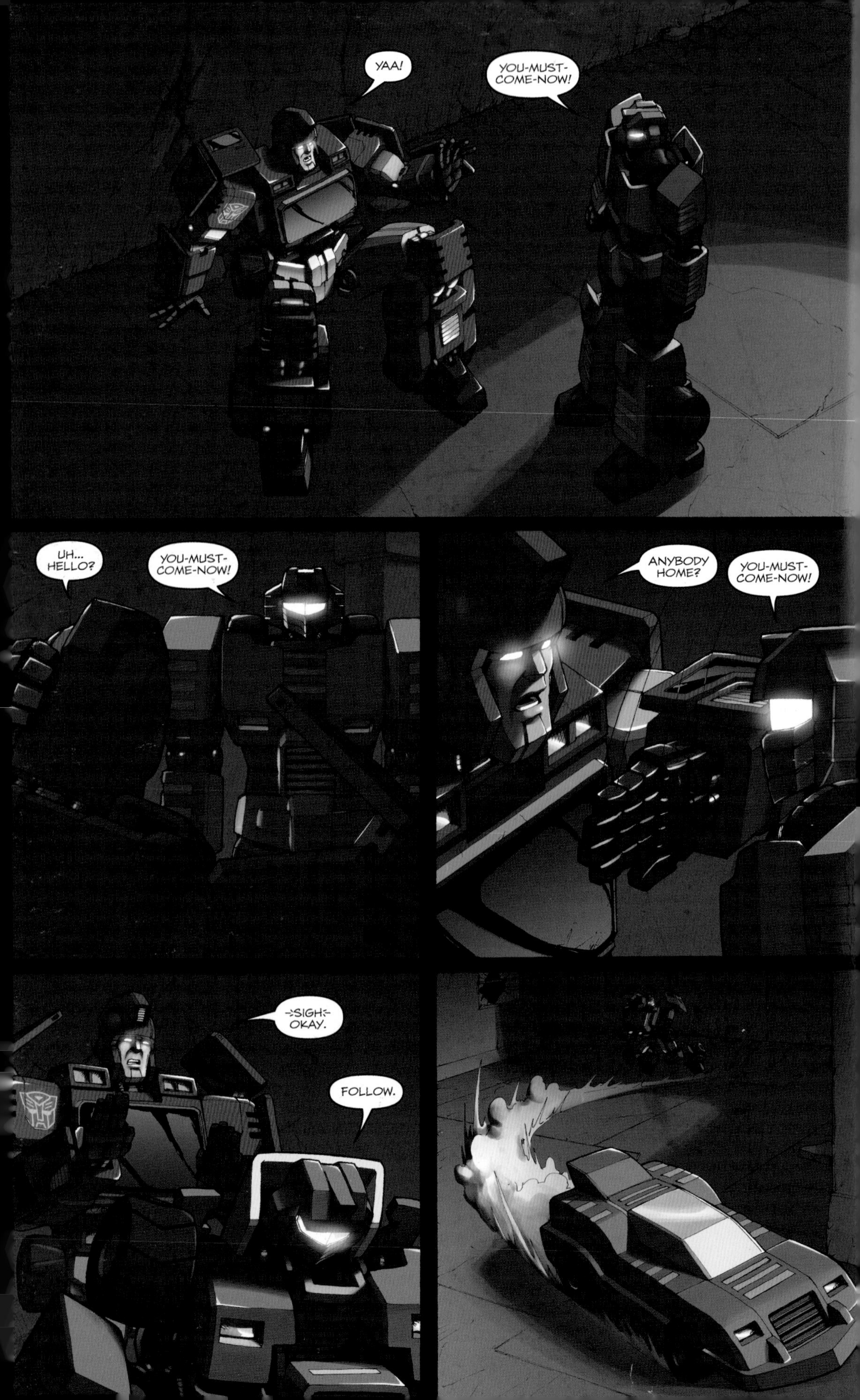
YAA!
YOU-MUST-COME-NOW!
UH... HELLO?
YOU-MUST-COME-NOW!
ANYBODY HOME?
YOU-MUST-COME-NOW!
-SIGH- OKAY.
FOLLOW.

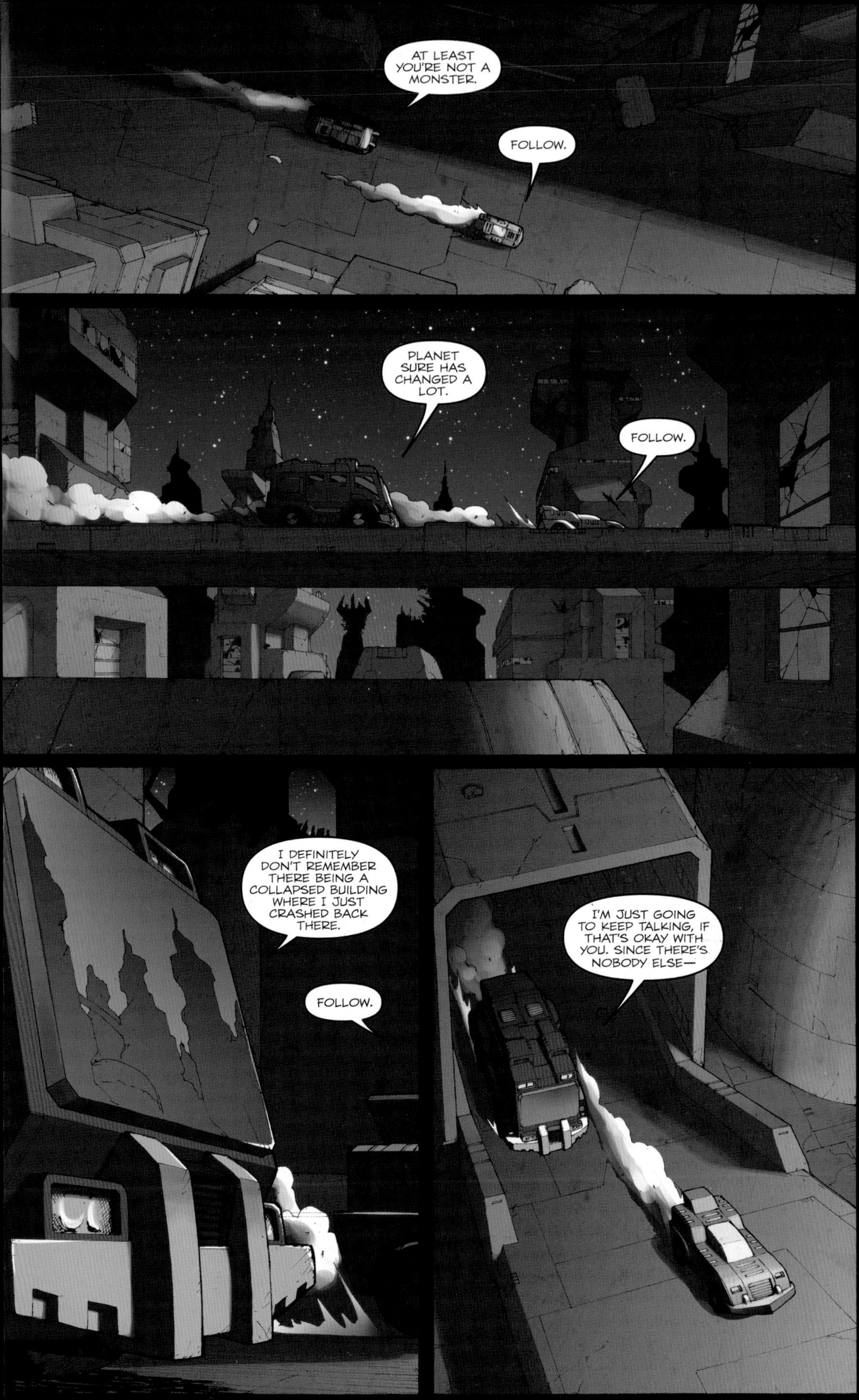
AT LEAST YOU'RE NOT A MONSTER.
FOLLOW.
PLANET SURE HAS CHANGED A LOT.
FOLLOW.
I DEFINITELY DON'T REMEMBER THERE BEING A COLLAPSED BUILDING WHERE I JUST CRASHED BACK THERE.
FOLLOW.
I'M JUST GOING TO KEEP TALKING, IF THAT'S OKAY WITH YOU. SINCE THERE'S NOBODY ELSE—

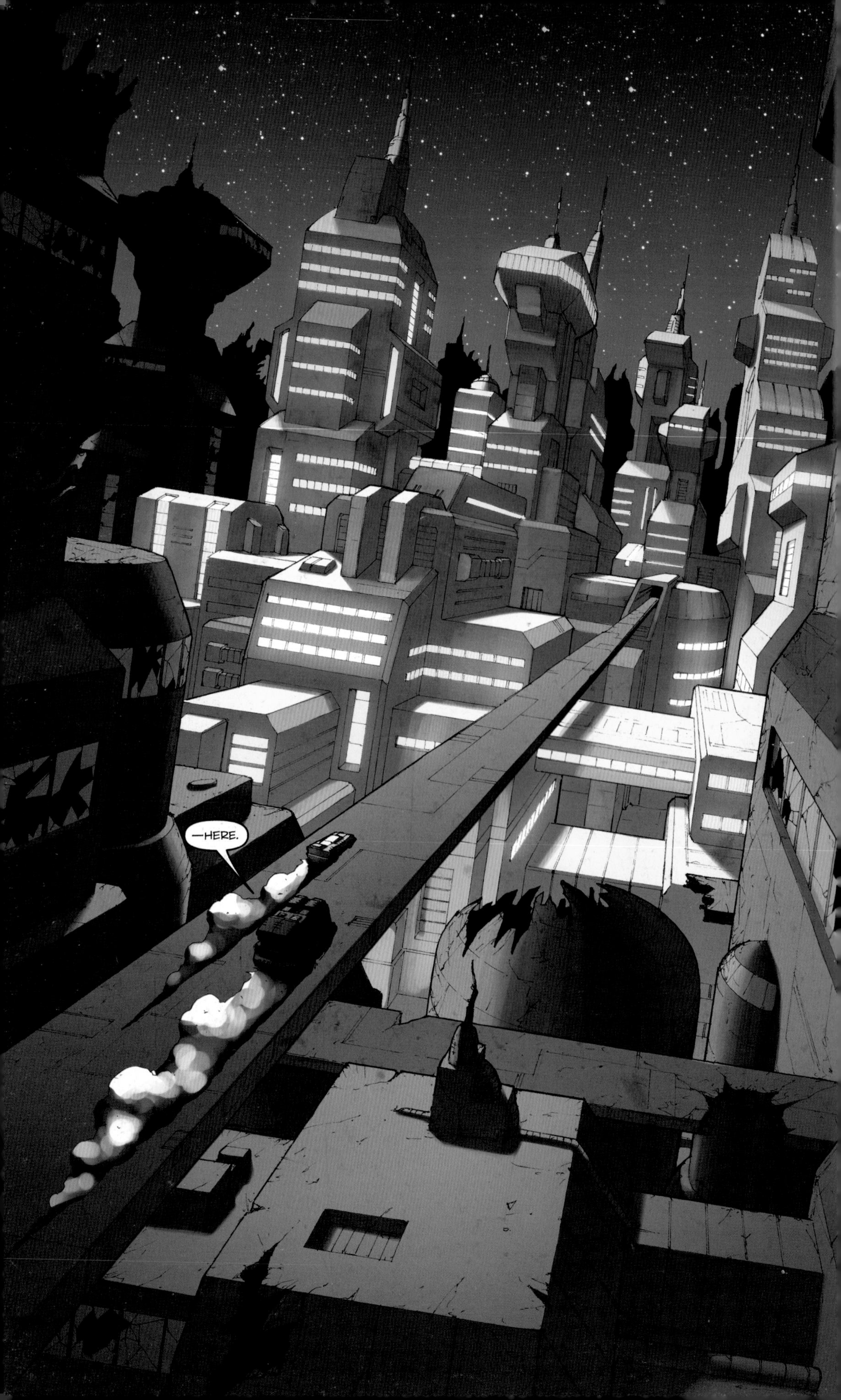
—HERE.

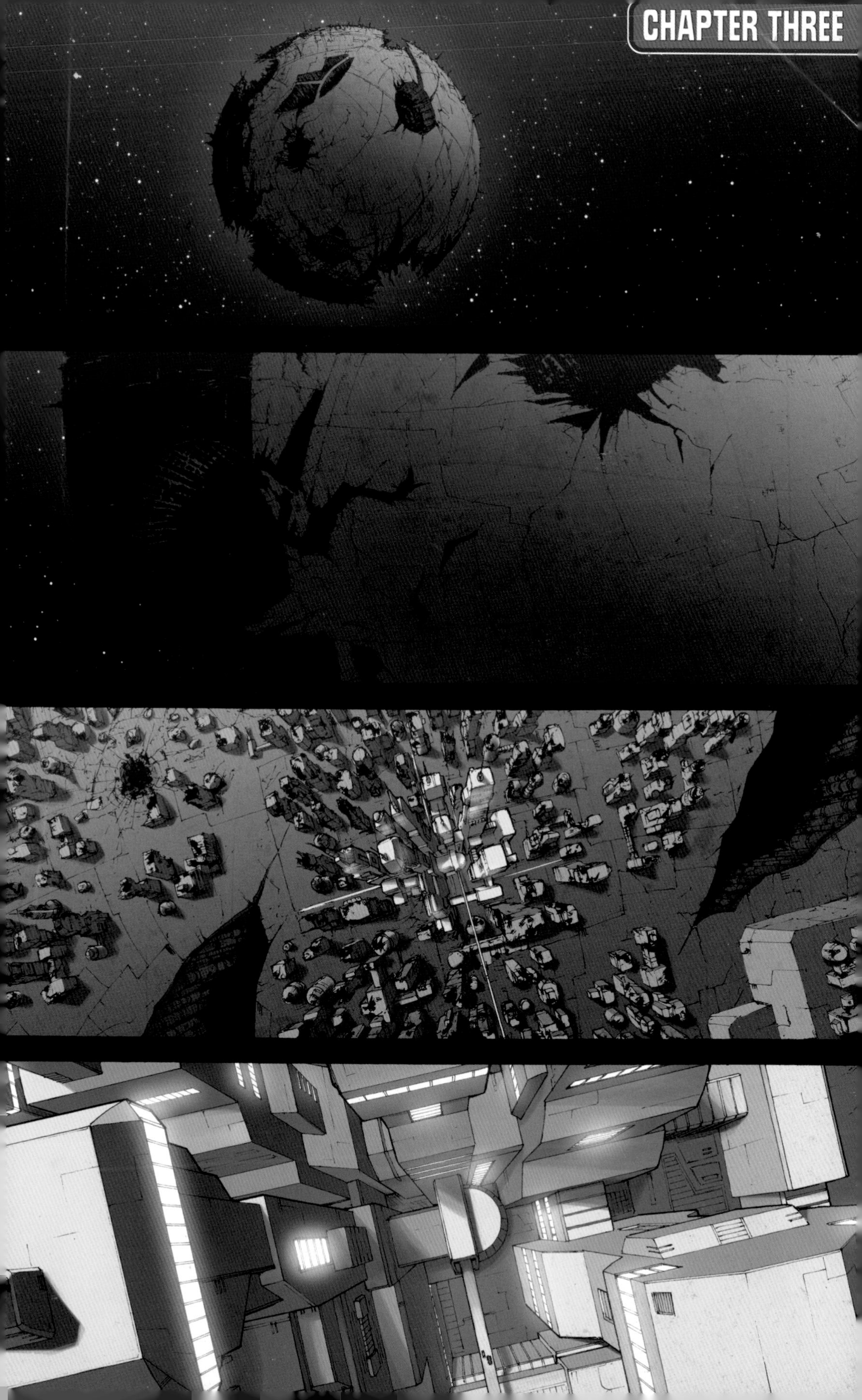
CHAPTER THREE

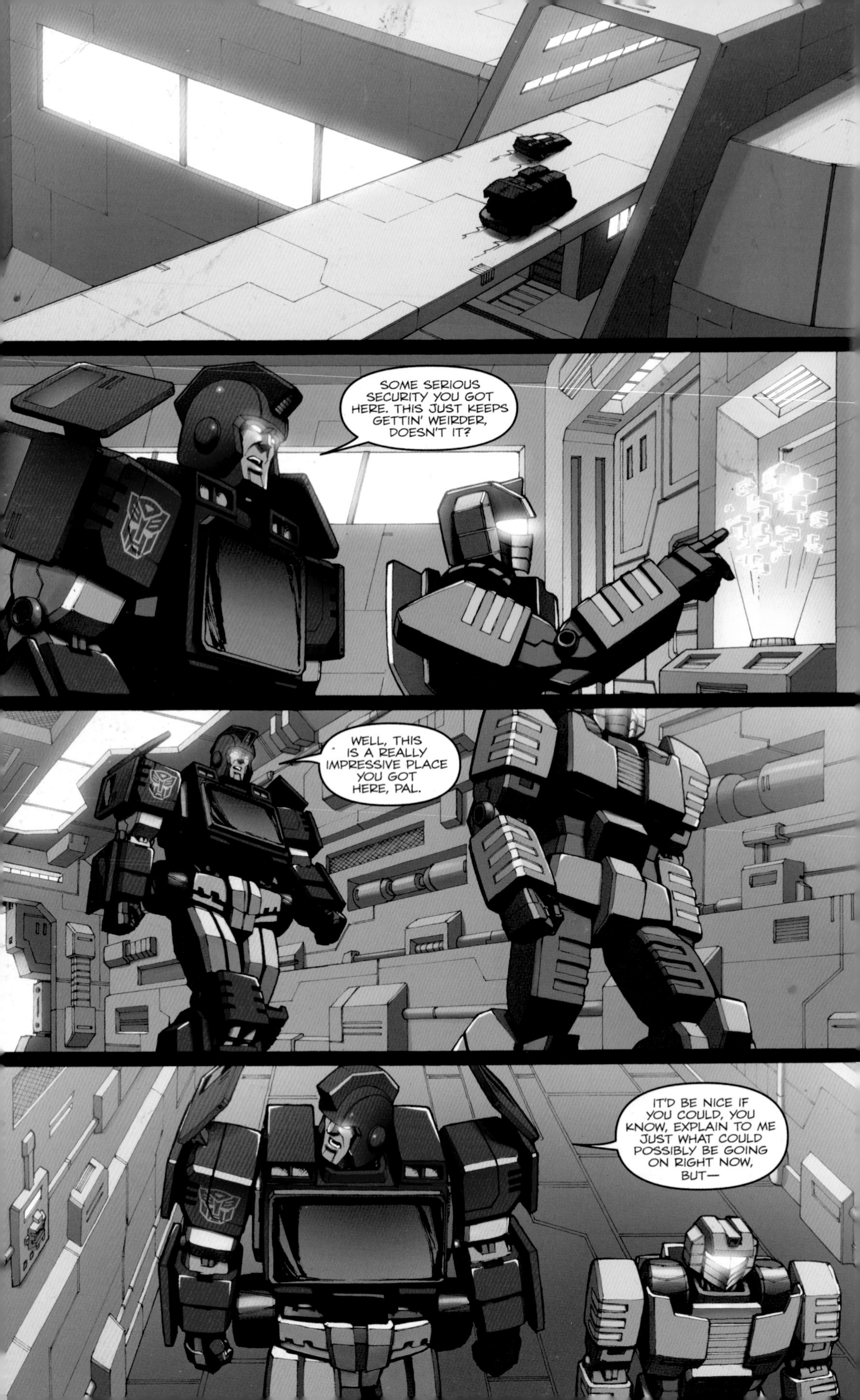
SOME SERIOUS SECURITY YOU GOT HERE. THIS JUST KEEPS GETTIN' WEIRDER, DOESN'T IT?
WELL, THIS IS A REALLY IMPRESSIVE PLACE YOU GOT HERE, PAL.
IT'D BE NICE IF YOU COULD, YOU KNOW, EXPLAIN TO ME JUST WHAT COULD POSSIBLY BE GOING ON RIGHT NOW, BUT—

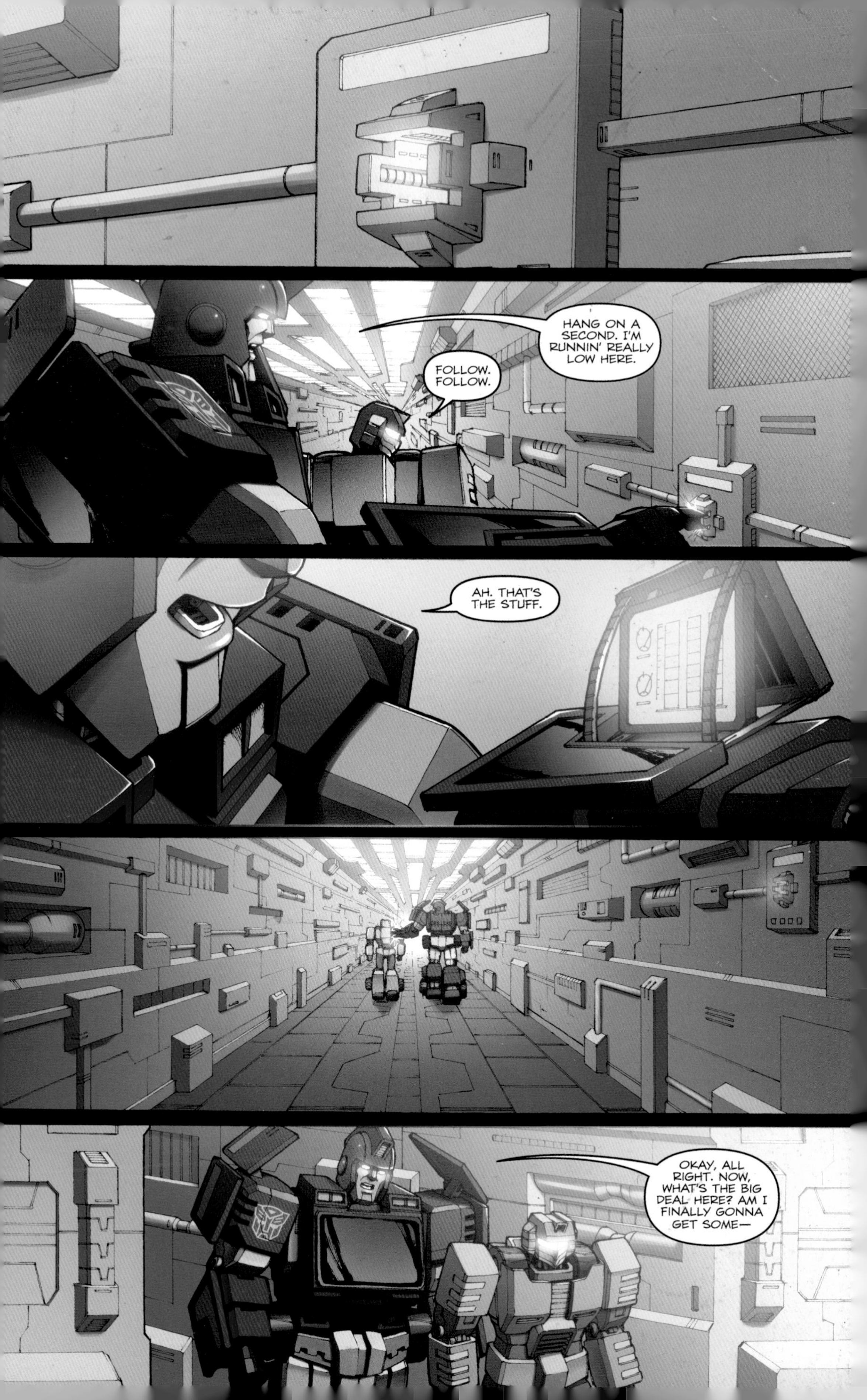
HANG ON A SECOND. I'M RUNNIN' REALLY LOW HERE.
FOLLOW. FOLLOW.
AH. THAT'S THE STUFF.
OKAY, ALL RIGHT. NOW, WHAT'S THE BIG DEAL HERE? AM I FINALLY GONNA GET SOME—

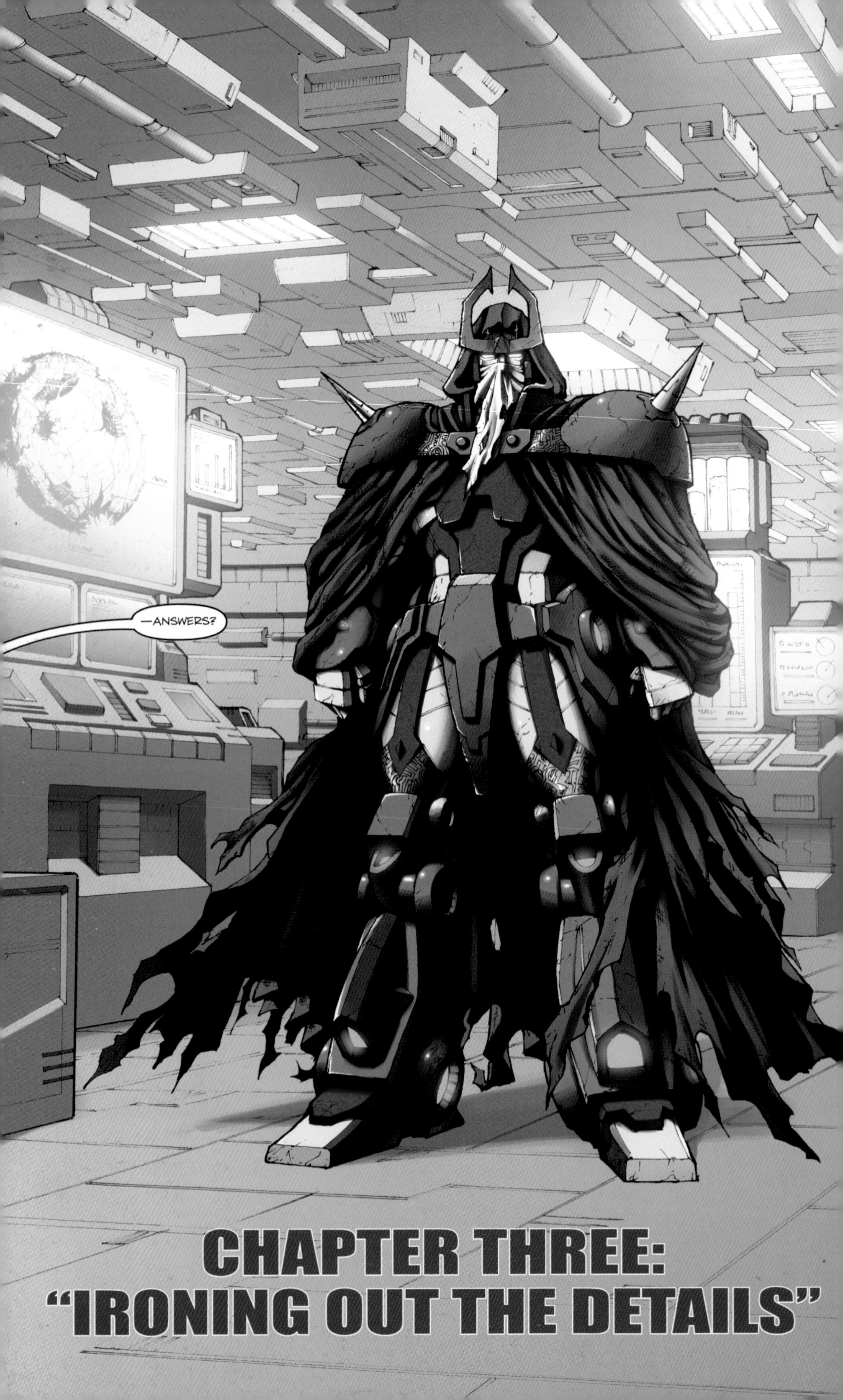
—ANSWERS?
CHAPTER THREE:
"IRONING OUT THE DETAILS"

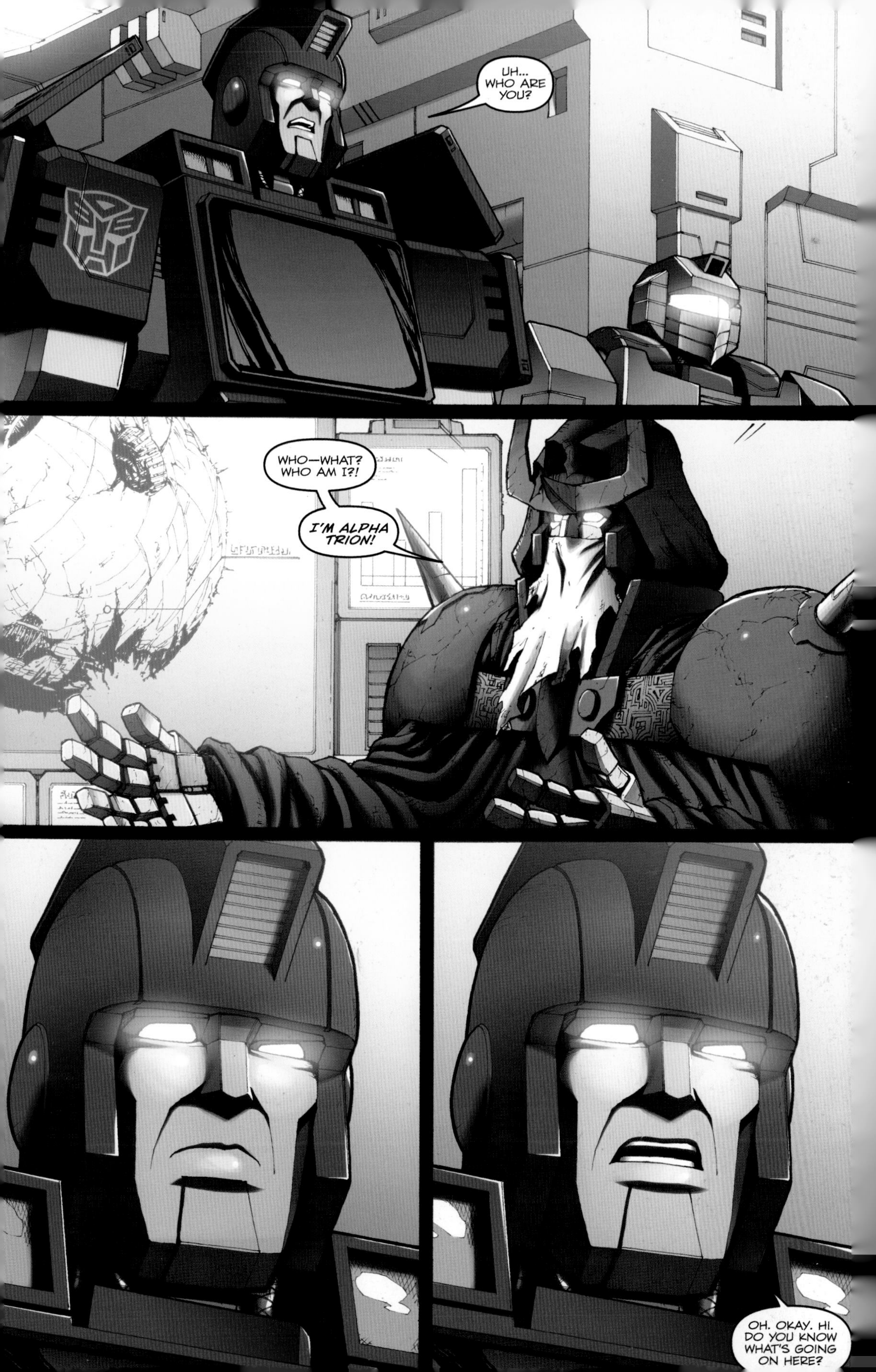
UH... WHO ARE YOU?
WHO—WHAT? WHO AM I?!
I'M ALPHA TRION!
OH. OKAY. HI. DO YOU KNOW WHAT'S GOING ON HERE?

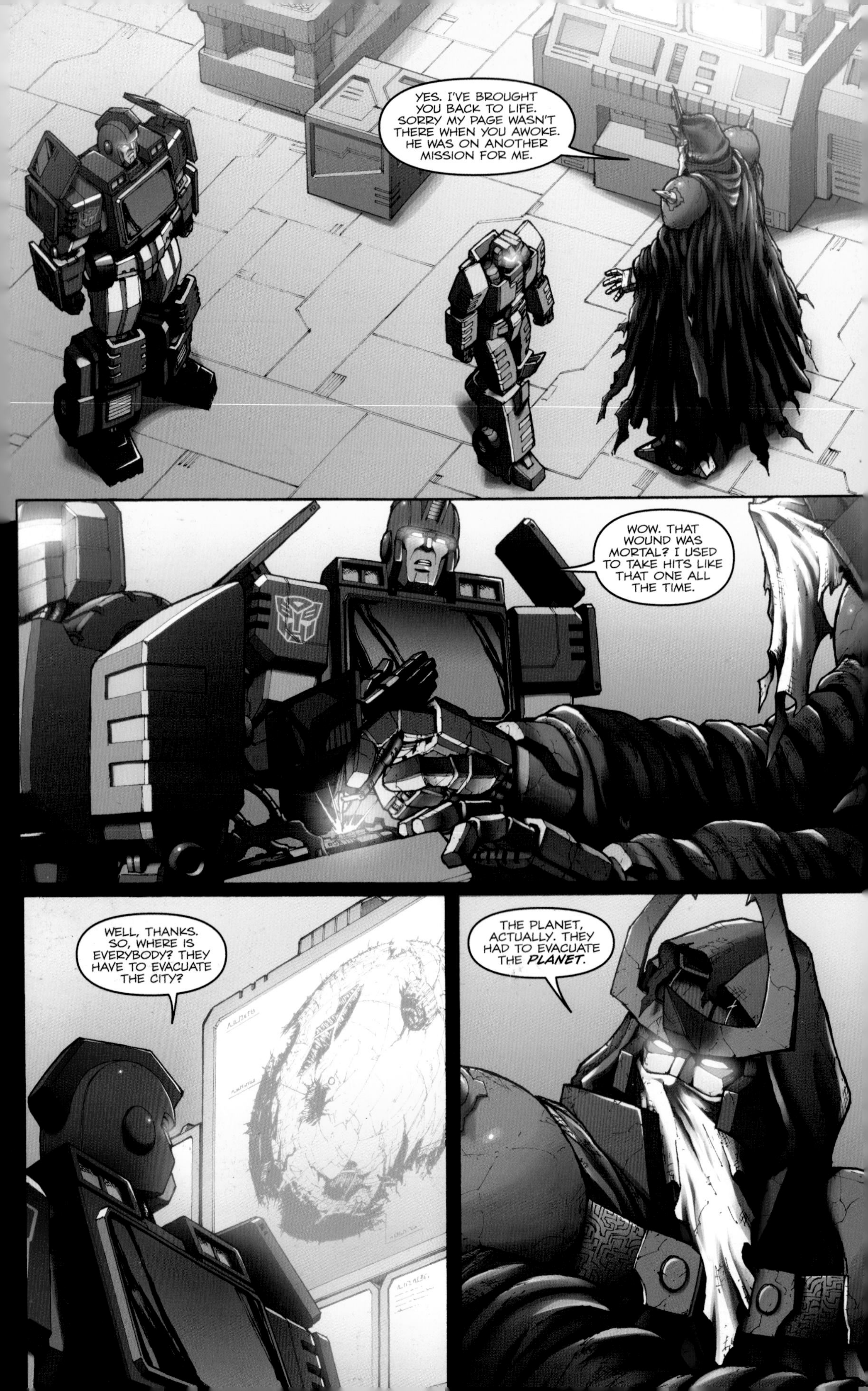
YES. I'VE BROUGHT YOU BACK TO LIFE. SORRY MY PAGE WASN'T THERE WHEN YOU AWOKE. HE WAS ON ANOTHER MISSION FOR ME.
WOW. THAT WOUND WAS MORTAL? I USED TO TAKE HITS LIKE THAT ONE ALL THE TIME.
WELL, THANKS. SO, WHERE IS EVERYBODY? THEY HAVE TO EVACUATE THE CITY?
THE PLANET, ACTUALLY. THEY HAD TO EVACUATE THE *PLANET*.

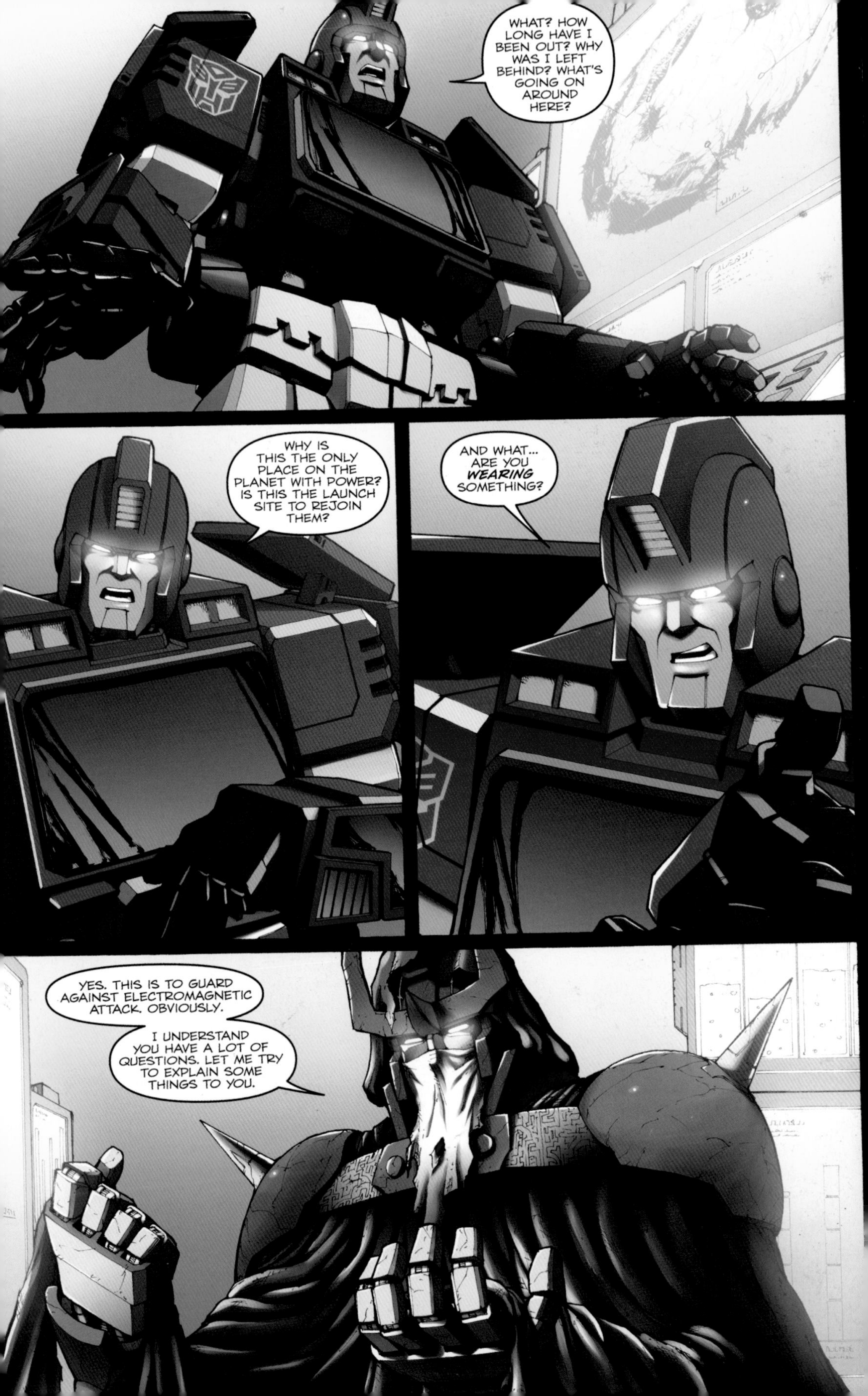
WHAT? HOW LONG HAVE I BEEN OUT? WHY WAS I LEFT BEHIND? WHAT'S GOING ON AROUND HERE?
WHY IS THIS THE ONLY PLACE ON THE PLANET WITH POWER? IS THIS THE LAUNCH SITE TO REJOIN THEM?
AND WHAT... ARE YOU *WEARING* SOMETHING?
YES. THIS IS TO GUARD AGAINST ELECTROMAGNETIC ATTACK. OBVIOUSLY.
I UNDERSTAND YOU HAVE A LOT OF QUESTIONS. LET ME TRY TO EXPLAIN SOME THINGS TO YOU.

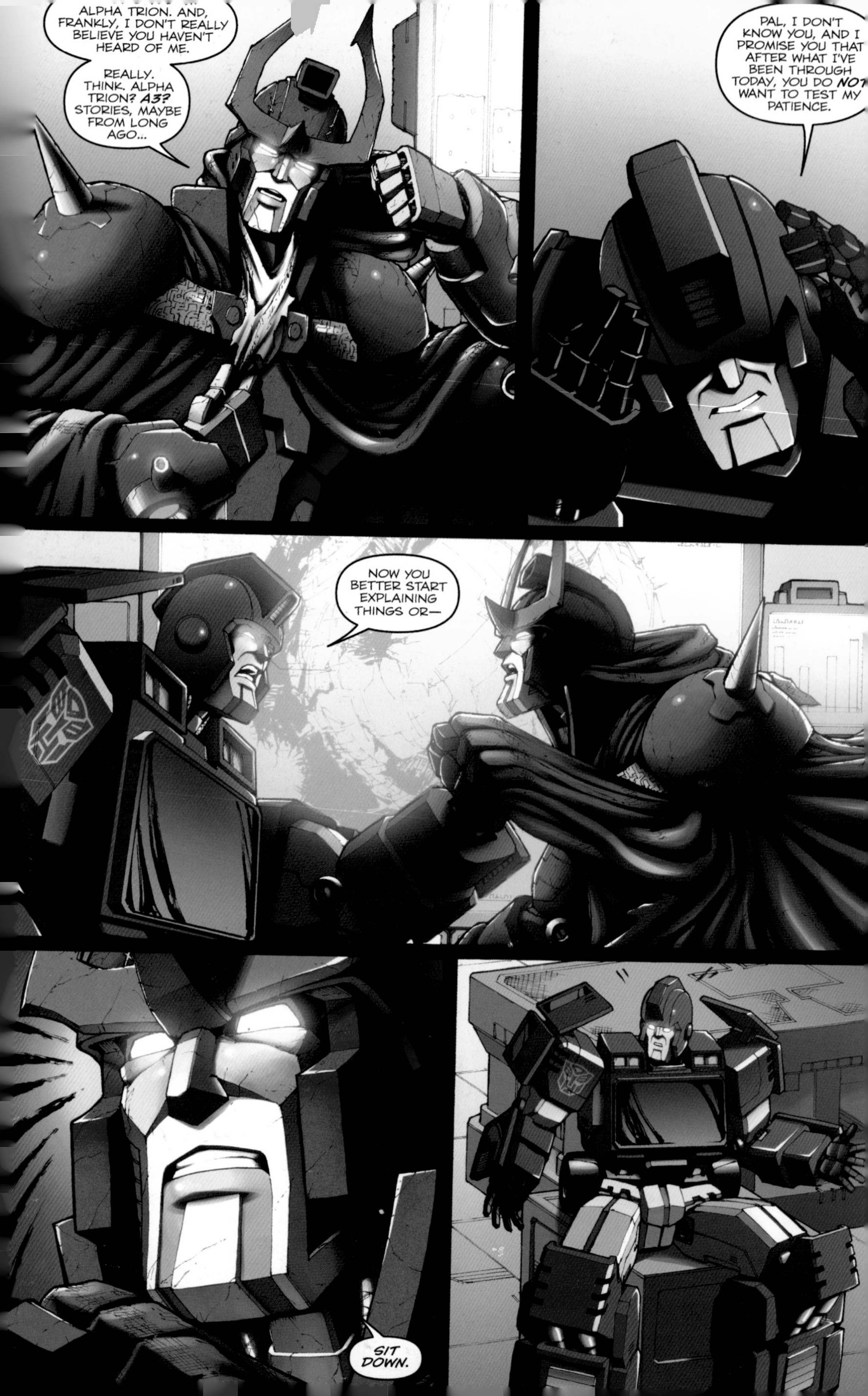
ALPHA TRION. AND, FRANKLY, I DON'T REALLY BELIEVE YOU HAVEN'T HEARD OF ME.
REALLY. THINK. ALPHA TRION? A3? STORIES, MAYBE FROM LONG AGO...
PAL, I DON'T KNOW YOU, AND I PROMISE YOU THAT AFTER WHAT I'VE BEEN THROUGH TODAY, YOU DO NOT WANT TO TEST MY PATIENCE.
NOW YOU BETTER START EXPLAINING THINGS OR—
SIT DOWN.

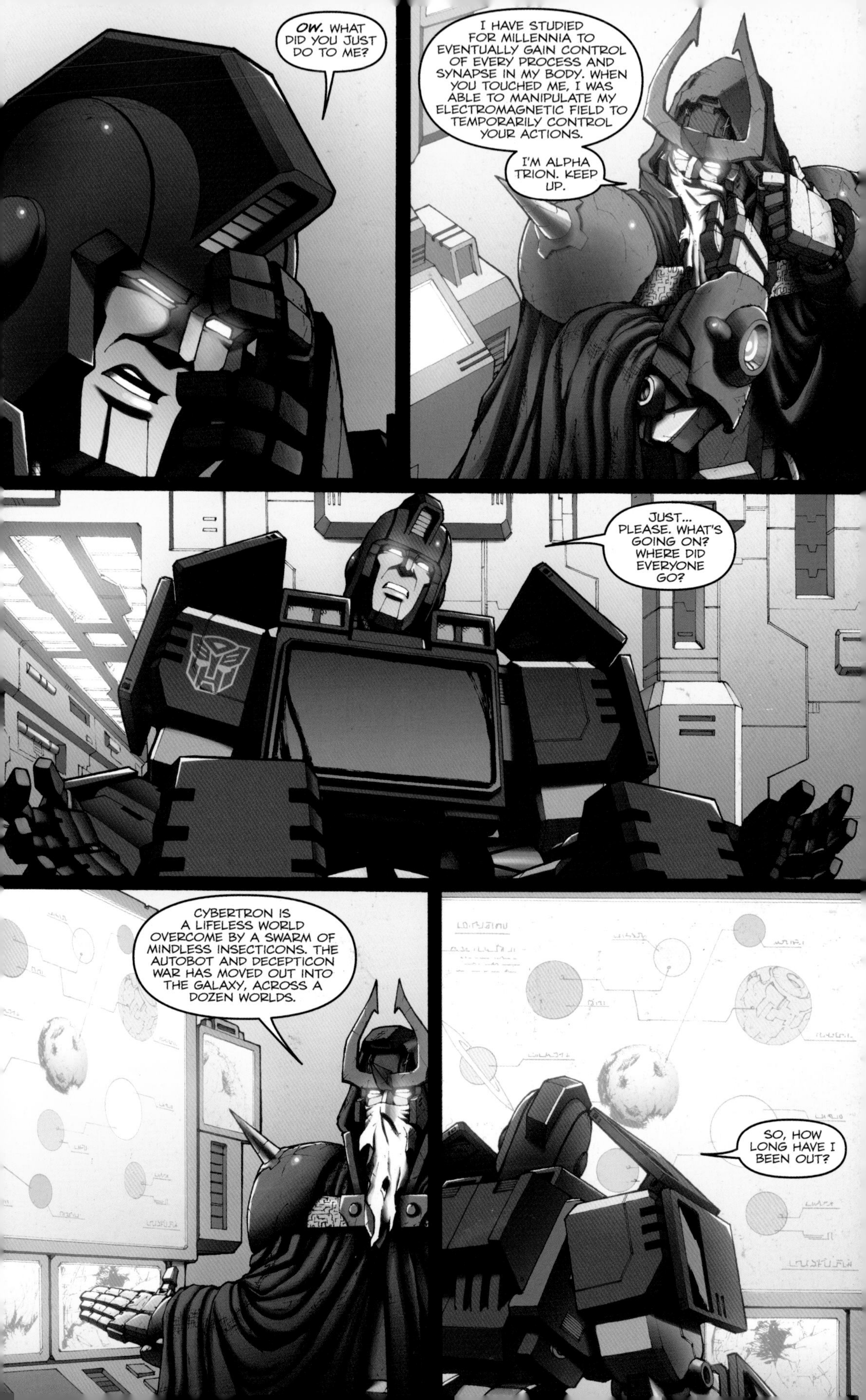

OW. WHAT DID YOU JUST DO TO ME?
I HAVE STUDIED FOR MILLENNIA TO EVENTUALLY GAIN CONTROL OF EVERY PROCESS AND SYNAPSE IN MY BODY. WHEN YOU TOUCHED ME, I WAS ABLE TO MANIPULATE MY ELECTROMAGNETIC FIELD TO TEMPORARILY CONTROL YOUR ACTIONS.
I'M ALPHA TRION. KEEP UP.
JUST... PLEASE. WHAT'S GOING ON? WHERE DID EVERYONE GO?
CYBERTRON IS A LIFELESS WORLD OVERCOME BY A SWARM OF MINDLESS INSECTICONS. THE AUTOBOT AND DECEPTICON WAR HAS MOVED OUT INTO THE GALAXY, ACROSS A DOZEN WORLDS.
SO, HOW LONG HAVE I BEEN OUT?

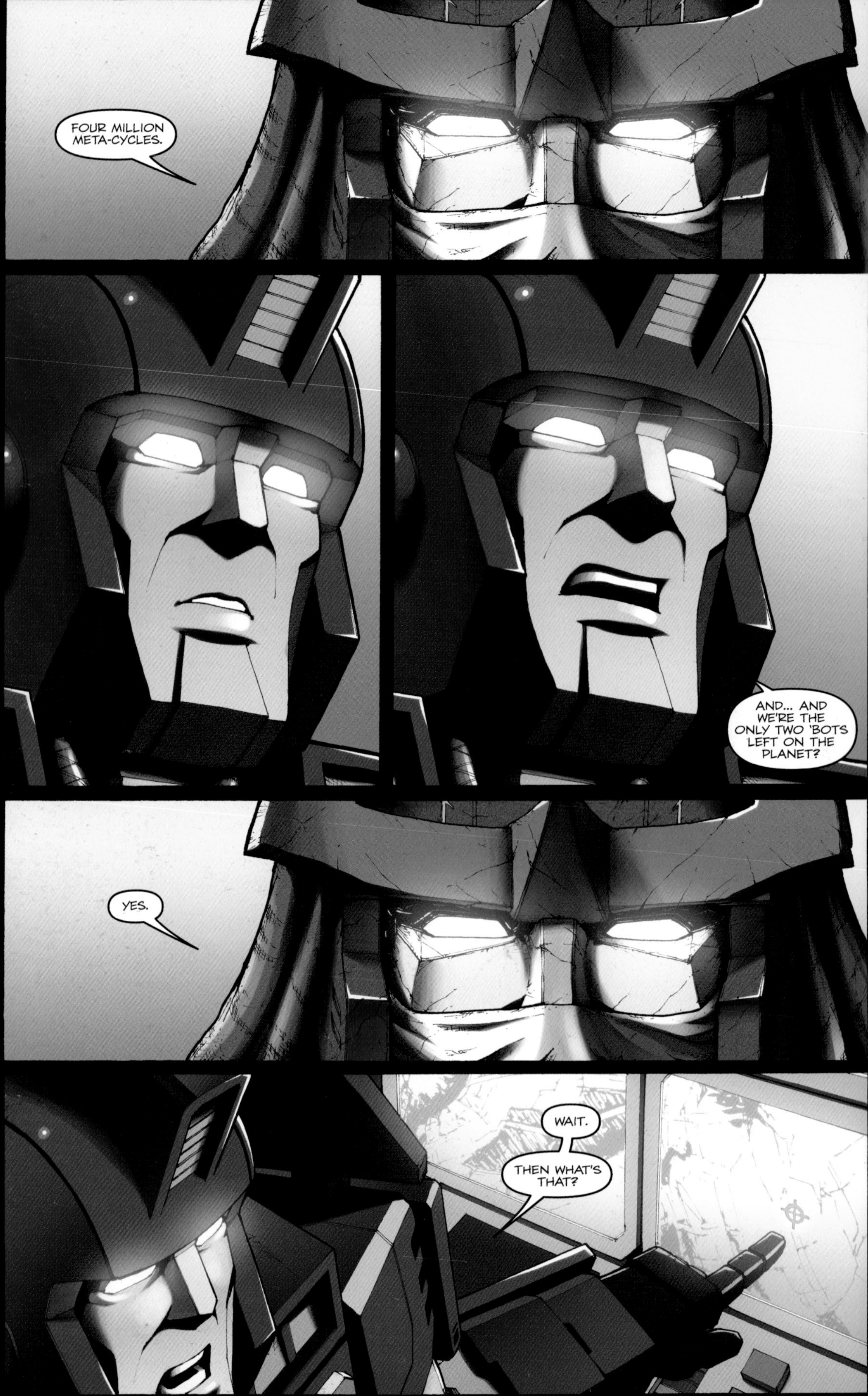
FOUR MILLION META-CYCLES.
AND... AND WE'RE THE ONLY TWO 'BOTS LEFT ON THE PLANET?
YES.
WAIT.
THEN WHAT'S THAT?

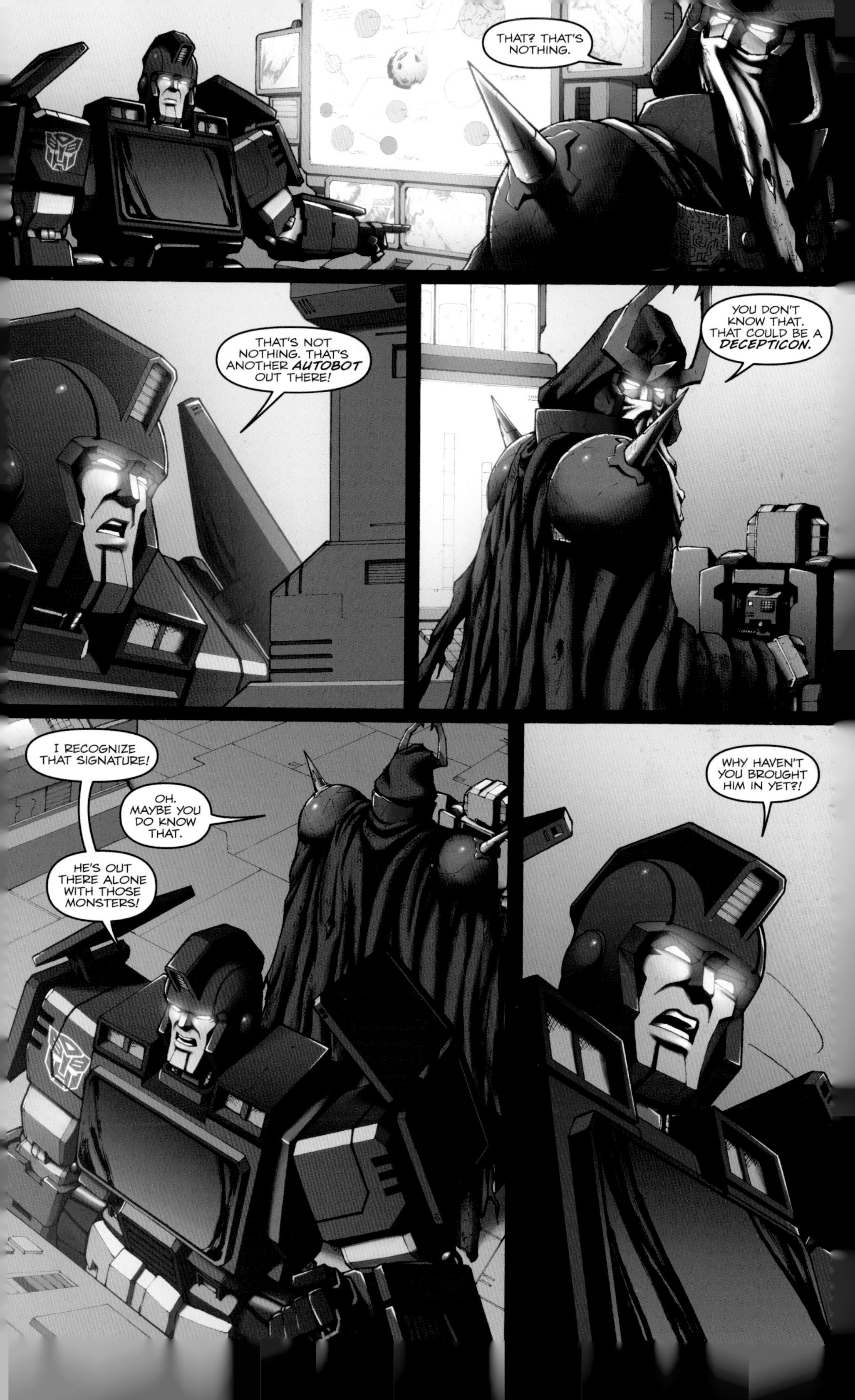
THAT? THAT'S NOTHING.
THAT'S NOT NOTHING. THAT'S ANOTHER AUTOBOT OUT THERE!
YOU DON'T KNOW THAT. THAT COULD BE A DECEPTICON.
I RECOGNIZE THAT SIGNATURE!
OH. MAYBE YOU DO KNOW THAT.
HE'S OUT THERE ALONE WITH THOSE MONSTERS!
WHY HAVEN'T YOU BROUGHT HIM IN YET?!

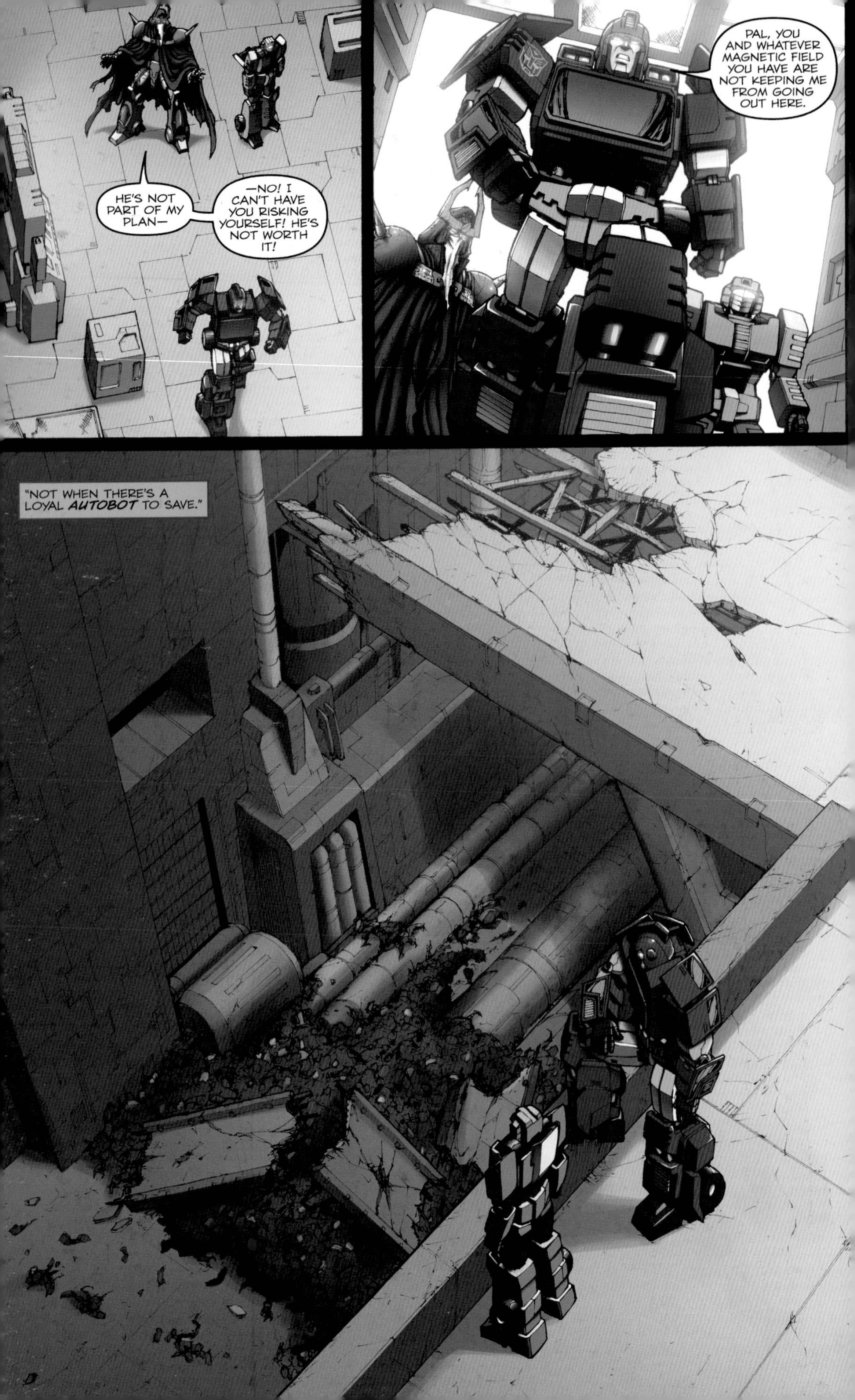
HE'S NOT PART OF MY PLAN—
—NO! I CAN'T HAVE YOU RISKING YOURSELF! HE'S NOT WORTH IT!
PAL, YOU AND WHATEVER MAGNETIC FIELD YOU HAVE ARE NOT KEEPING ME FROM GOING OUT HERE.
"NOT WHEN THERE'S A LOYAL AUTOBOT TO SAVE."

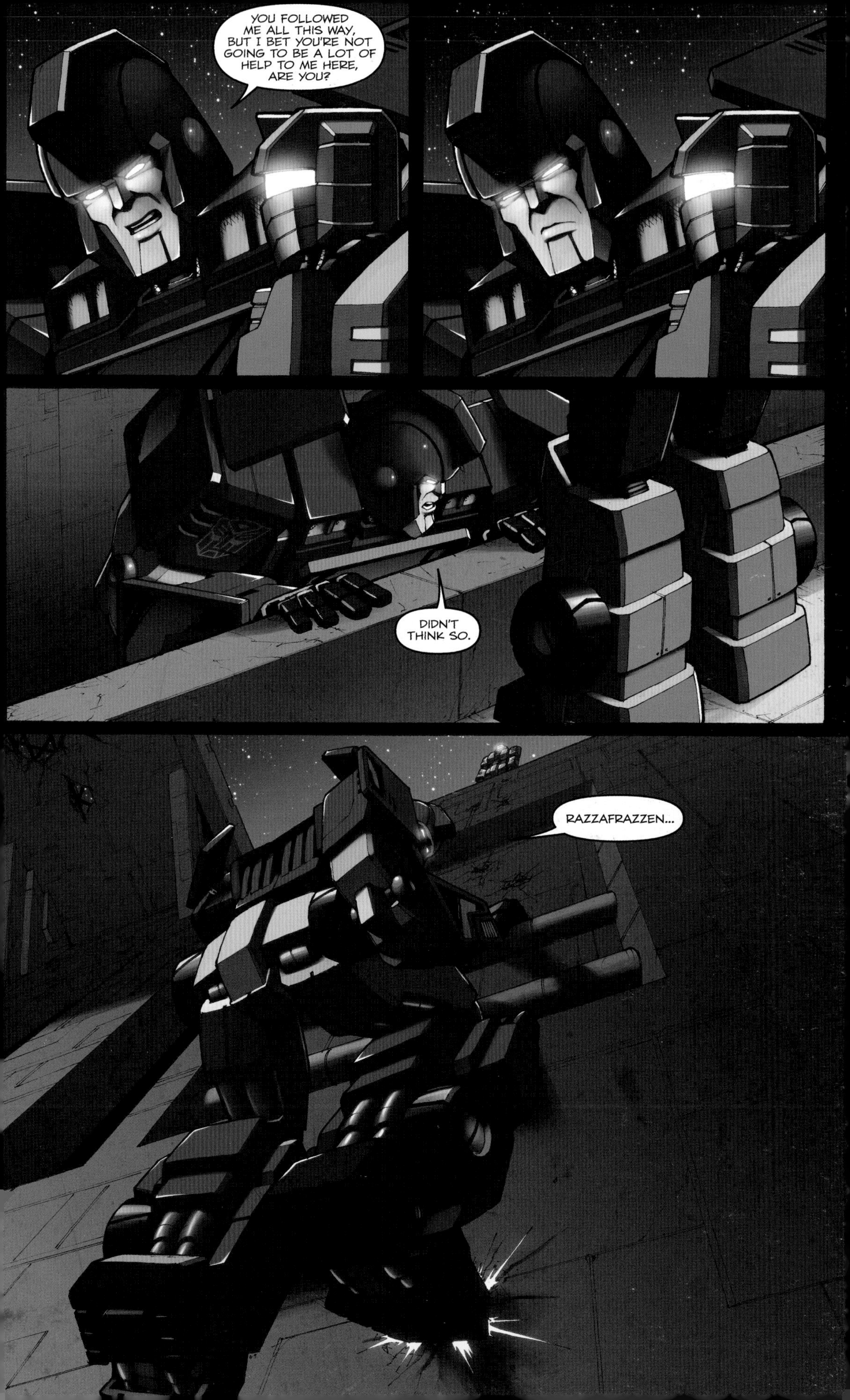
YOU FOLLOWED ME ALL THIS WAY, BUT I BET YOU'RE NOT GOING TO BE A LOT OF HELP TO ME HERE, ARE YOU?
DIDN'T THINK SO.
RAZZAFRAZZEN...

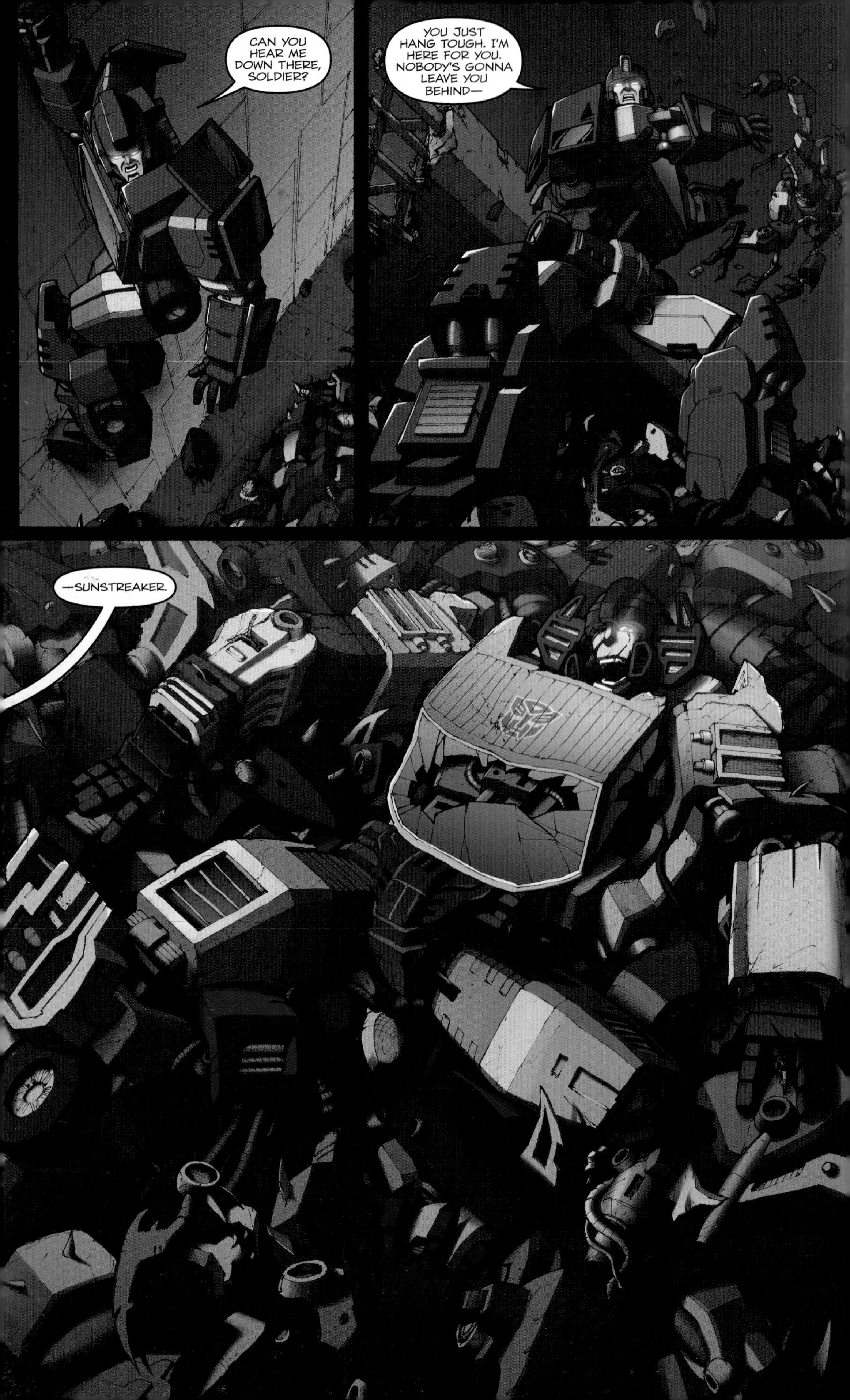
CAN YOU HEAR ME DOWN THERE, SOLDIER?
YOU JUST HANG TOUGH. I'M HERE FOR YOU. NOBODY'S GONNA LEAVE YOU BEHIND—
—SUNSTREAKER.

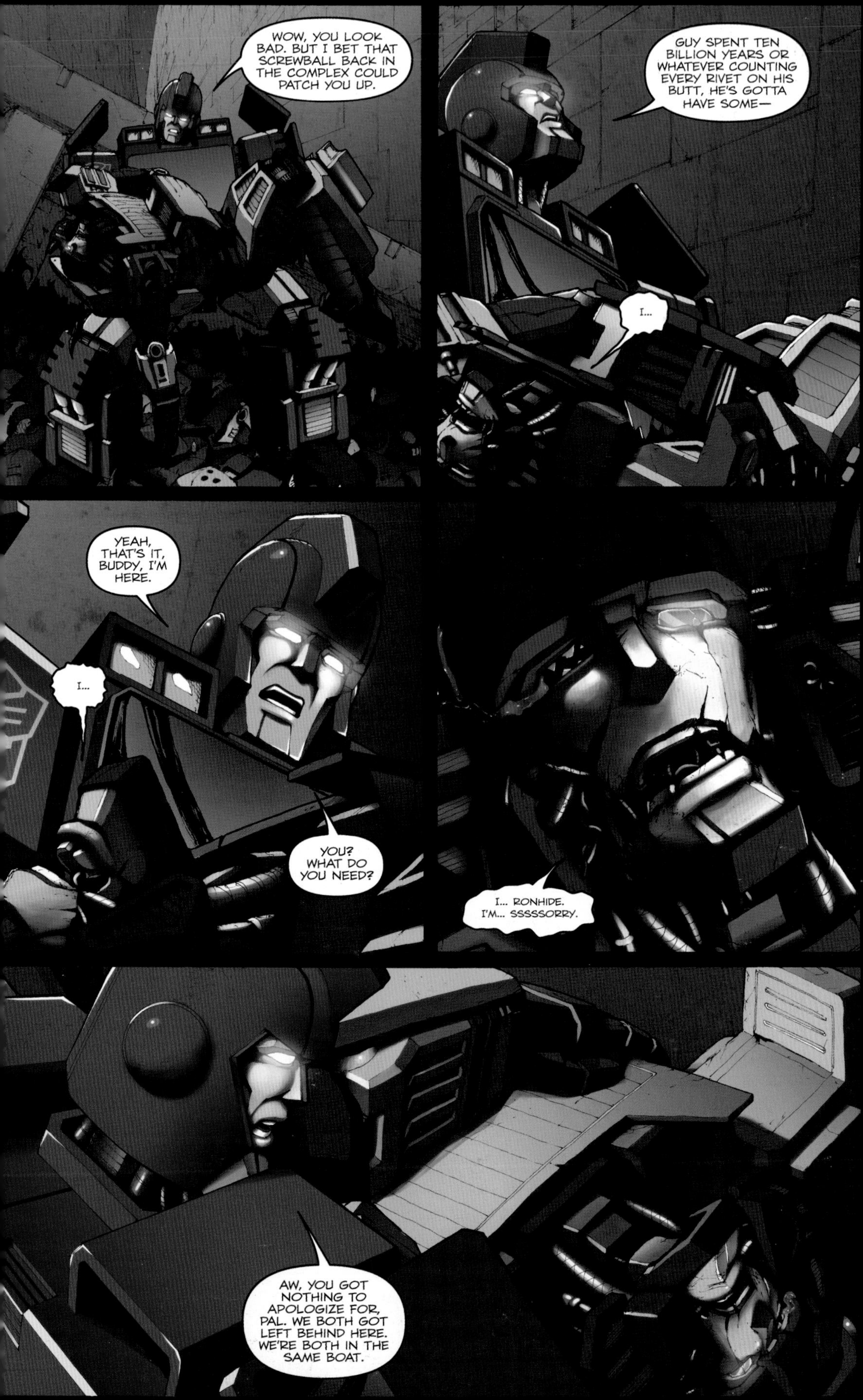
WOW, YOU LOOK BAD. BUT I BET THAT SCREWBALL BACK IN THE COMPLEX COULD PATCH YOU UP.
GUY SPENT TEN BILLION YEARS OR WHATEVER COUNTING EVERY RIVET ON HIS BUTT, HE'S GOTTA HAVE SOME—
I...
YEAH, THAT'S IT, BUDDY, I'M HERE.
I...
YOU? WHAT DO YOU NEED?
I... RONHIDE. I'M... SSSSSORRY.
AW, YOU GOT NOTHING TO APOLOGIZE FOR, PAL. WE BOTH GOT LEFT BEHIND HERE. WE'RE BOTH IN THE SAME BOAT.

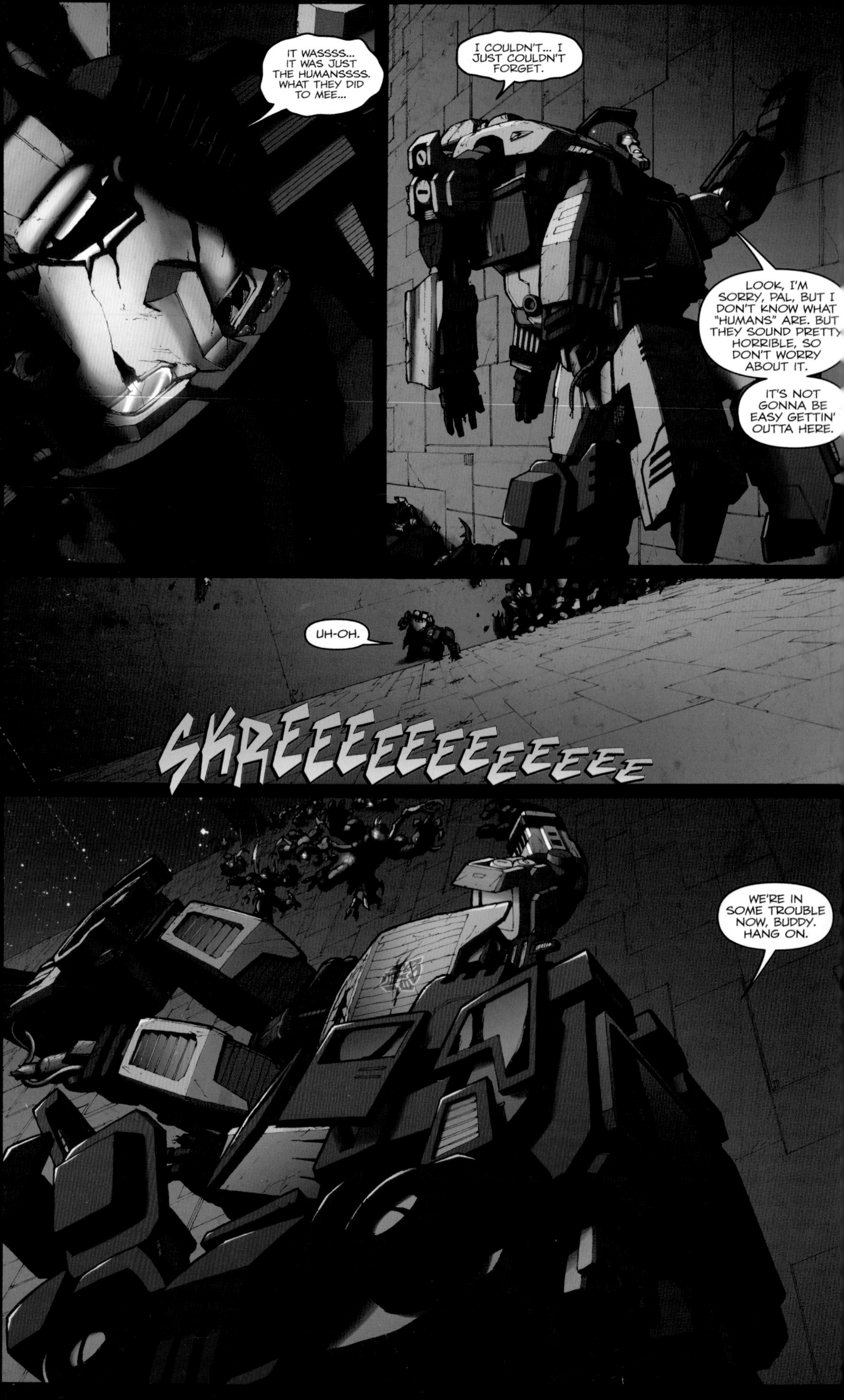
IT WASSSS... IT WAS JUST THE HUMANSSSS. WHAT THEY DID TO MEE...
I COULDN'T... I JUST COULDN'T FORGET.
LOOK, I'M SORRY, PAL, BUT I DON'T KNOW WHAT "HUMANS" ARE. BUT THEY SOUND PRETTY HORRIBLE, SO DON'T WORRY ABOUT IT.
IT'S NOT GONNA BE EASY GETTIN' OUTTA HERE.
UH-OH.
SKREEEEEEEEEEEE
WE'RE IN SOME TROUBLE NOW, BUDDY. HANG ON.

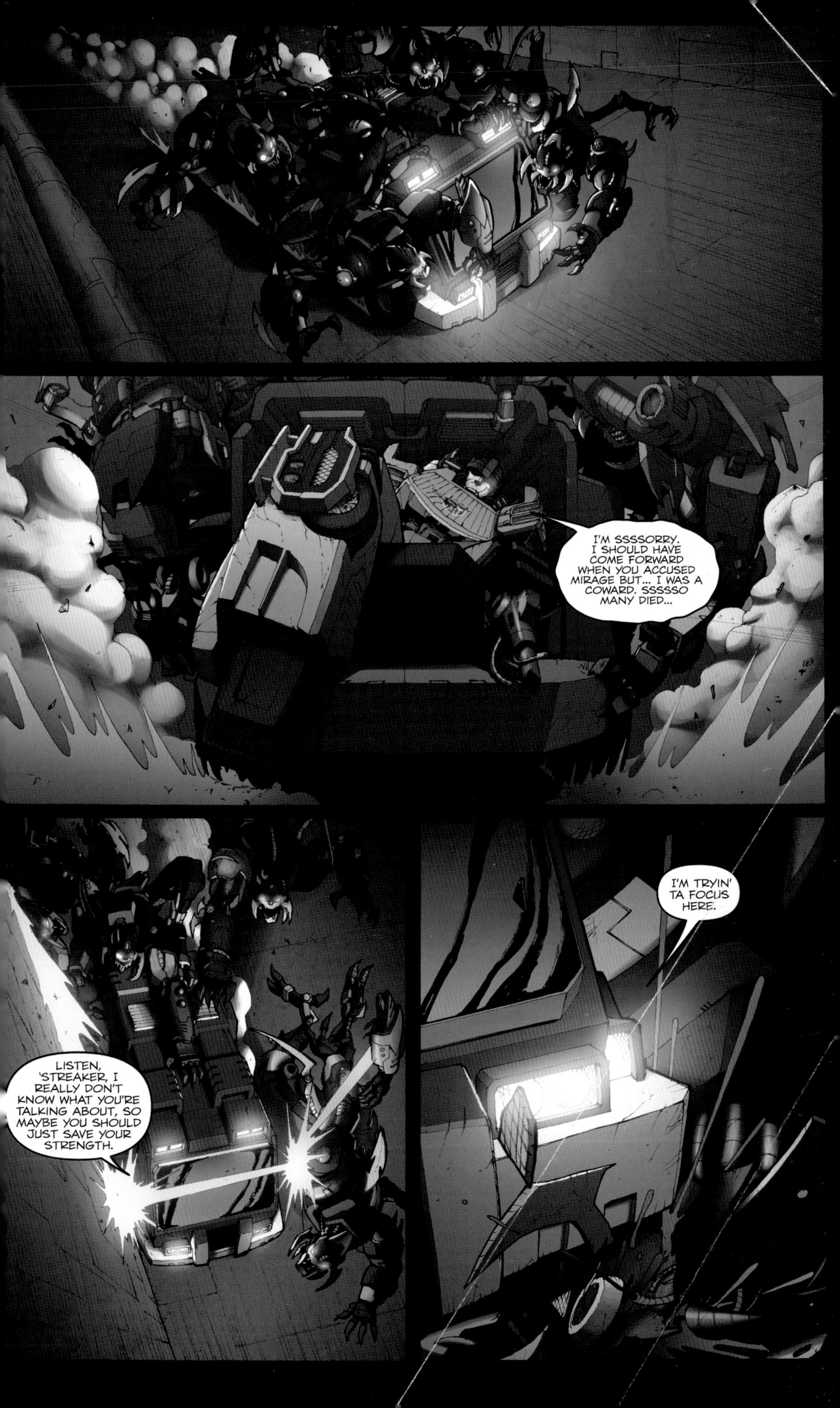
I'M SSSSORRY. I SHOULD HAVE COME FORWARD WHEN YOU ACCUSED MIRAGE BUT... I WAS A COWARD. SSSSSO MANY DIED...
LISTEN, 'STREAKER, I REALLY DON'T KNOW WHAT YOU'RE TALKING ABOUT, SO MAYBE YOU SHOULD JUST SAVE YOUR STRENGTH.
I'M TRYIN' TA FOCUS HERE.

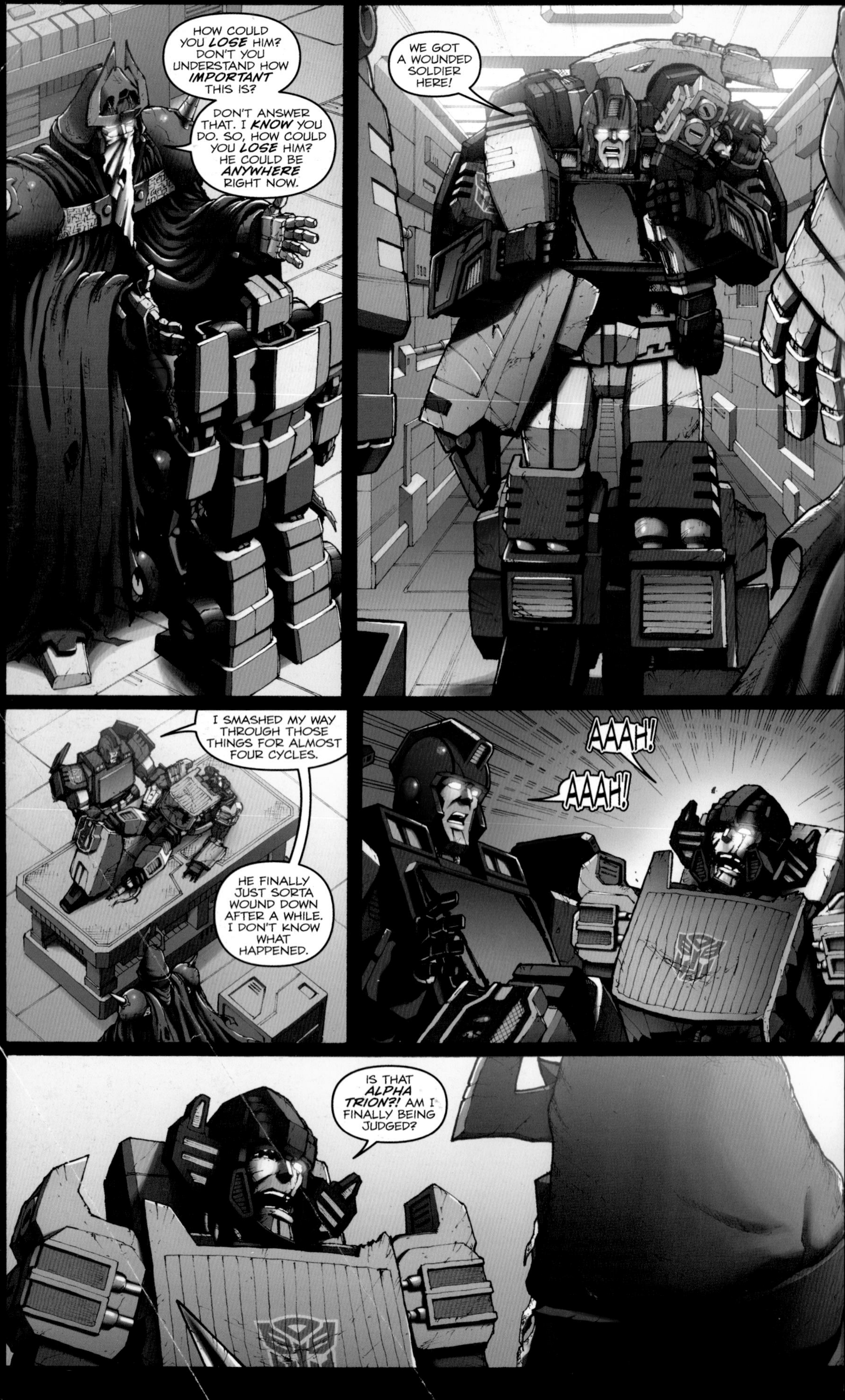
HOW COULD YOU LOSE HIM? DON'T YOU UNDERSTAND HOW IMPORTANT THIS IS?
DON'T ANSWER THAT. I KNOW YOU DO. SO, HOW COULD YOU LOSE HIM? HE COULD BE ANYWHERE RIGHT NOW.
WE GOT A WOUNDED SOLDIER HERE!
I SMASHED MY WAY THROUGH THOSE THINGS FOR ALMOST FOUR CYCLES.
HE FINALLY JUST SORTA WOUND DOWN AFTER A WHILE. I DON'T KNOW WHAT HAPPENED.
AAAH!
AAAH!
IS THAT ALPHA TRION?! AM I FINALLY BEING JUDGED?

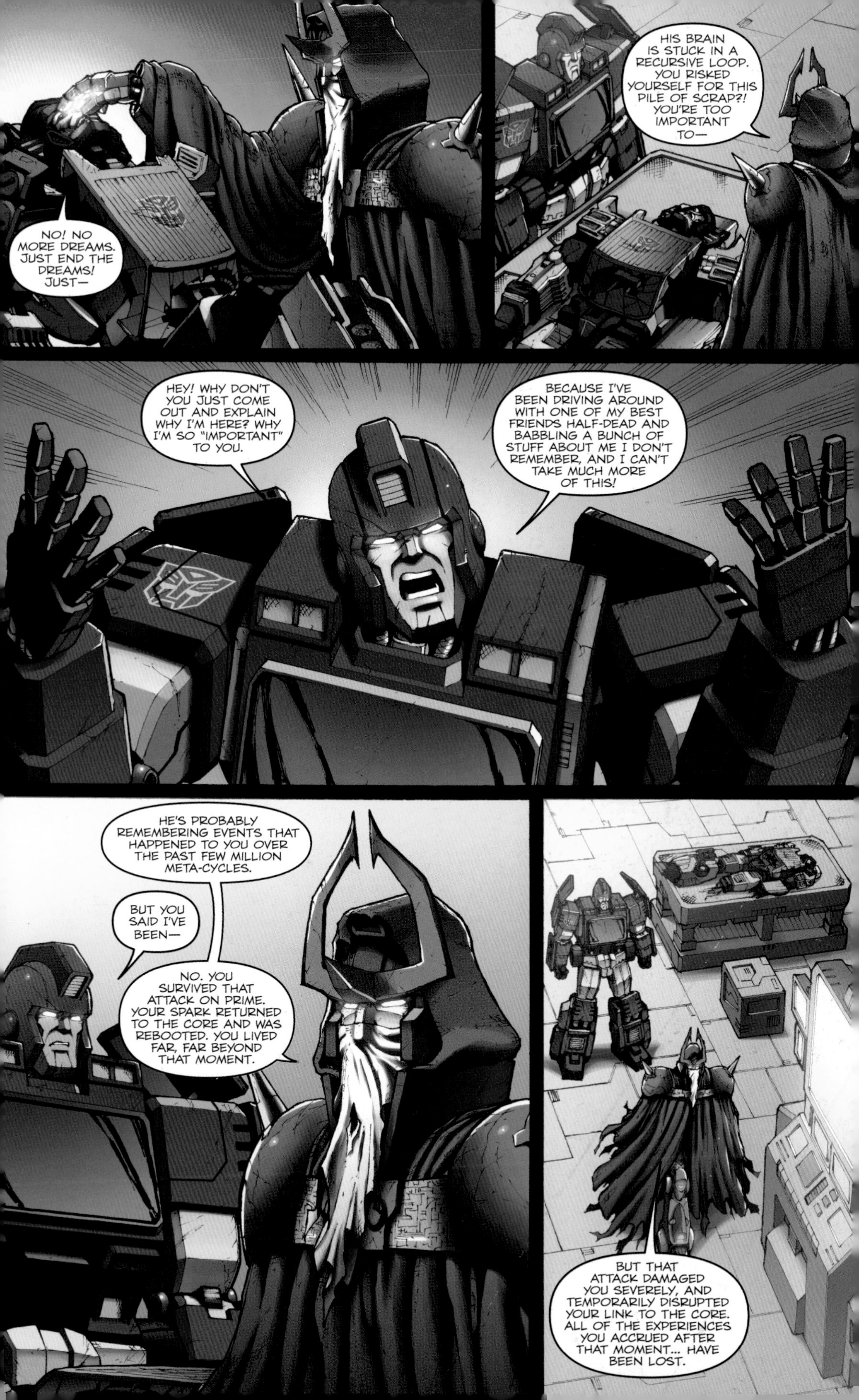
NO! NO MORE DREAMS. JUST END THE DREAMS! JUST—
HIS BRAIN IS STUCK IN A RECURSIVE LOOP. YOU RISKED YOURSELF FOR THIS PILE OF SCRAP?! YOU'RE TOO IMPORTANT TO—
HEY! WHY DON'T YOU JUST COME OUT AND EXPLAIN WHY I'M HERE? WHY I'M SO "IMPORTANT" TO YOU.
BECAUSE I'VE BEEN DRIVING AROUND WITH ONE OF MY BEST FRIENDS HALF-DEAD AND BABBLING A BUNCH OF STUFF ABOUT ME I DON'T REMEMBER, AND I CAN'T TAKE MUCH MORE OF THIS!
HE'S PROBABLY REMEMBERING EVENTS THAT HAPPENED TO YOU OVER THE PAST FEW MILLION META-CYCLES.
BUT YOU SAID I'VE BEEN—
NO. YOU SURVIVED THAT ATTACK ON PRIME. YOUR SPARK RETURNED TO THE CORE AND WAS REBOOTED. YOU LIVED FAR, FAR BEYOND THAT MOMENT.
BUT THAT ATTACK DAMAGED YOU SEVERELY, AND TEMPORARILY DISRUPTED YOUR LINK TO THE CORE. ALL OF THE EXPERIENCES YOU ACCRUED AFTER THAT MOMENT... HAVE BEEN LOST.

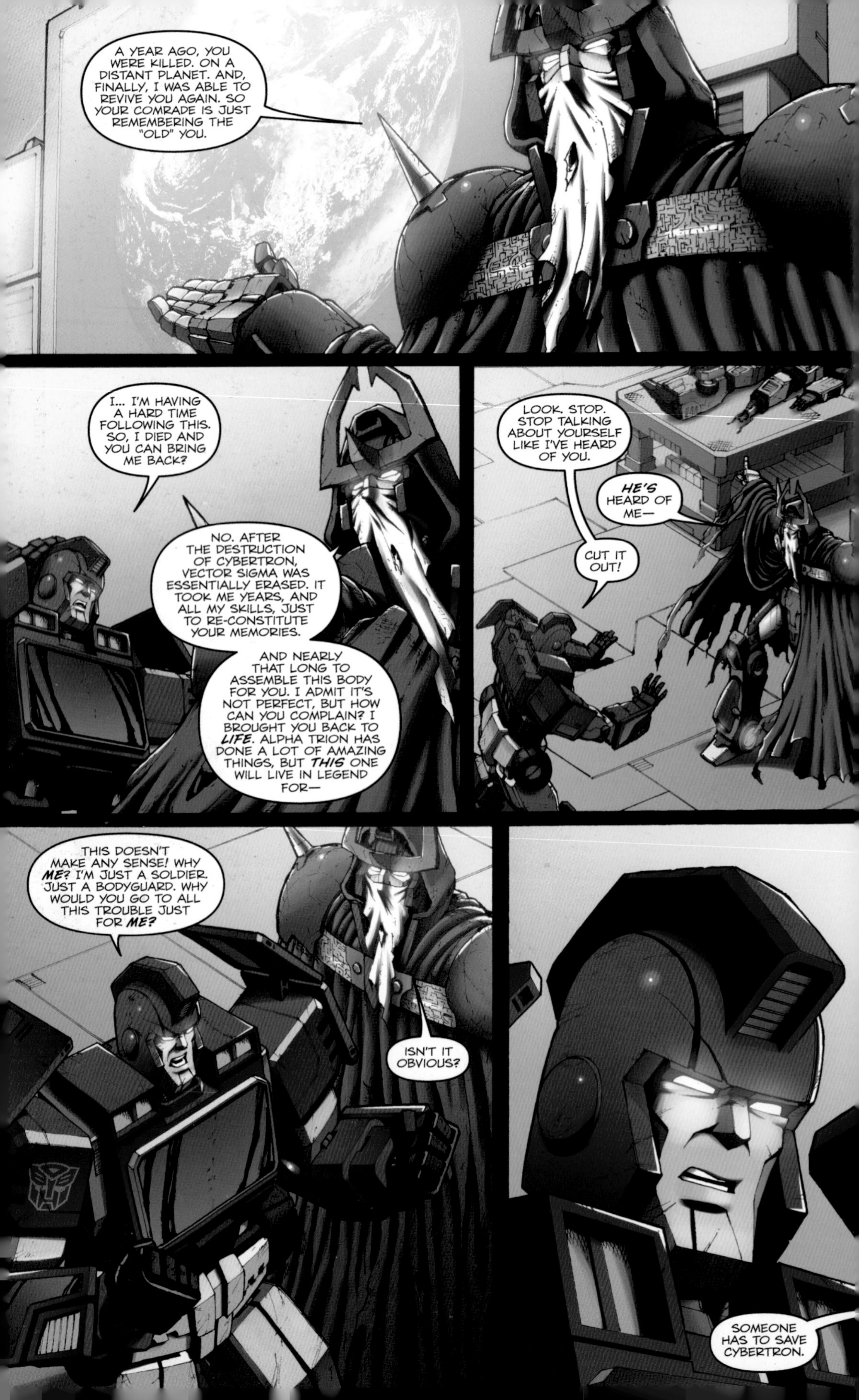
A YEAR AGO, YOU WERE KILLED. ON A DISTANT PLANET. AND, FINALLY, I WAS ABLE TO REVIVE YOU AGAIN. SO YOUR COMRADE IS JUST REMEMBERING THE "OLD" YOU.
I... I'M HAVING A HARD TIME FOLLOWING THIS. SO, I DIED AND YOU CAN BRING ME BACK?
NO. AFTER THE DESTRUCTION OF CYBERTRON, VECTOR SIGMA WAS ESSENTIALLY ERASED. IT TOOK ME YEARS, AND ALL MY SKILLS, JUST TO RE-CONSTITUTE YOUR MEMORIES.
AND NEARLY THAT LONG TO ASSEMBLE THIS BODY FOR YOU. I ADMIT IT'S NOT PERFECT, BUT HOW CAN YOU COMPLAIN? I BROUGHT YOU BACK TO *LIFE*. ALPHA TRION HAS DONE A LOT OF AMAZING THINGS, BUT *THIS* ONE WILL LIVE IN LEGEND FOR—
LOOK. STOP. STOP TALKING ABOUT YOURSELF LIKE I'VE HEARD OF YOU.
HE'S HEARD OF ME—
CUT IT OUT!
THIS DOESN'T MAKE ANY SENSE! WHY *ME*? I'M JUST A SOLDIER. JUST A BODYGUARD. WHY WOULD YOU GO TO ALL THIS TROUBLE JUST FOR *ME*?
ISN'T IT OBVIOUS?
SOMEONE HAS TO SAVE CYBERTRON.

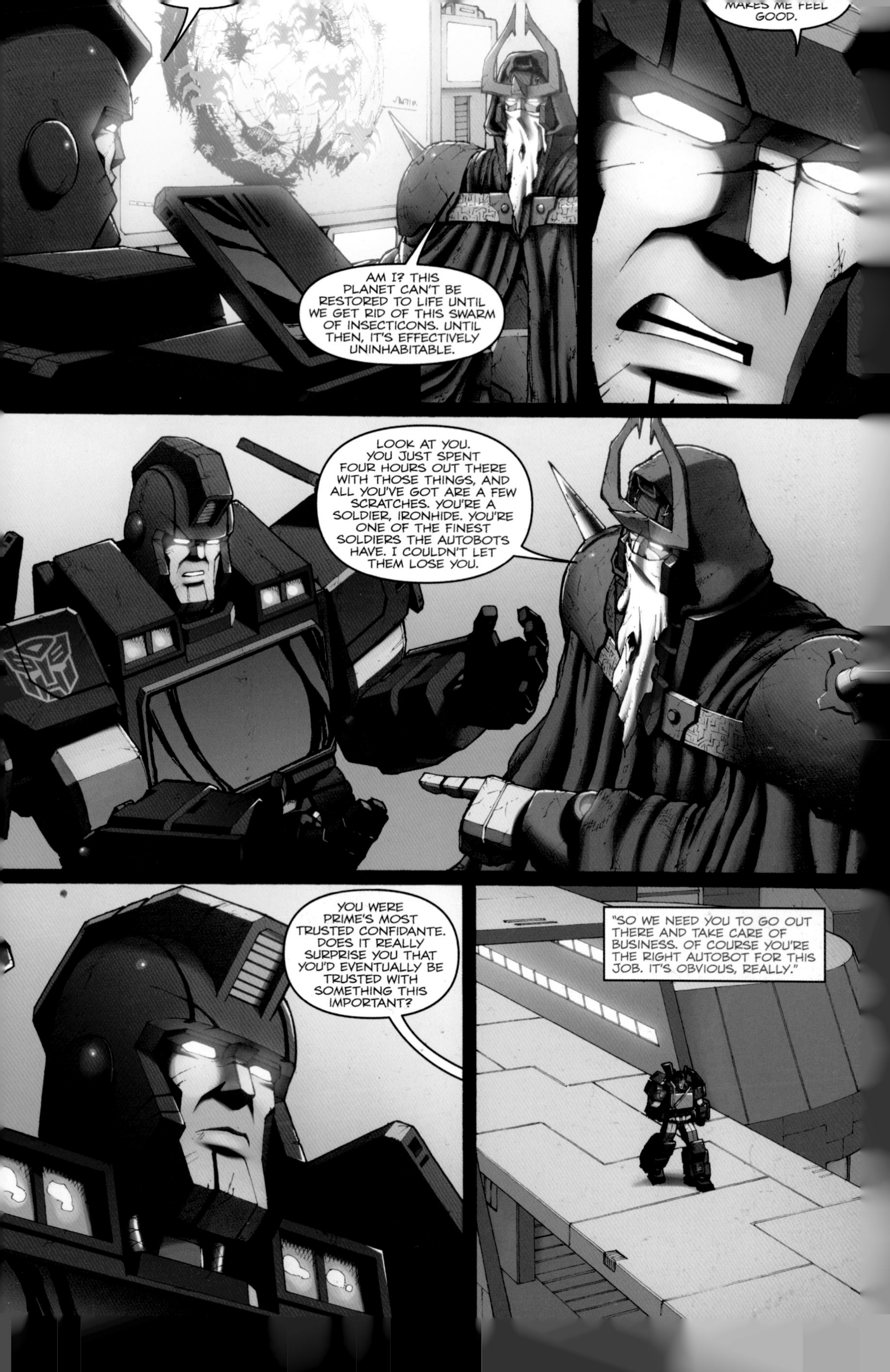
MAKES ME FEEL GOOD.
AM I? THIS PLANET CAN'T BE RESTORED TO LIFE UNTIL WE GET RID OF THIS SWARM OF INSECTICONS. UNTIL THEN, IT'S EFFECTIVELY UNINHABITABLE.
LOOK AT YOU. YOU JUST SPENT FOUR HOURS OUT THERE WITH THOSE THINGS, AND ALL YOU'VE GOT ARE A FEW SCRATCHES. YOU'RE A SOLDIER, IRONHIDE. YOU'RE ONE OF THE FINEST SOLDIERS THE AUTOBOTS HAVE. I COULDN'T LET THEM LOSE YOU.
YOU WERE PRIME'S MOST TRUSTED CONFIDANTE. DOES IT REALLY SURPRISE YOU THAT YOU'D EVENTUALLY BE TRUSTED WITH SOMETHING THIS IMPORTANT?
"SO WE NEED YOU TO GO OUT THERE AND TAKE CARE OF BUSINESS. OF COURSE YOU'RE THE RIGHT AUTOBOT FOR THIS JOB. IT'S OBVIOUS, REALLY."

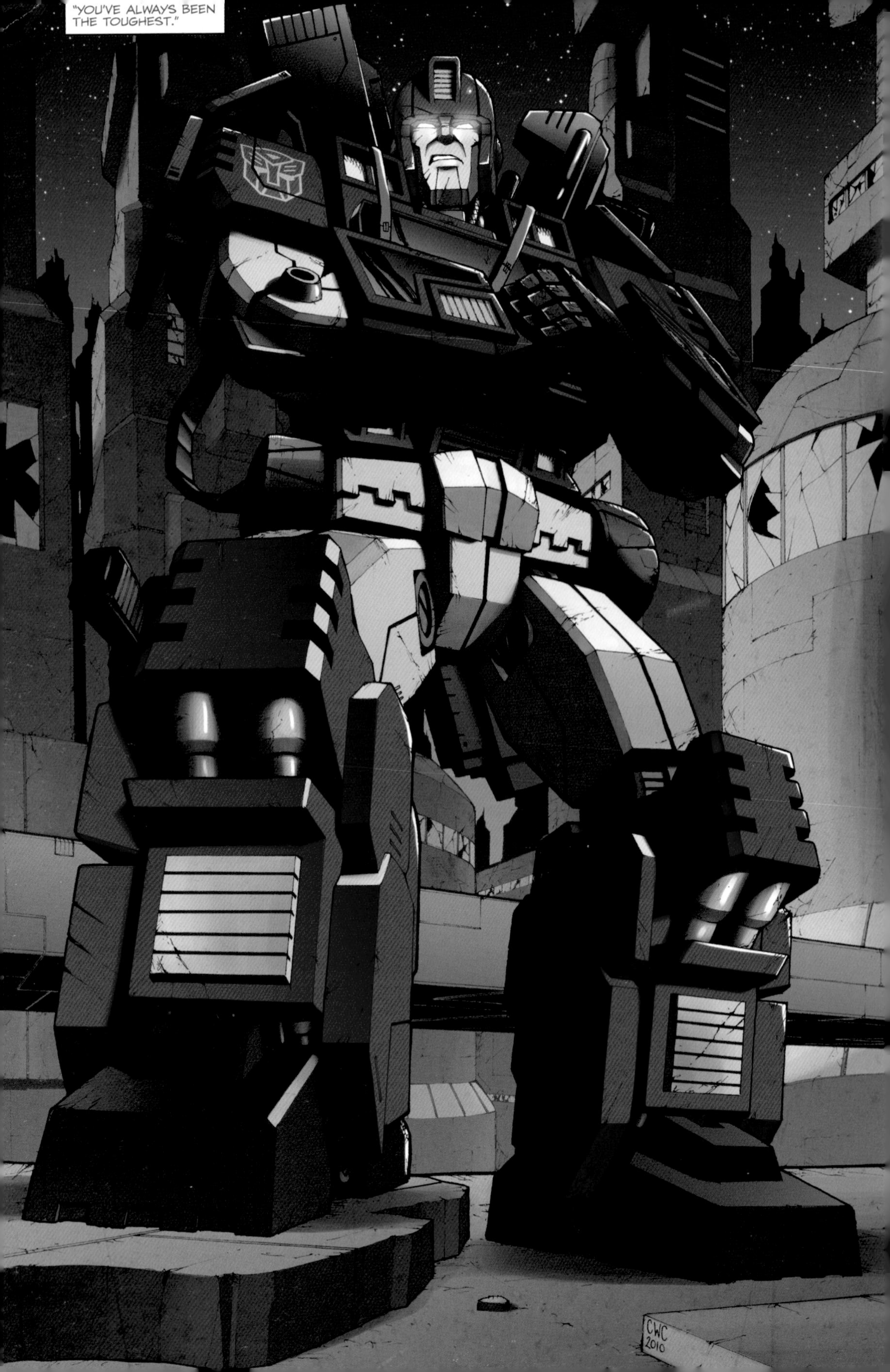
"YOU'VE ALWAYS BEEN THE TOUGHEST."
CWC 2010

CHAPTER FOUR

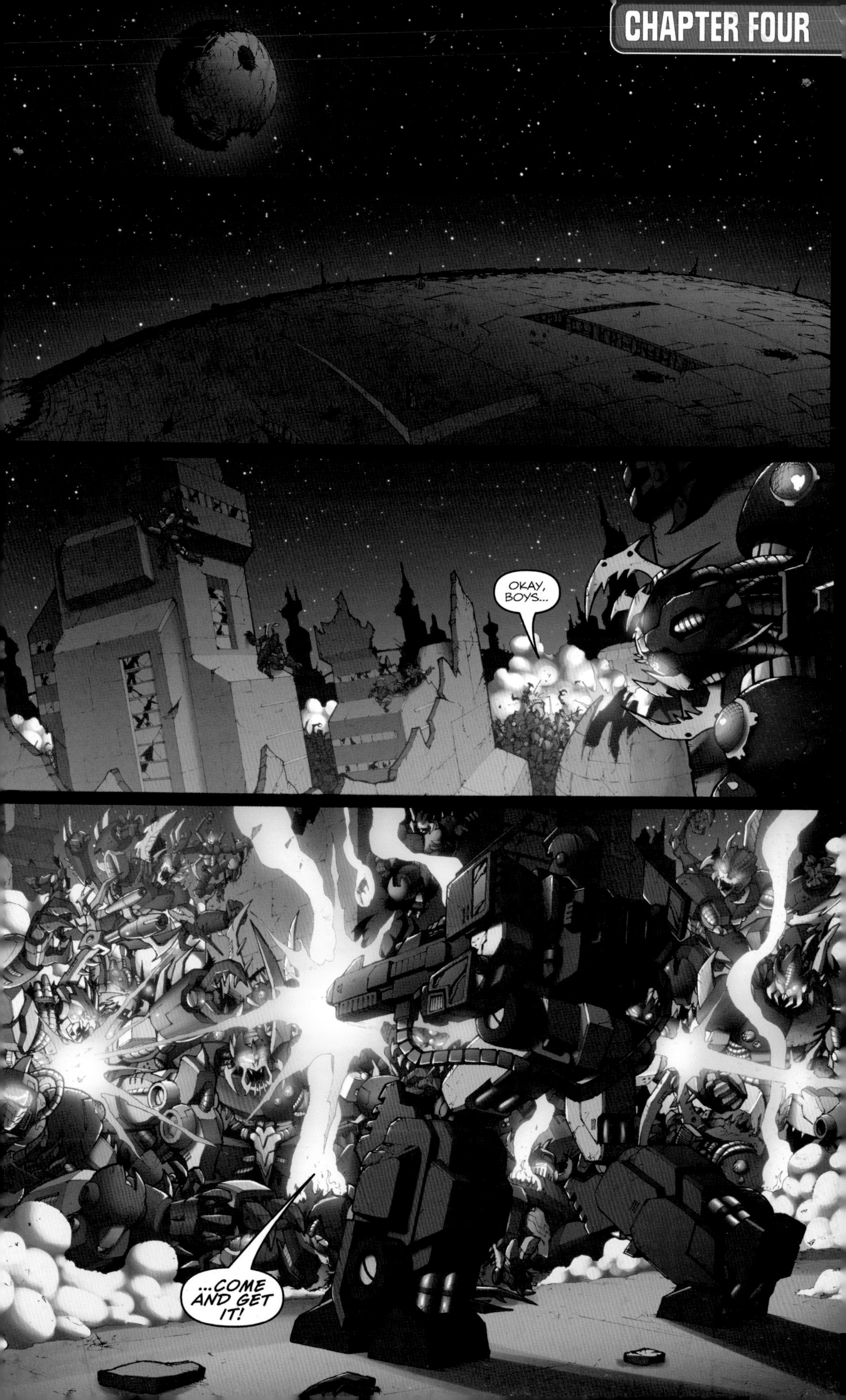
OKAY, BOYS...
...COME AND GET IT!

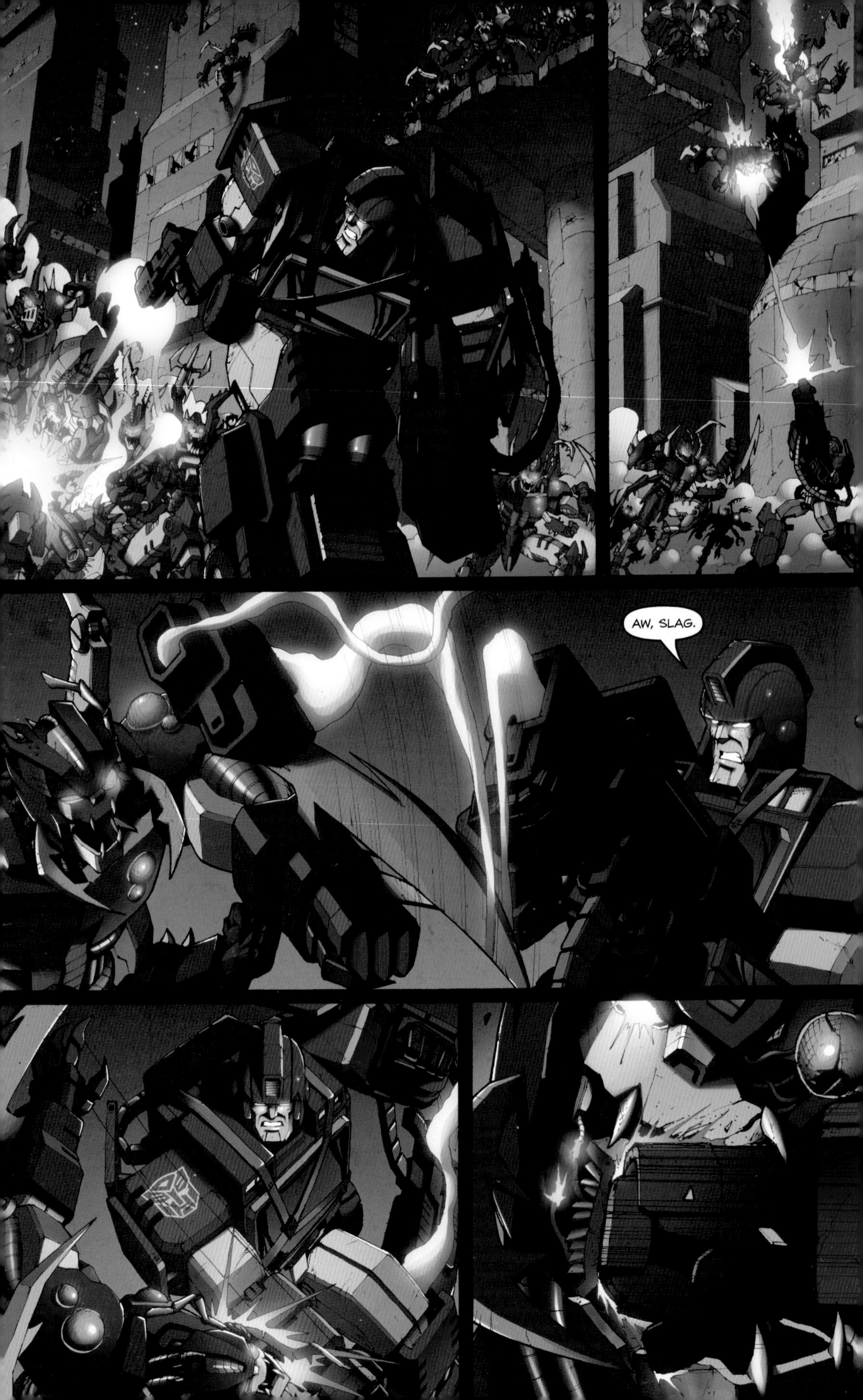
AW, SLAG.

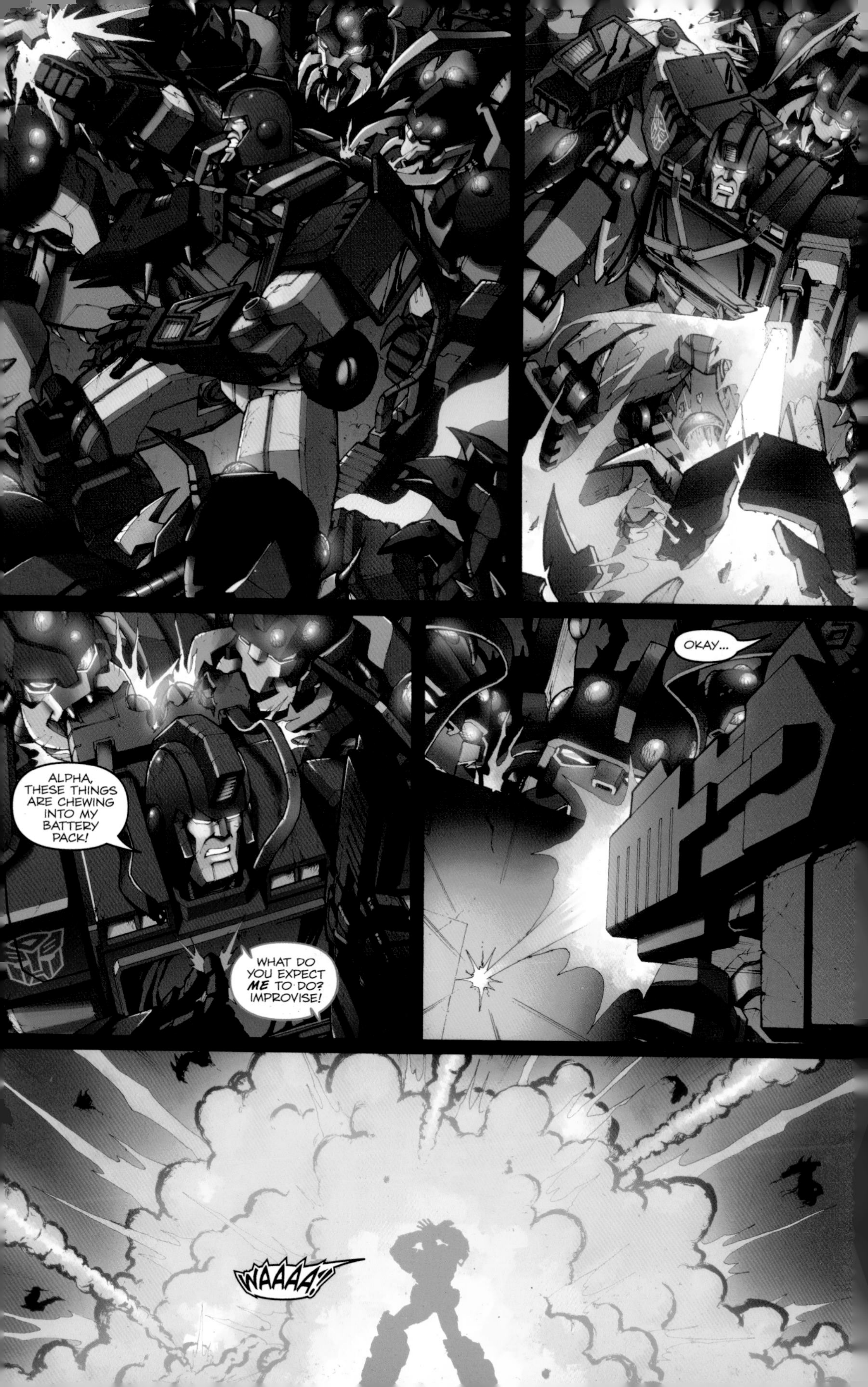
ALPHA, THESE THINGS ARE CHEWING INTO MY BATTERY PACK!
WHAT DO YOU EXPECT *ME* TO DO? IMPROVISE!
OKAY...
WAAAA!

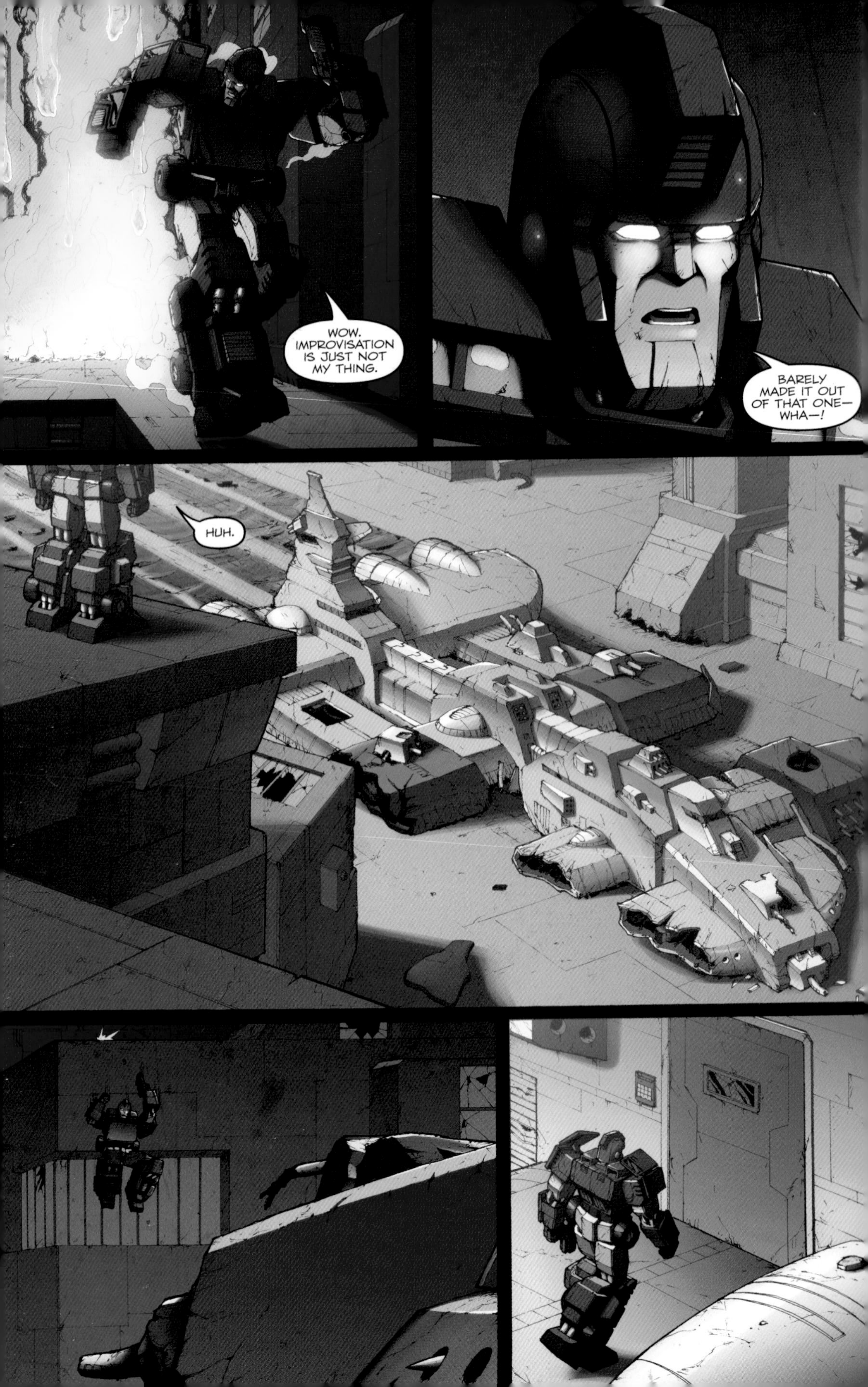
WOW. IMPROVISATION IS JUST NOT MY THING.
BARELY MADE IT OUT OF THAT ONE— WHA—!
HUH.

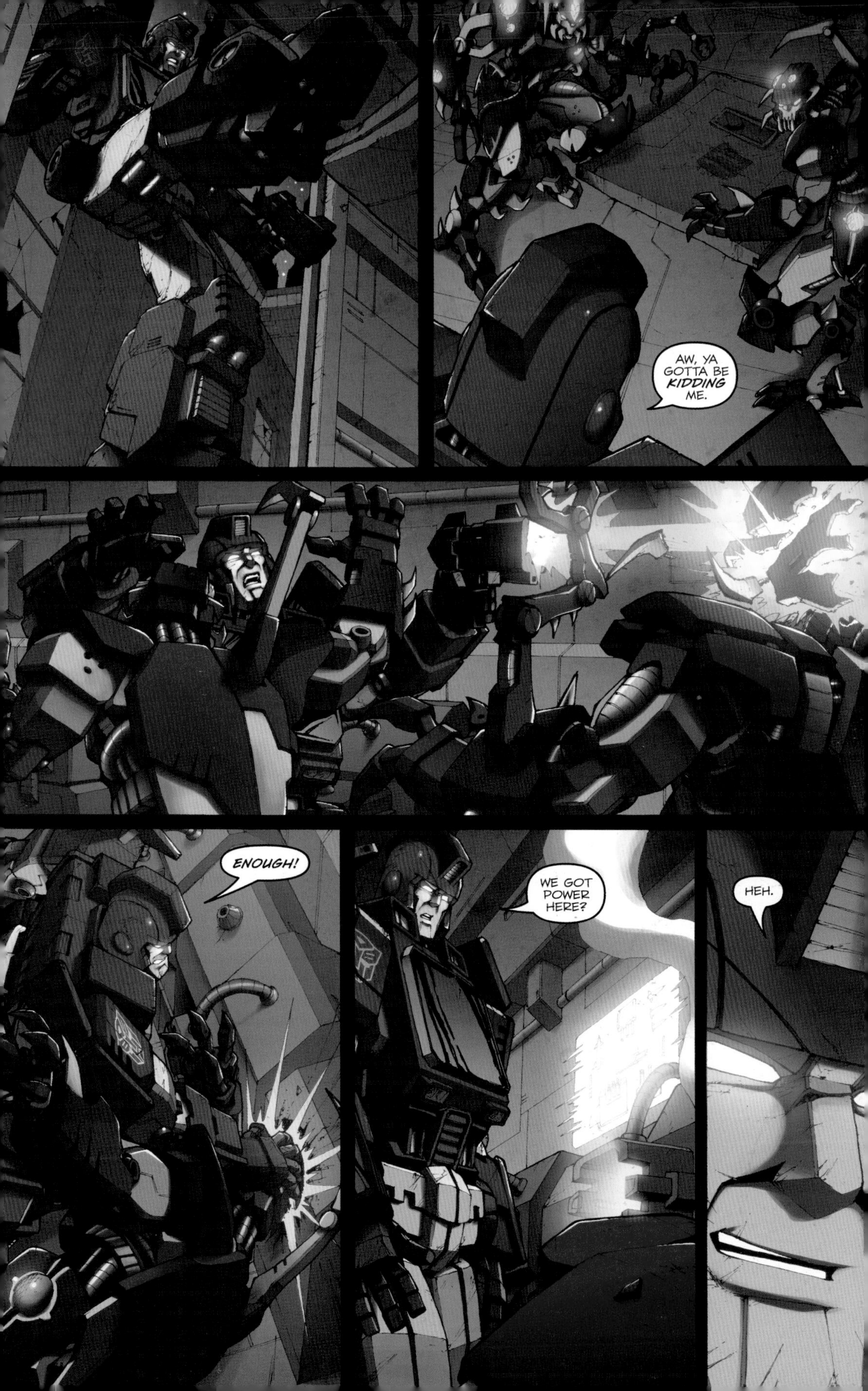
AW, YA GOTTA BE *KIDDING* ME.
ENOUGH!
WE GOT POWER HERE?
HEH.

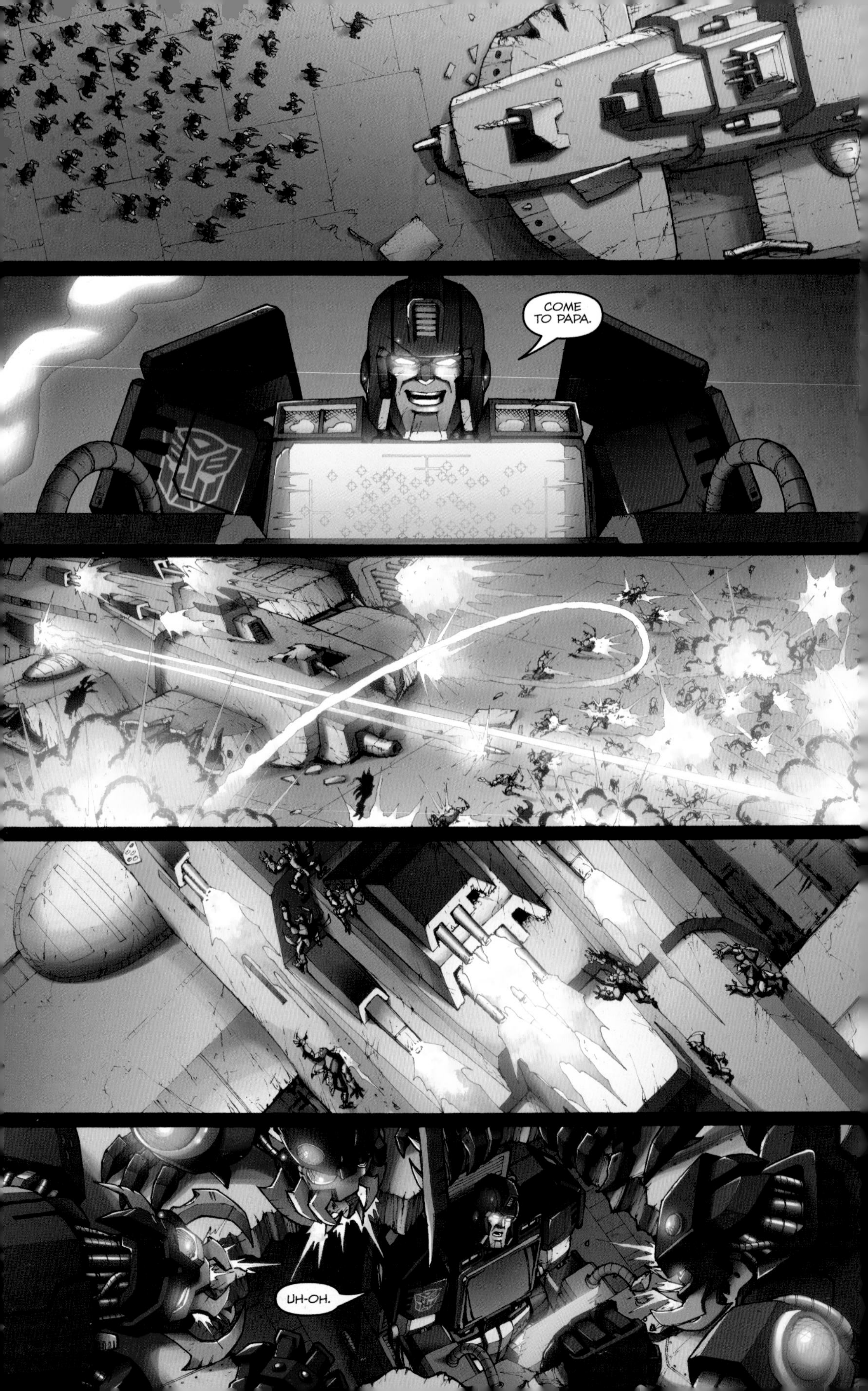
COME TO PAPA.
UH-OH.

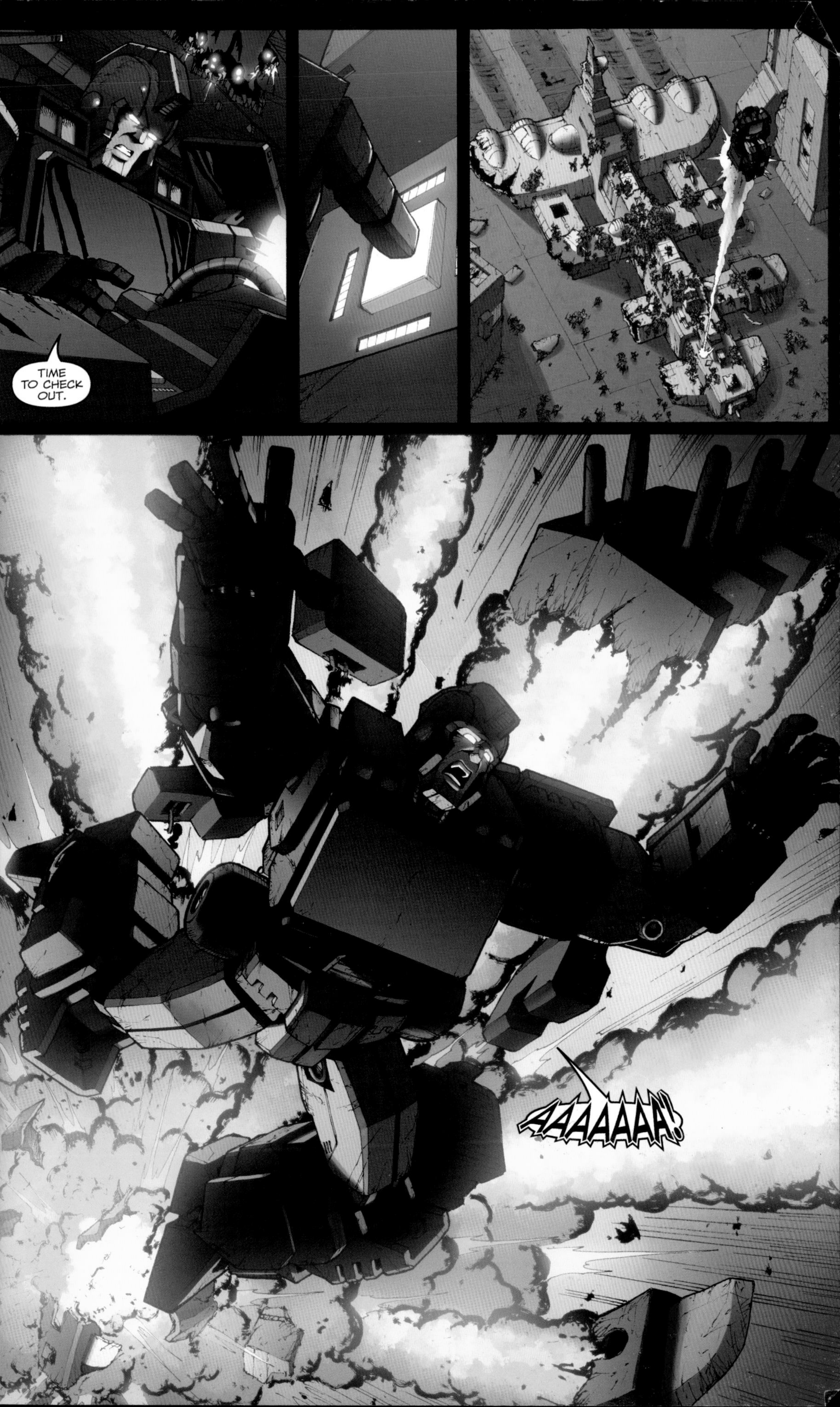
TIME TO CHECK OUT.
AAAAAAA!

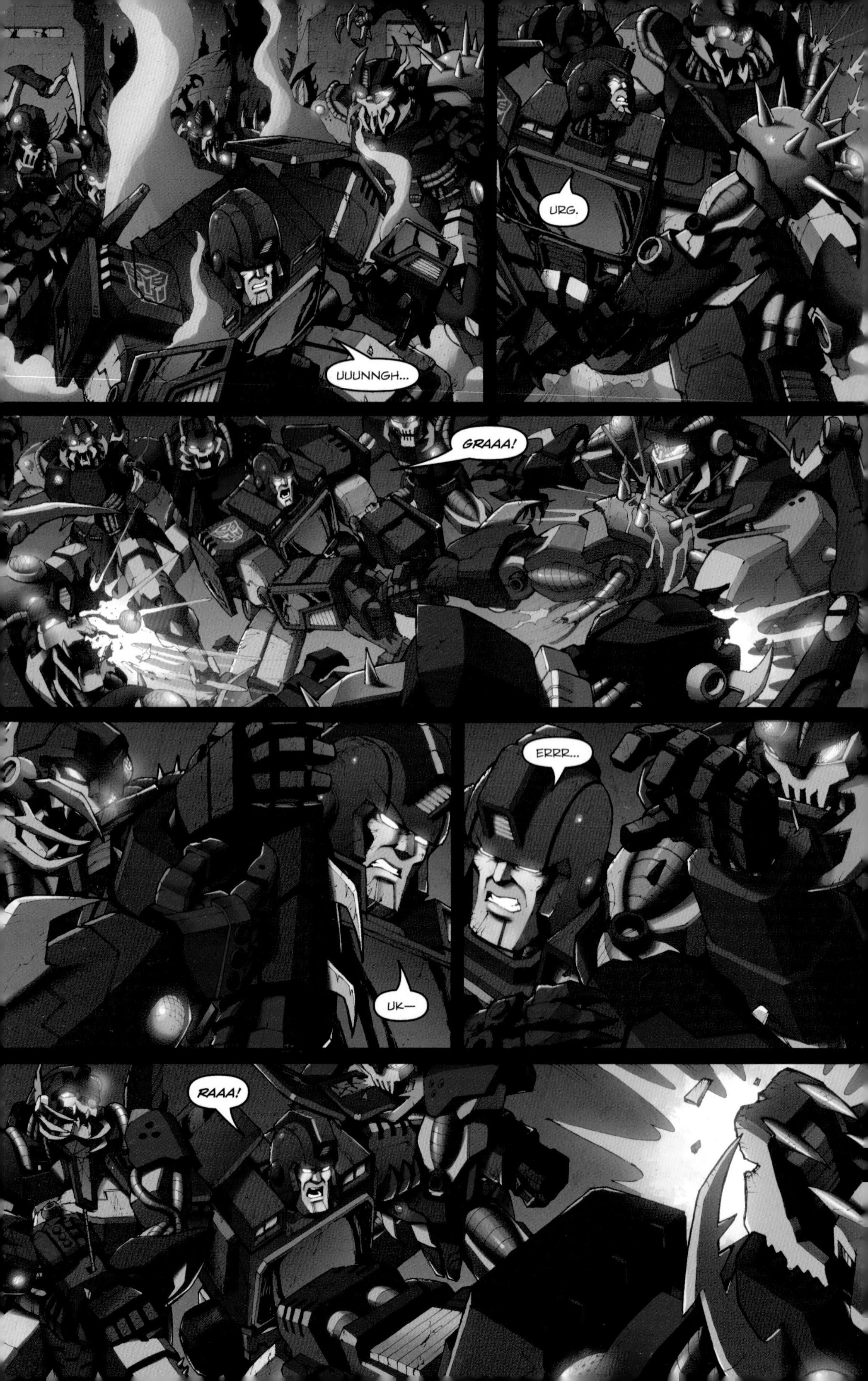
UUUNNGH...
URG.
GRAAA!
UK—
ERRR...
RAAA!

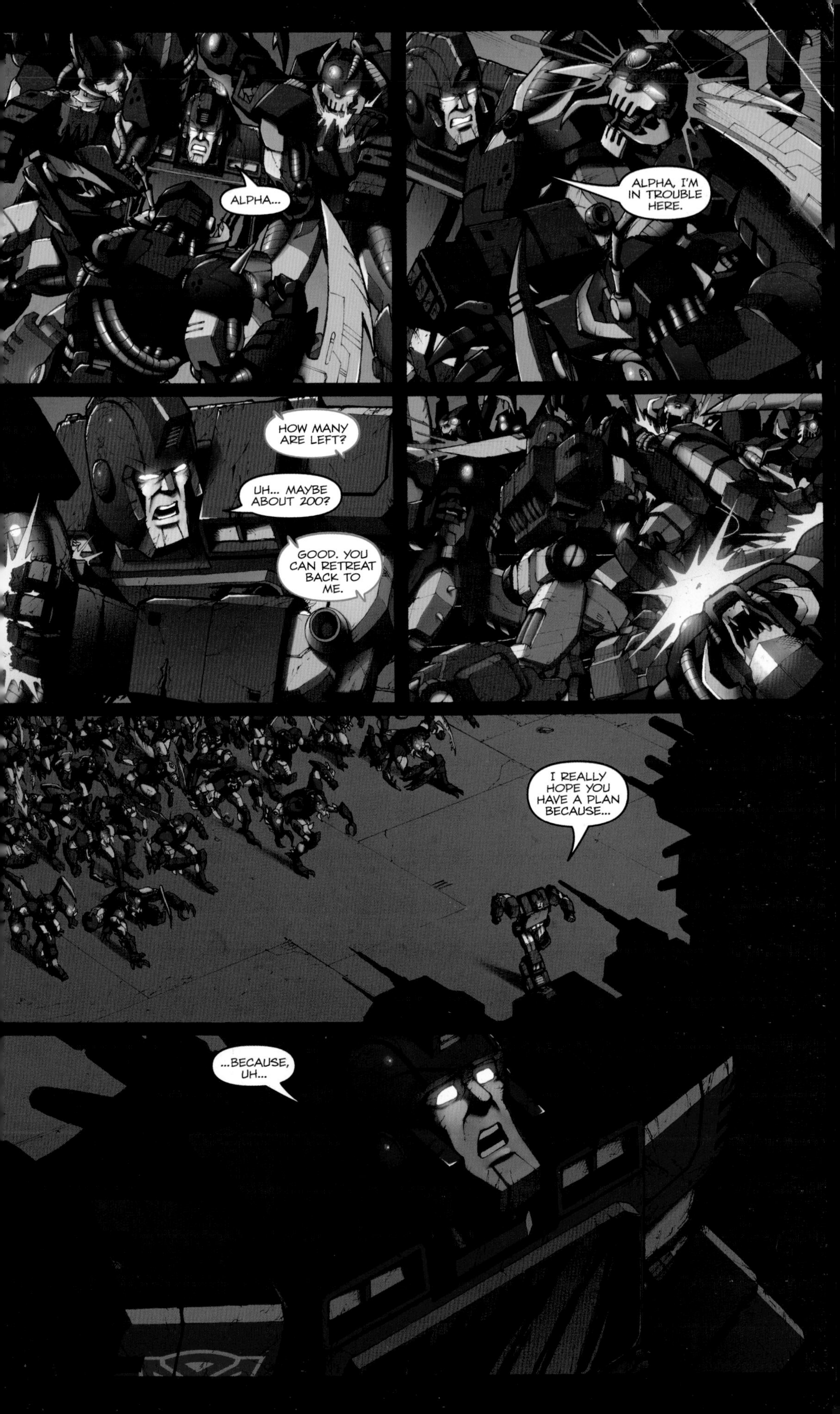
ALPHA...
ALPHA, I'M IN TROUBLE HERE.
HOW MANY ARE LEFT?
UH... MAYBE ABOUT 200?
GOOD. YOU CAN RETREAT BACK TO ME.
I REALLY HOPE YOU HAVE A PLAN BECAUSE...
...BECAUSE, UH...

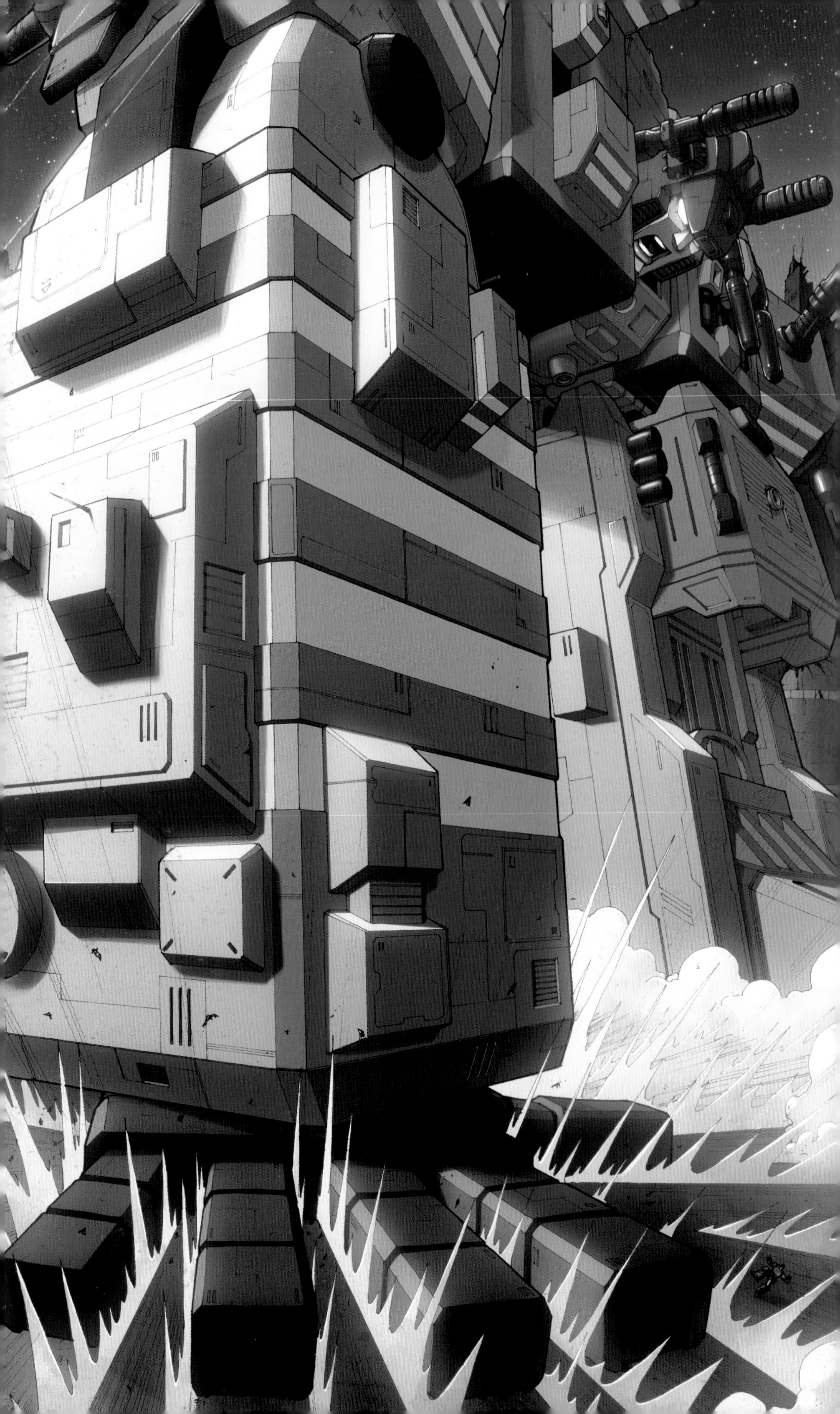

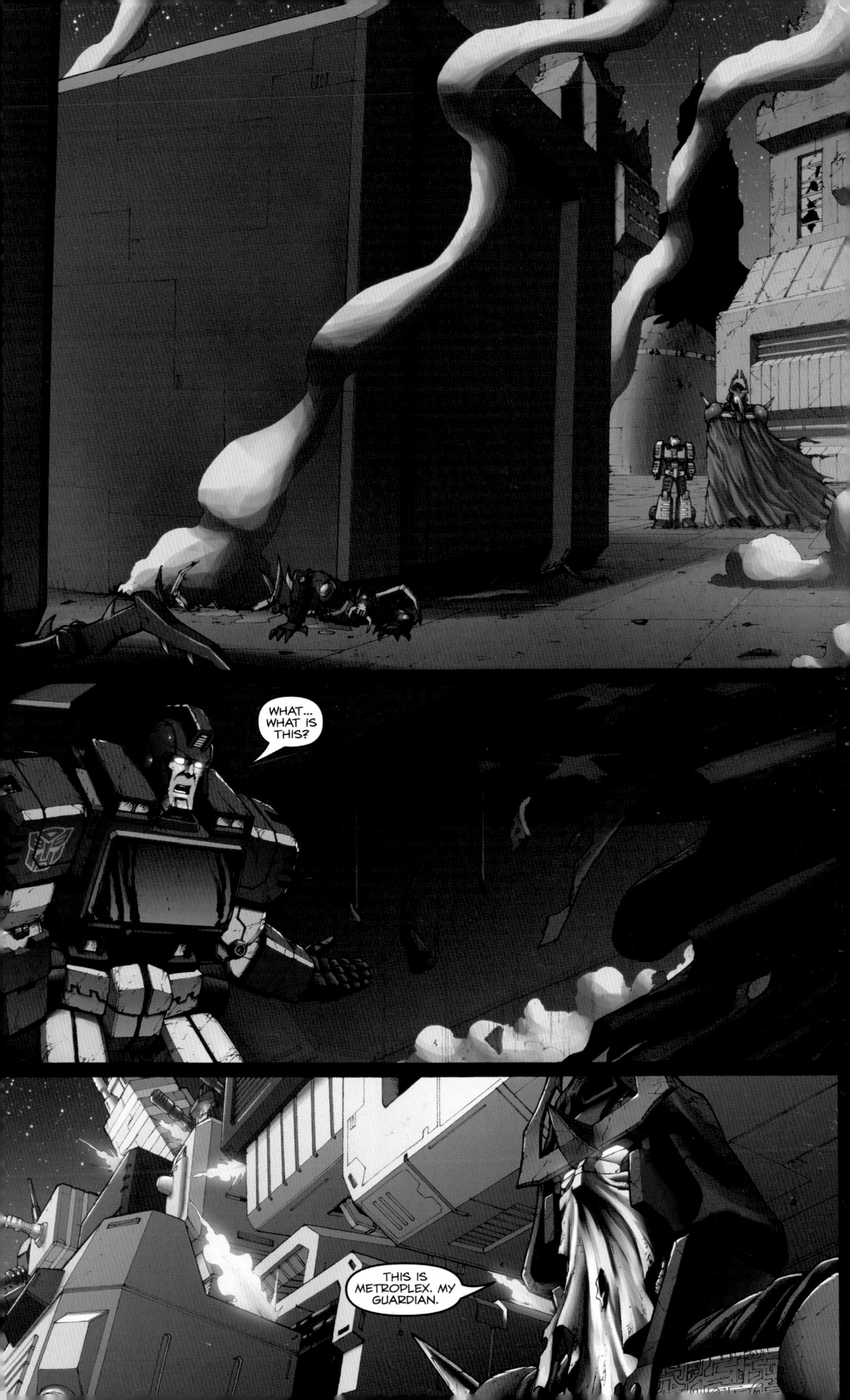
WHAT... WHAT IS THIS?
THIS IS METROPLEX. MY GUARDIAN.

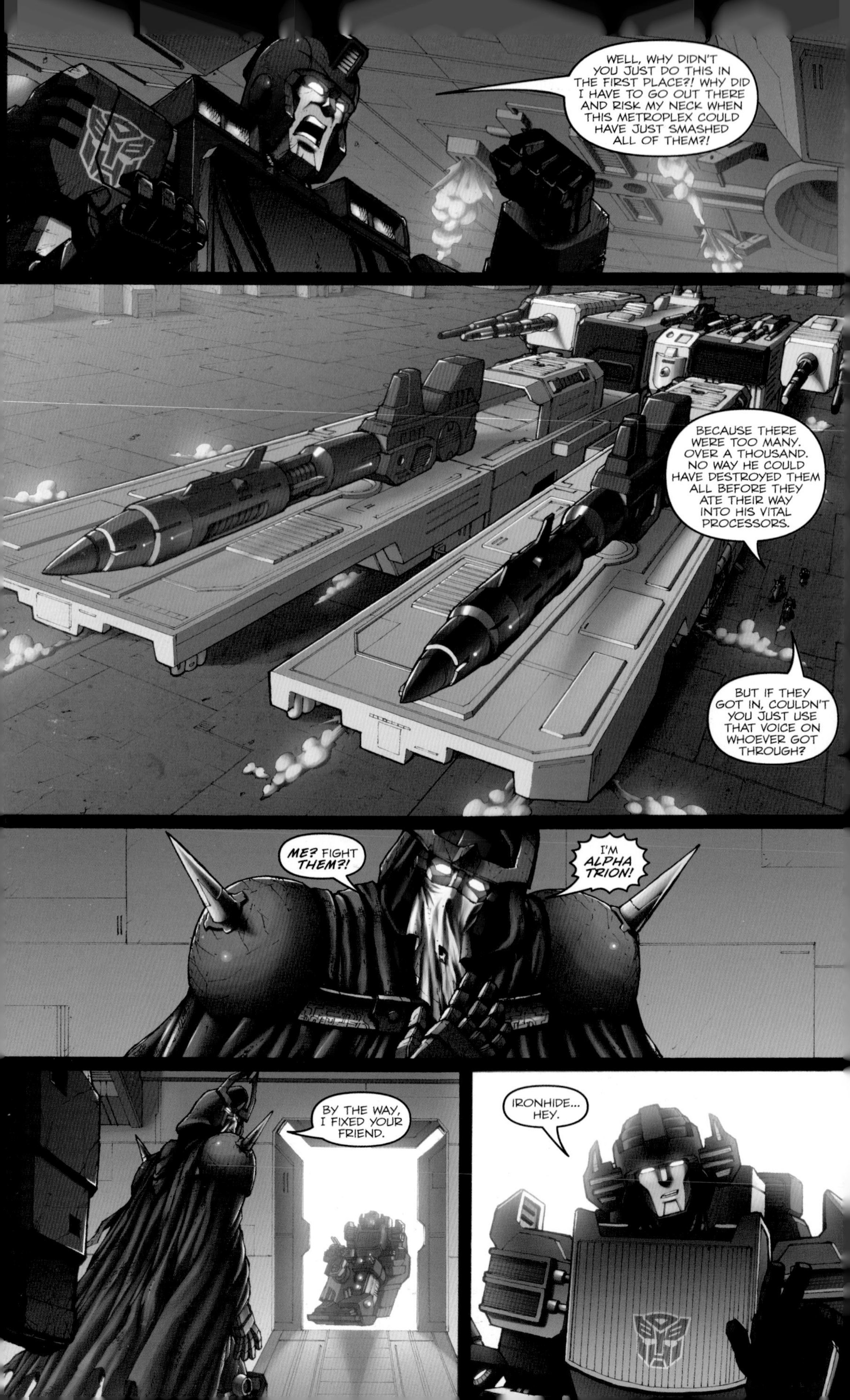
WELL, WHY DIDN'T YOU JUST DO THIS IN THE FIRST PLACE?! WHY DID I HAVE TO GO OUT THERE AND RISK MY NECK WHEN THIS METROPLEX COULD HAVE JUST SMASHED ALL OF THEM?!
BECAUSE THERE WERE TOO MANY. OVER A THOUSAND. NO WAY HE COULD HAVE DESTROYED THEM ALL BEFORE THEY ATE THEIR WAY INTO HIS VITAL PROCESSORS.
BUT IF THEY GOT IN, COULDN'T YOU JUST USE THAT VOICE ON WHOEVER GOT THROUGH?
ME? FIGHT THEM?!
I'M ALPHA TRION!
BY THE WAY, I FIXED YOUR FRIEND.
IRONHIDE... HEY.

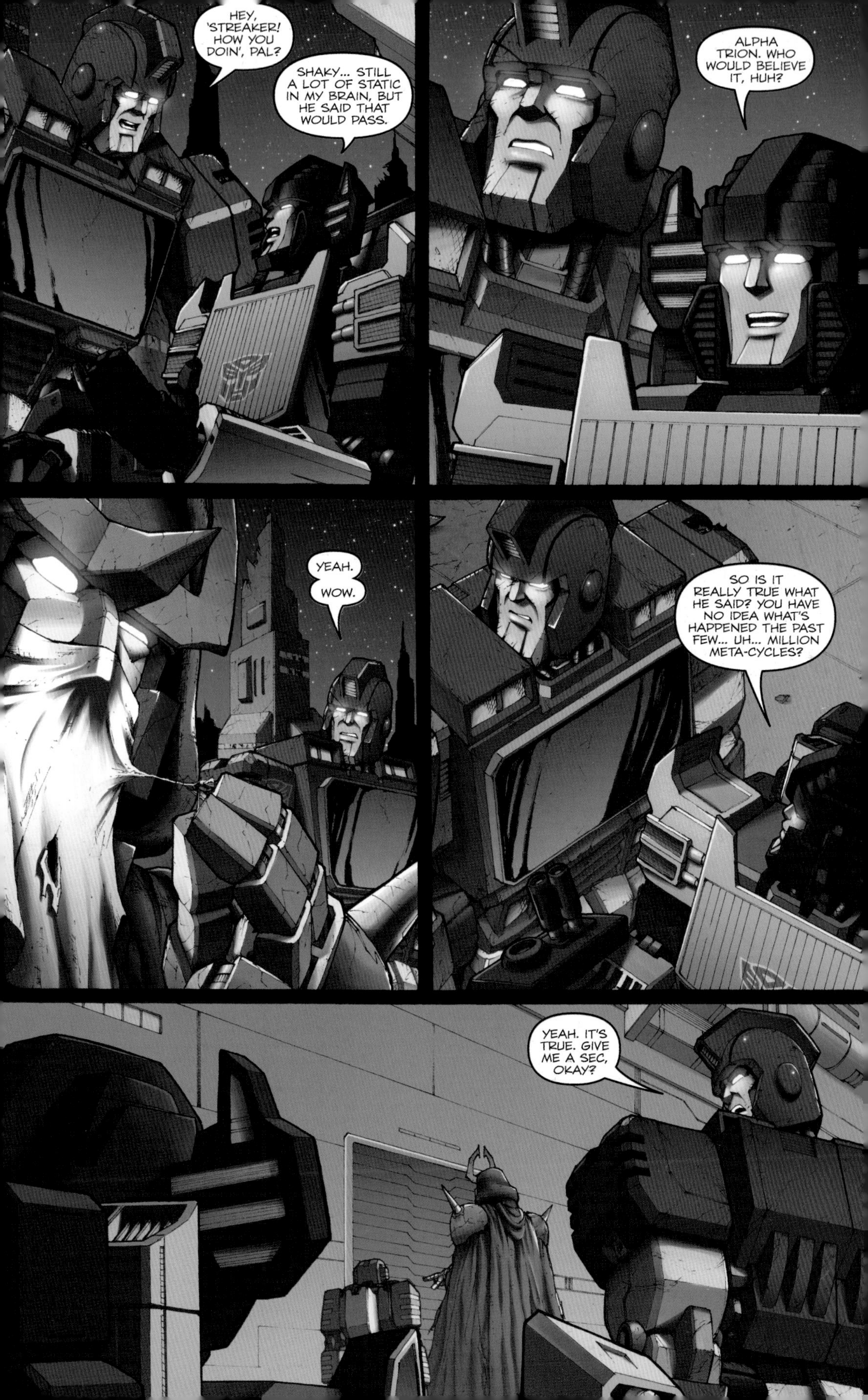
HEY, 'STREAKER! HOW YOU DOIN', PAL?
SHAKY... STILL A LOT OF STATIC IN MY BRAIN, BUT HE SAID THAT WOULD PASS.
ALPHA TRION. WHO WOULD BELIEVE IT, HUH?
YEAH.
WOW.
SO IS IT REALLY TRUE WHAT HE SAID? YOU HAVE NO IDEA WHAT'S HAPPENED THE PAST FEW... UH... MILLION META-CYCLES?
YEAH. IT'S TRUE. GIVE ME A SEC, OKAY?

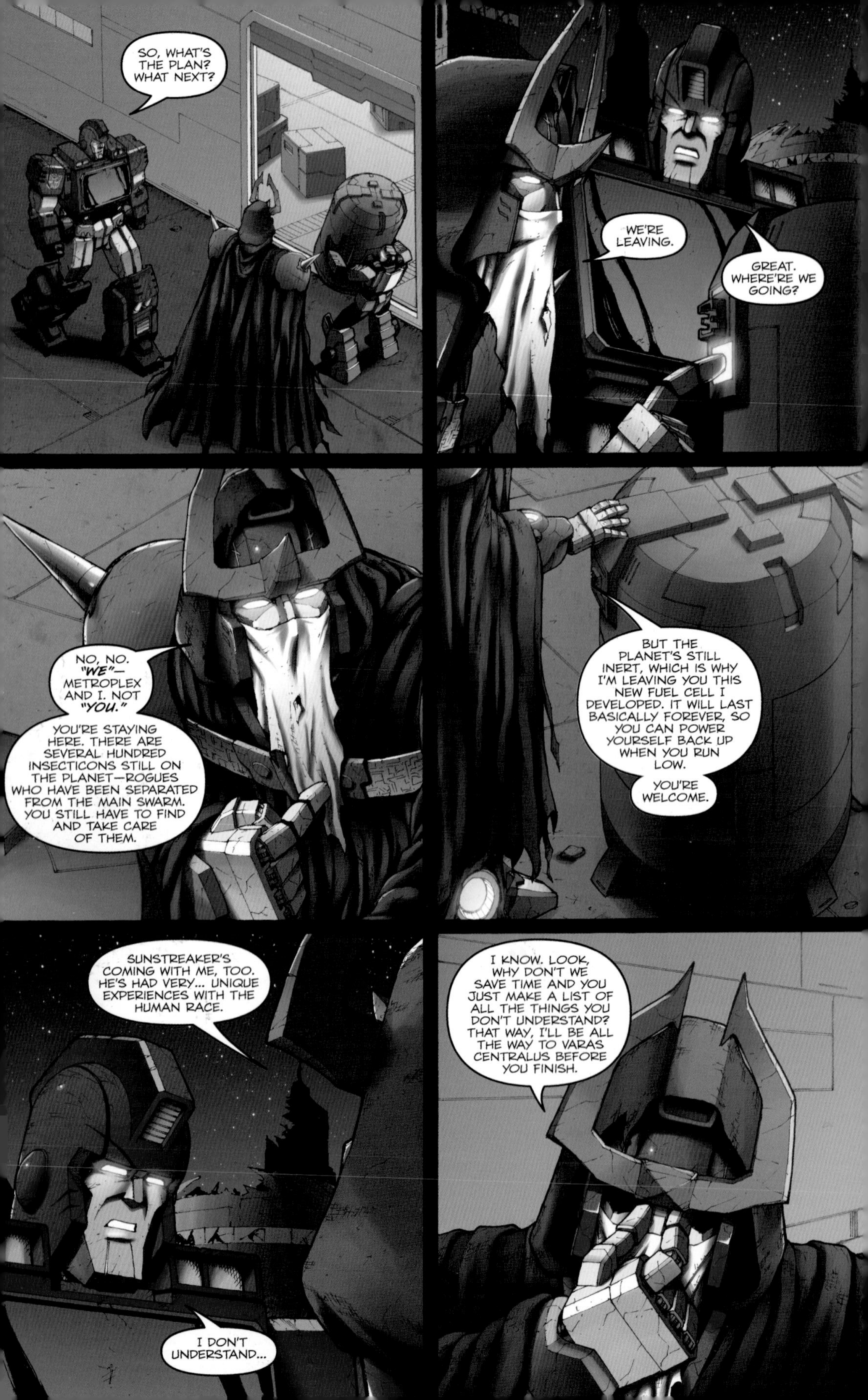
SO, WHAT'S THE PLAN? WHAT NEXT?
WE'RE LEAVING.
GREAT. WHERE'RE WE GOING?
NO, NO. "WE"—METROPLEX AND I. NOT "YOU."
YOU'RE STAYING HERE. THERE ARE SEVERAL HUNDRED INSECTICONS STILL ON THE PLANET—ROGUES WHO HAVE BEEN SEPARATED FROM THE MAIN SWARM. YOU STILL HAVE TO FIND AND TAKE CARE OF THEM.
BUT THE PLANET'S STILL INERT, WHICH IS WHY I'M LEAVING YOU THIS NEW FUEL CELL I DEVELOPED. IT WILL LAST BASICALLY FOREVER, SO YOU CAN POWER YOURSELF BACK UP WHEN YOU RUN LOW.
YOU'RE WELCOME.
SUNSTREAKER'S COMING WITH ME, TOO. HE'S HAD VERY... UNIQUE EXPERIENCES WITH THE HUMAN RACE.
I DON'T UNDERSTAND...
I KNOW. LOOK, WHY DON'T WE SAVE TIME AND YOU JUST MAKE A LIST OF ALL THE THINGS YOU DON'T UNDERSTAND? THAT WAY, I'LL BE ALL THE WAY TO VARAS CENTRALUS BEFORE YOU FINISH.

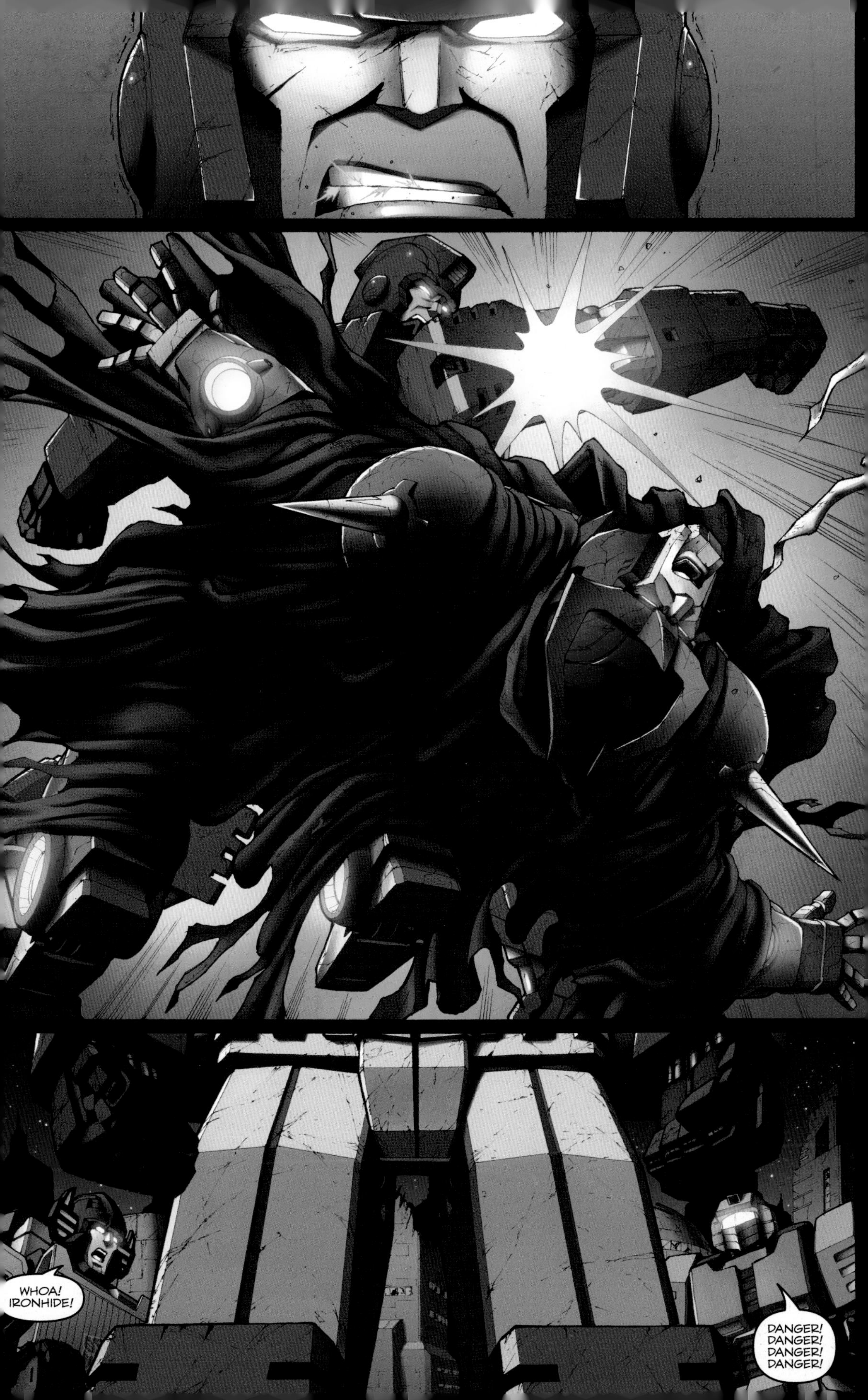
WHOA! IRONHIDE!
DANGER! DANGER! DANGER! DANGER!

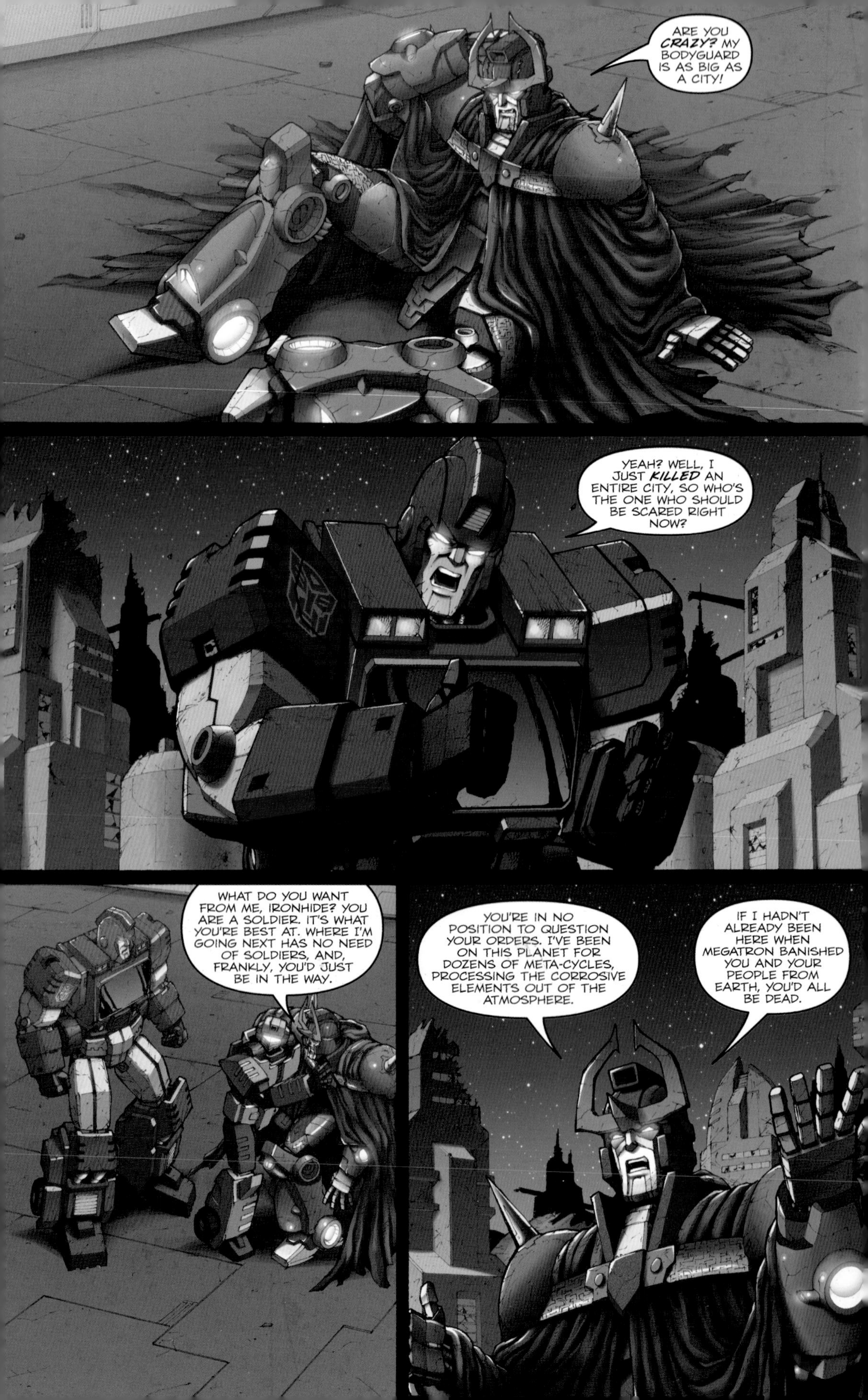
ARE YOU CRAZY? MY BODYGUARD IS AS BIG AS A CITY!
YEAH? WELL, I JUST KILLED AN ENTIRE CITY, SO WHO'S THE ONE WHO SHOULD BE SCARED RIGHT NOW?
WHAT DO YOU WANT FROM ME, IRONHIDE? YOU ARE A SOLDIER. IT'S WHAT YOU'RE BEST AT. WHERE I'M GOING NEXT HAS NO NEED OF SOLDIERS, AND, FRANKLY, YOU'D JUST BE IN THE WAY.
YOU'RE IN NO POSITION TO QUESTION YOUR ORDERS. I'VE BEEN ON THIS PLANET FOR DOZENS OF META-CYCLES, PROCESSING THE CORROSIVE ELEMENTS OUT OF THE ATMOSPHERE.
IF I HADN'T ALREADY BEEN HERE WHEN MEGATRON BANISHED YOU AND YOUR PEOPLE FROM EARTH, YOU'D ALL BE DEAD.

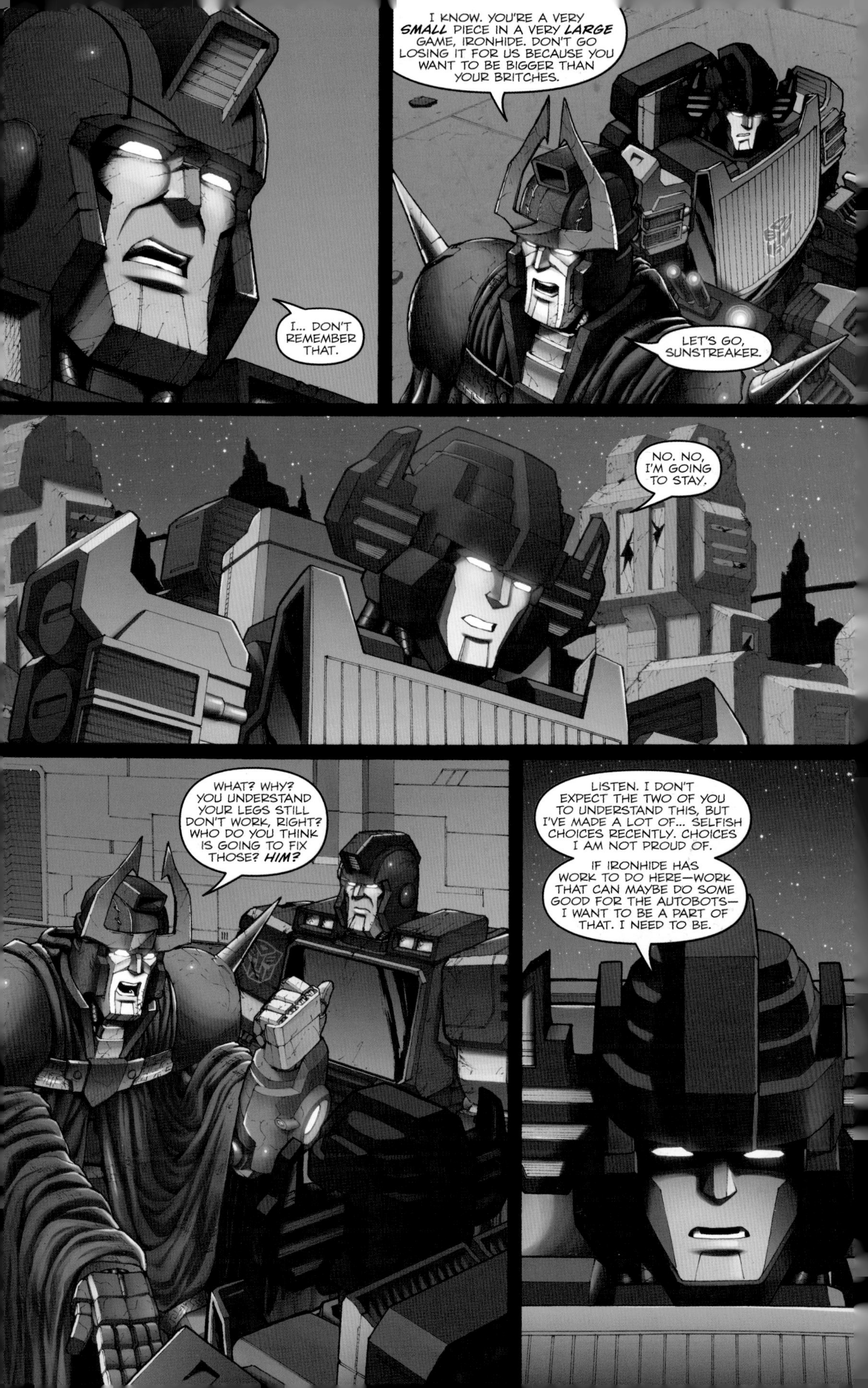
I KNOW. YOU'RE A VERY SMALL PIECE IN A VERY LARGE GAME, IRONHIDE. DON'T GO LOSING IT FOR US BECAUSE YOU WANT TO BE BIGGER THAN YOUR BRITCHES.
I... DON'T REMEMBER THAT.
LET'S GO, SUNSTREAKER.
NO. NO, I'M GOING TO STAY.
WHAT? WHY? YOU UNDERSTAND YOUR LEGS STILL DON'T WORK, RIGHT? WHO DO YOU THINK IS GOING TO FIX THOSE? HIM?
LISTEN. I DON'T EXPECT THE TWO OF YOU TO UNDERSTAND THIS, BUT I'VE MADE A LOT OF... SELFISH CHOICES RECENTLY. CHOICES I AM NOT PROUD OF.
IF IRONHIDE HAS WORK TO DO HERE—WORK THAT CAN MAYBE DO SOME GOOD FOR THE AUTOBOTS—I WANT TO BE A PART OF THAT. I NEED TO BE.

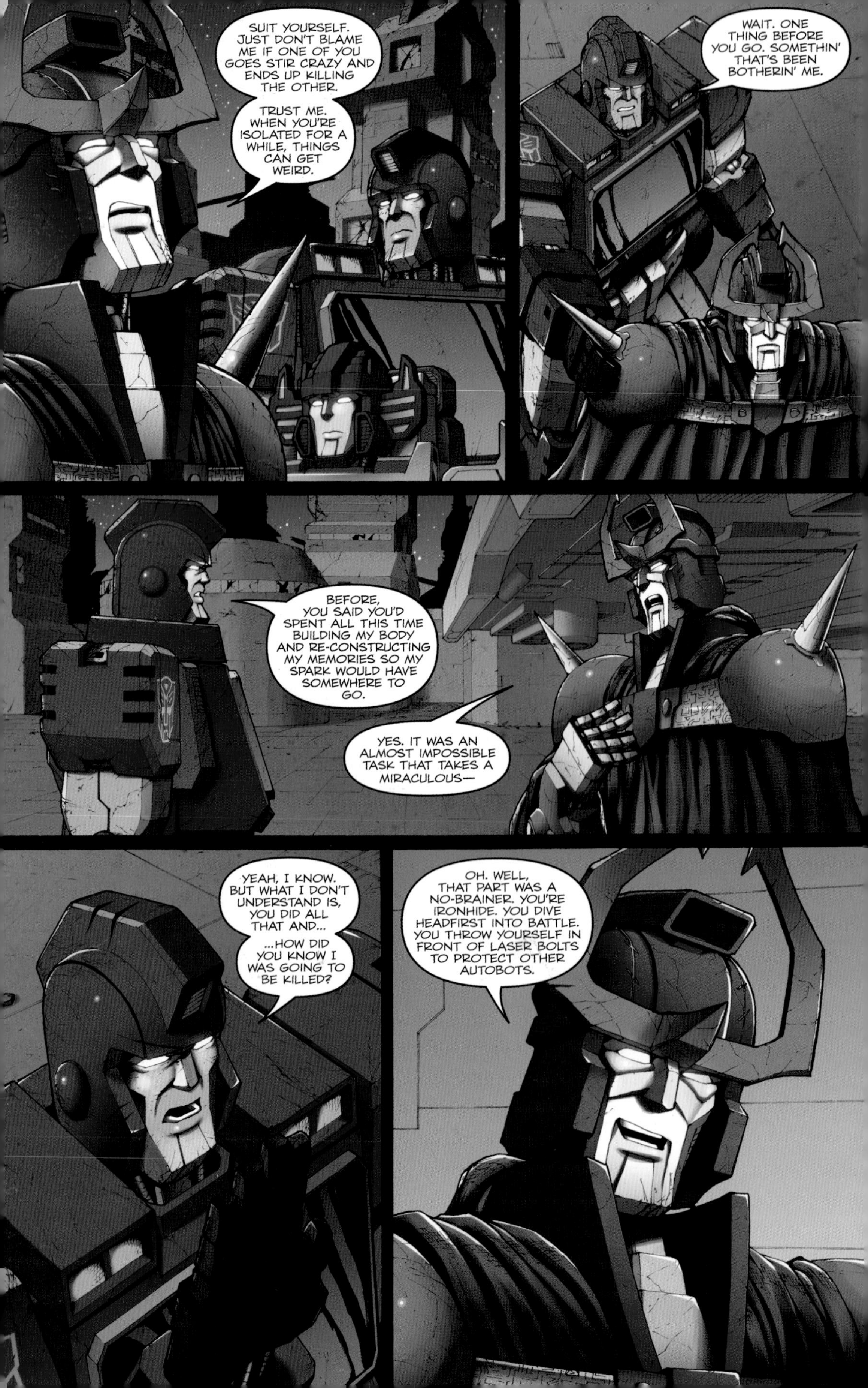
SUIT YOURSELF. JUST DON'T BLAME ME IF ONE OF YOU GOES STIR CRAZY AND ENDS UP KILLING THE OTHER.
TRUST ME. WHEN YOU'RE ISOLATED FOR A WHILE, THINGS CAN GET WEIRD.
WAIT. ONE THING BEFORE YOU GO. SOMETHIN' THAT'S BEEN BOTHERIN' ME.
BEFORE, YOU SAID YOU'D SPENT ALL THIS TIME BUILDING MY BODY AND RE-CONSTRUCTING MY MEMORIES SO MY SPARK WOULD HAVE SOMEWHERE TO GO.
YES. IT WAS AN ALMOST IMPOSSIBLE TASK THAT TAKES A MIRACULOUS—
YEAH, I KNOW. BUT WHAT I DON'T UNDERSTAND IS, YOU DID ALL THAT AND...
...HOW DID YOU KNOW I WAS GOING TO BE KILLED?
OH. WELL, THAT PART WAS A NO-BRAINER. YOU'RE IRONHIDE. YOU DIVE HEADFIRST INTO BATTLE. YOU THROW YOURSELF IN FRONT OF LASER BOLTS TO PROTECT OTHER AUTOBOTS.

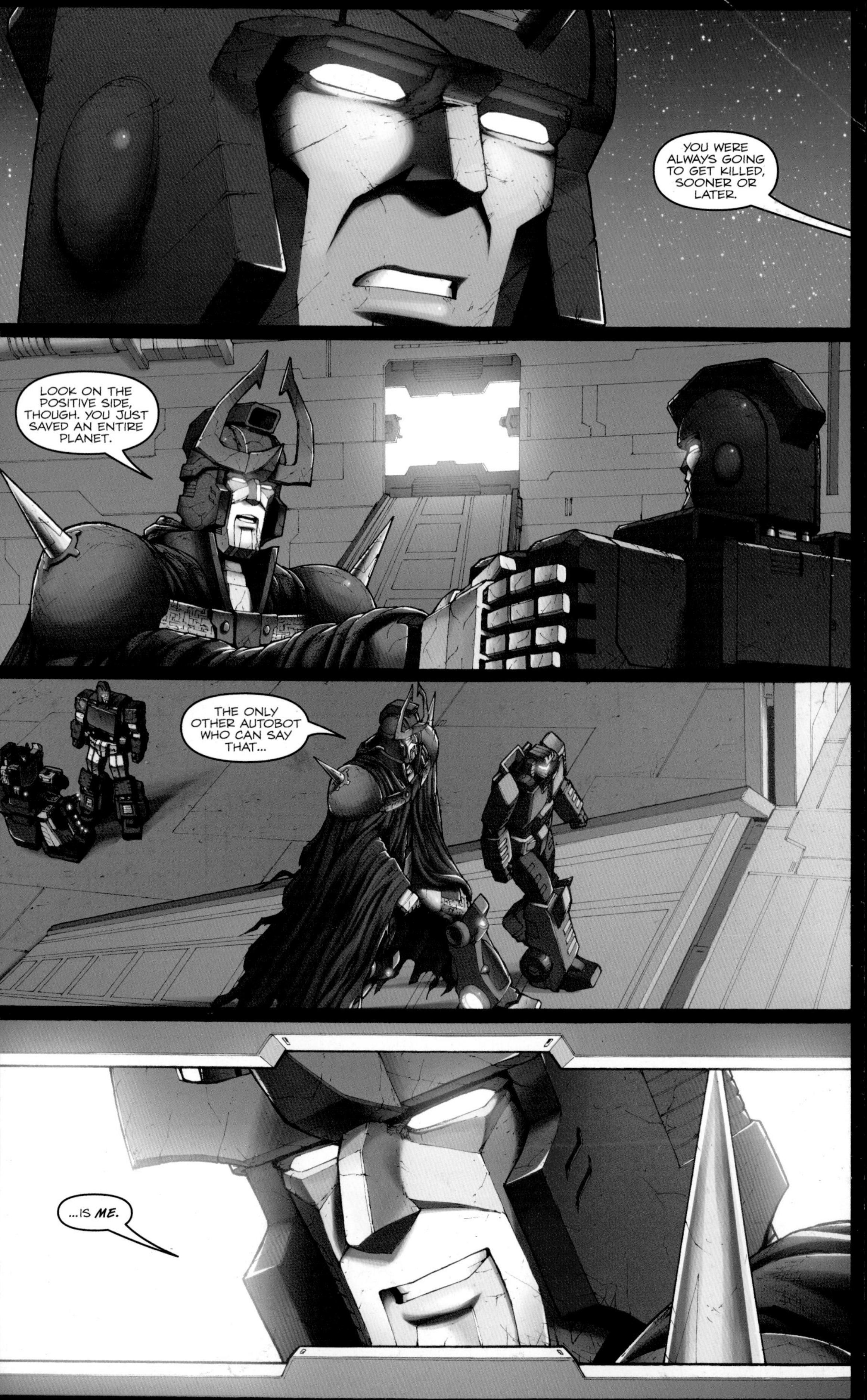
YOU WERE ALWAYS GOING TO GET KILLED, SOONER OR LATER.
LOOK ON THE POSITIVE SIDE, THOUGH. YOU JUST SAVED AN ENTIRE PLANET.
THE ONLY OTHER AUTOBOT WHO CAN SAY THAT...
...IS *ME.*

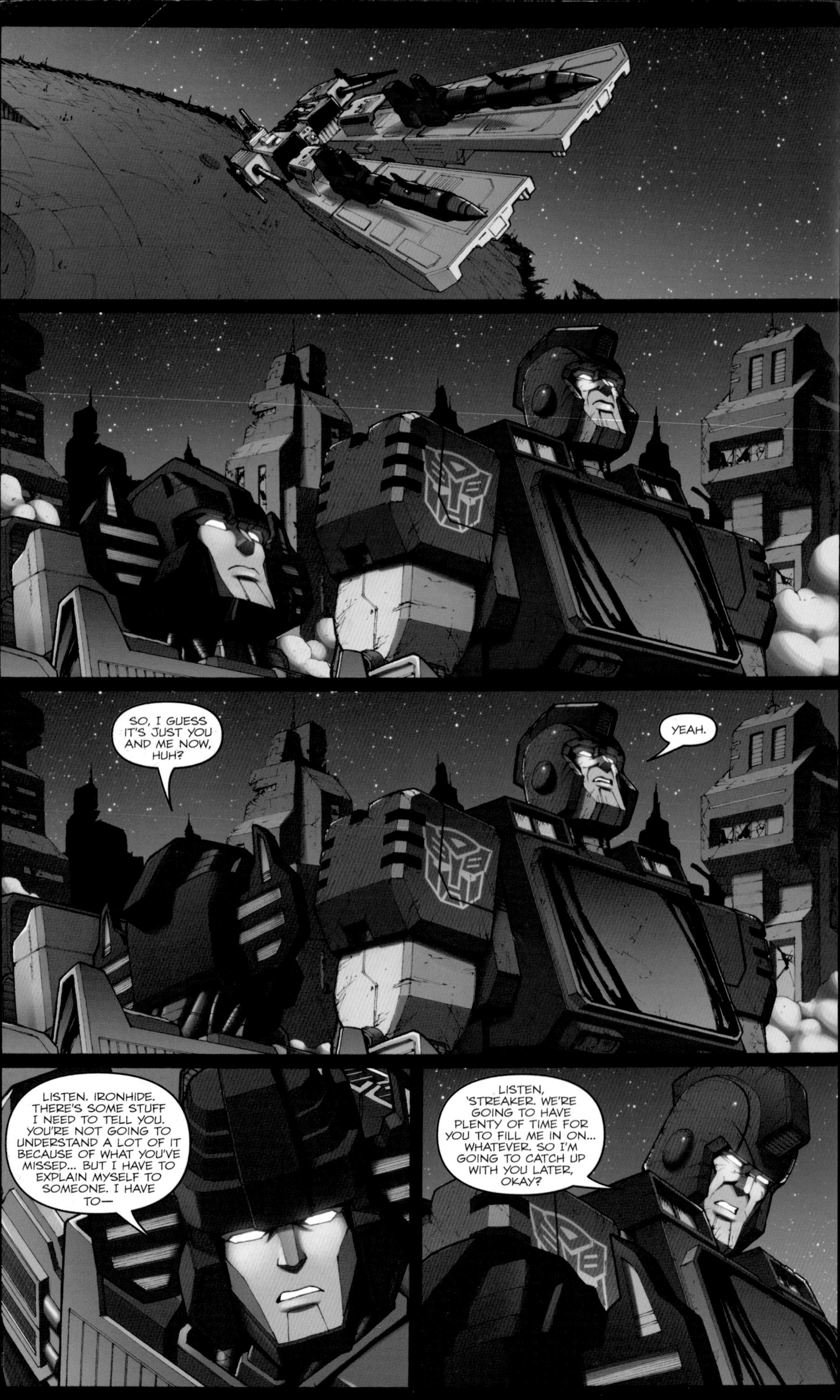
SO, I GUESS IT'S JUST YOU AND ME NOW, HUH?
YEAH.
LISTEN. IRONHIDE. THERE'S SOME STUFF I NEED TO TELL YOU. YOU'RE NOT GOING TO UNDERSTAND A LOT OF IT BECAUSE OF WHAT YOU'VE MISSED... BUT I HAVE TO EXPLAIN MYSELF TO SOMEONE. I HAVE TO—
LISTEN, 'STREAKER. WE'RE GOING TO HAVE PLENTY OF TIME FOR YOU TO FILL ME IN ON... WHATEVER. SO I'M GOING TO CATCH UP WITH YOU LATER, OKAY?

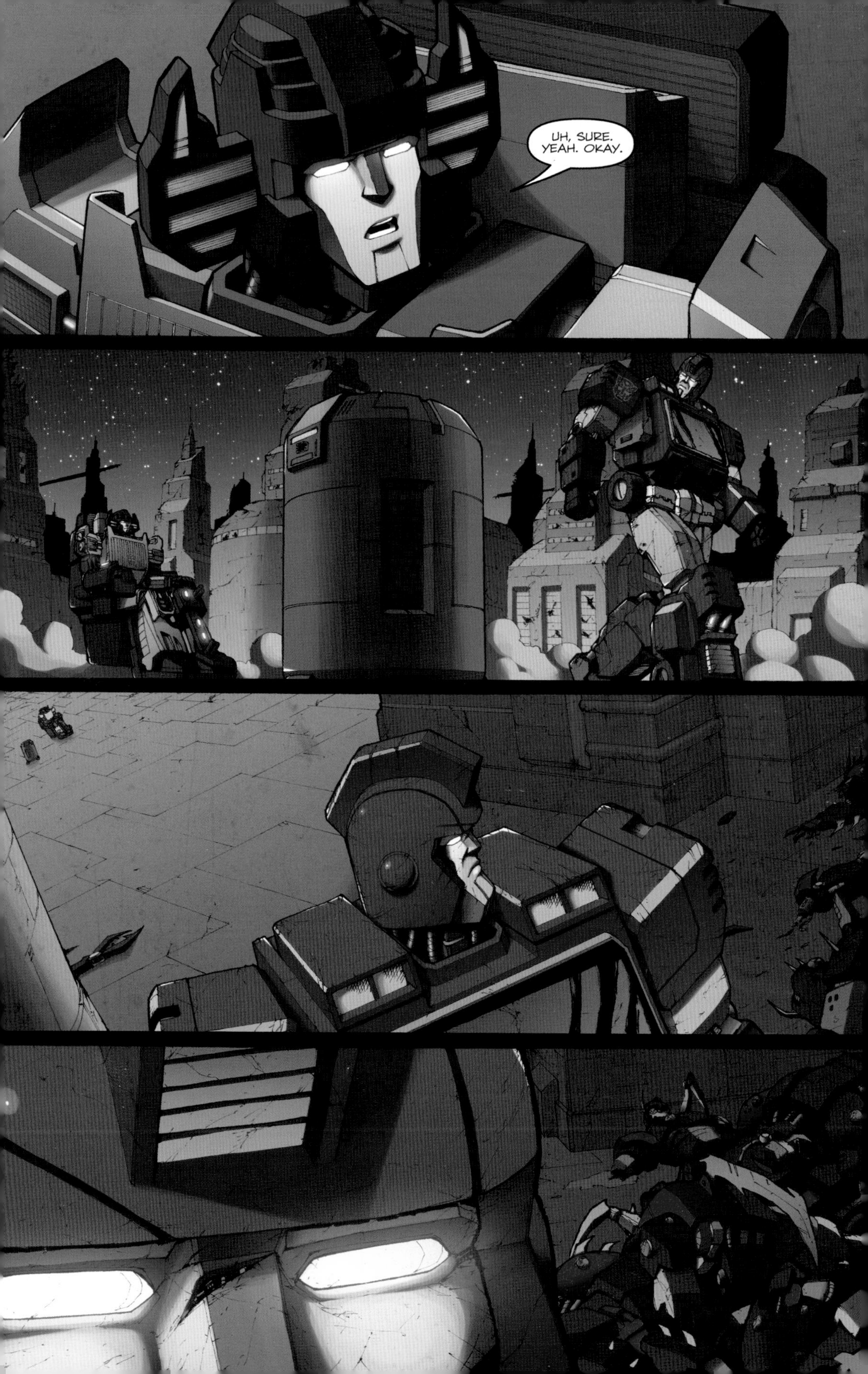
UH, SURE. YEAH. OKAY.

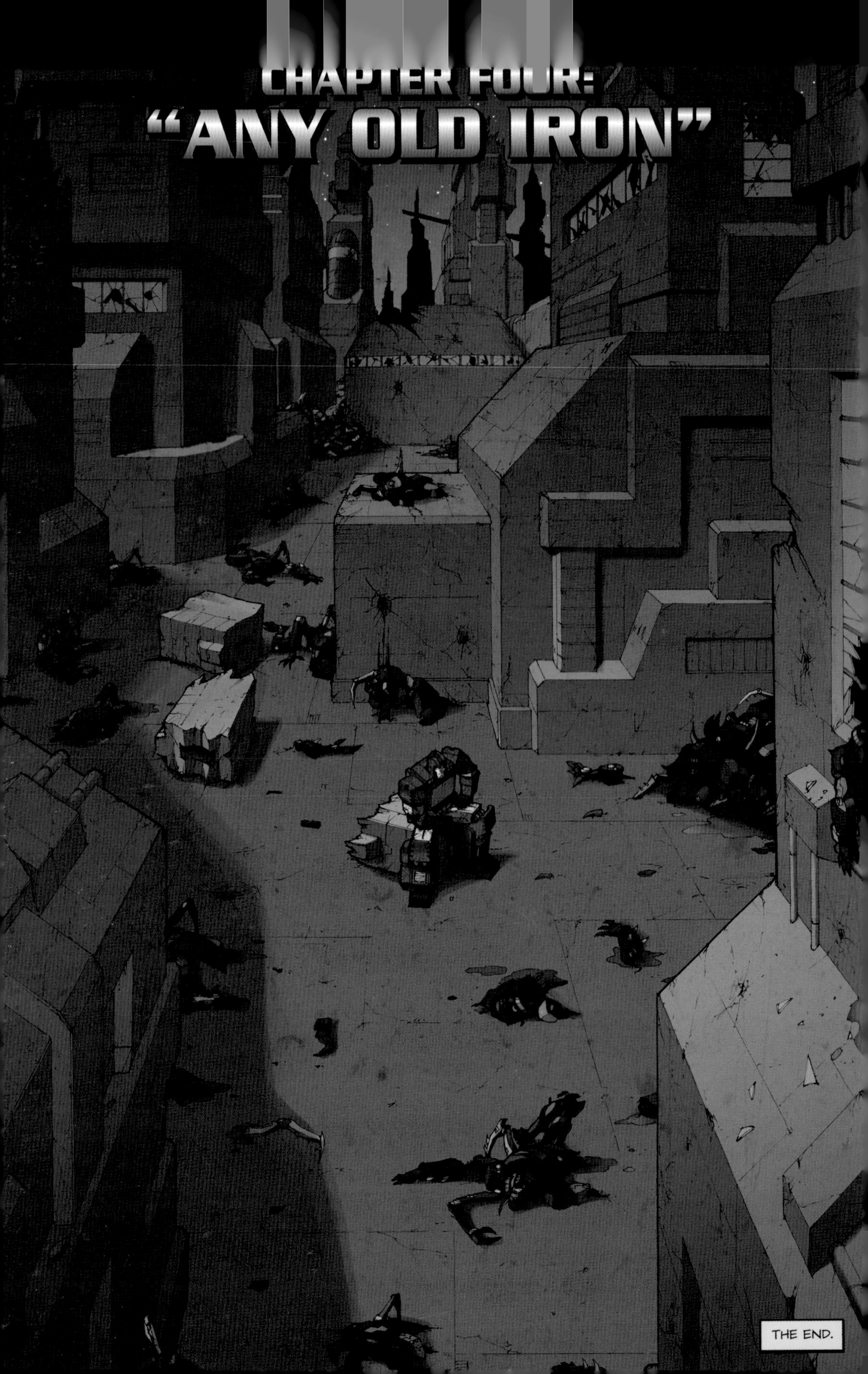
CHAPTER FOUR:
"ANY OLD IRON"
THE END.

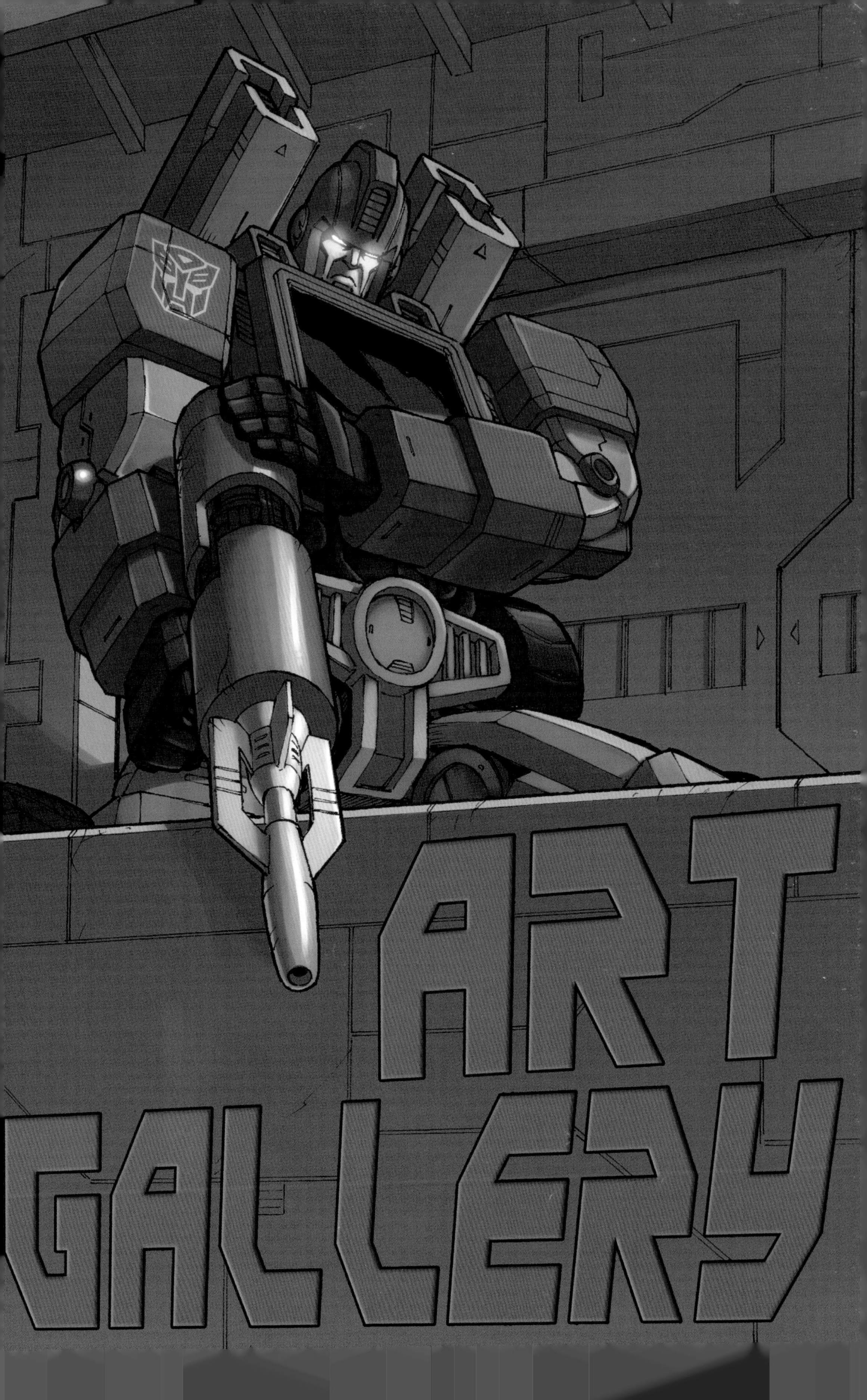
ART
GALLERY

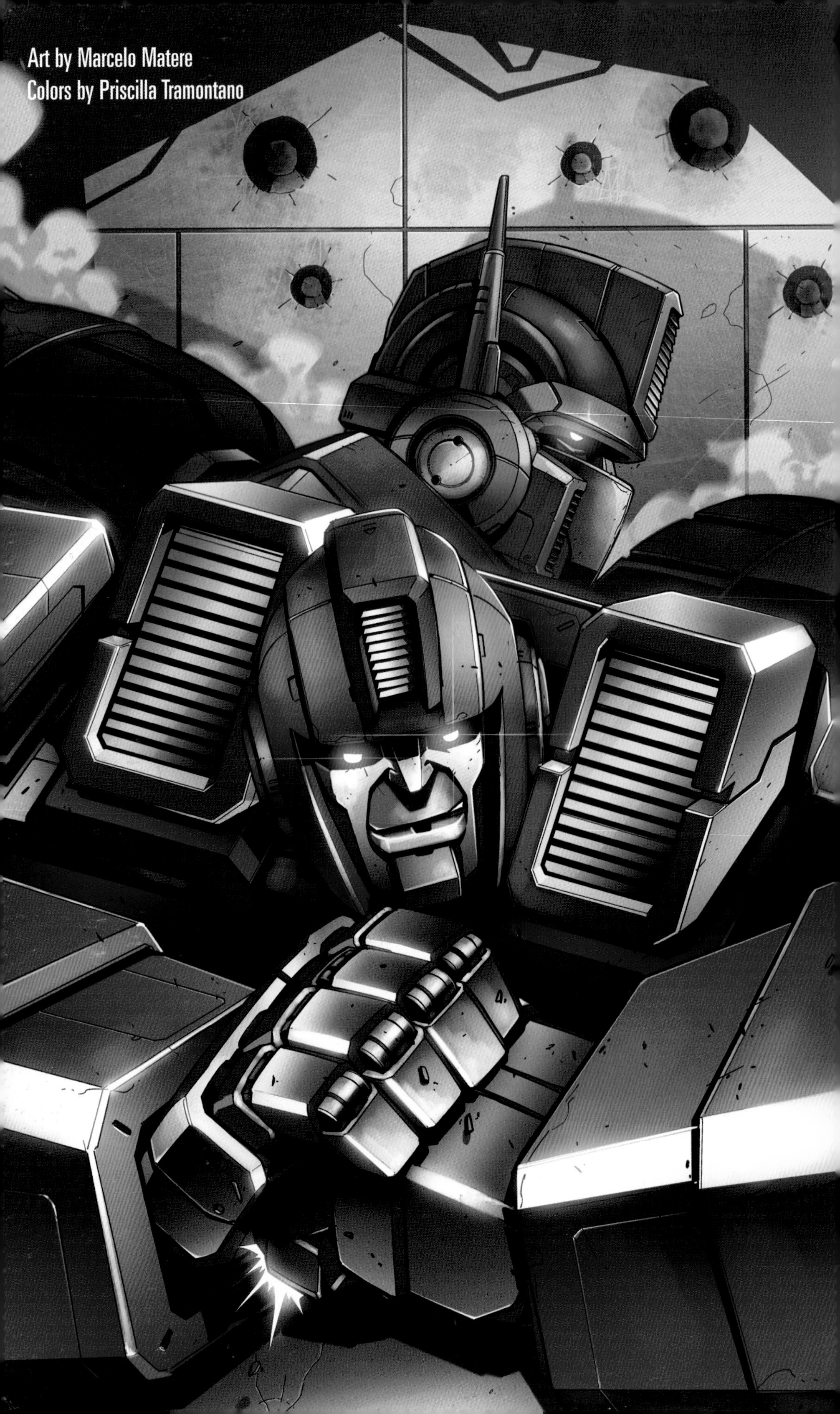

Art by Marcelo Matere
Colors by Priscilla Tramontano

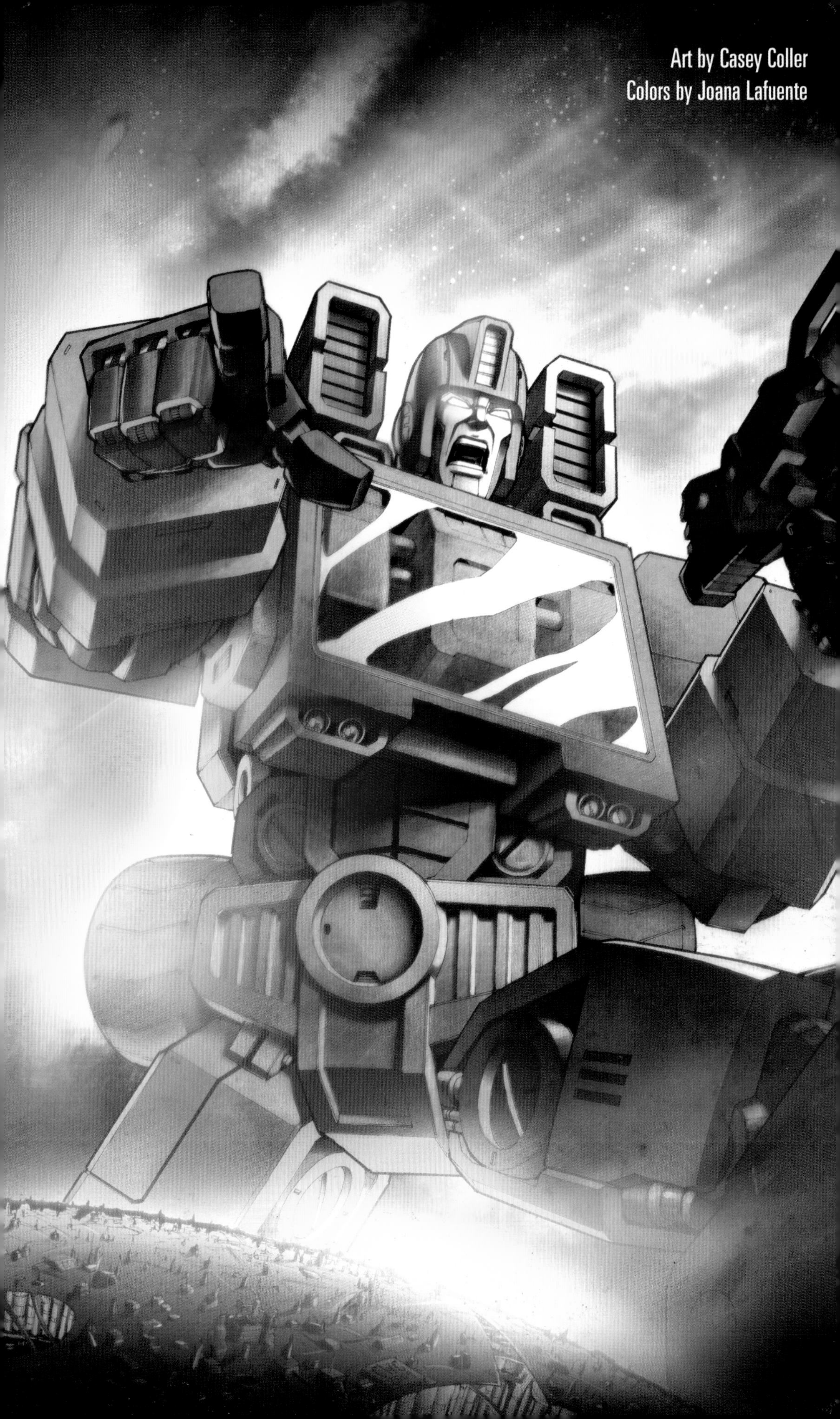

Art by Casey Coller
Colors by Joana Lafuente

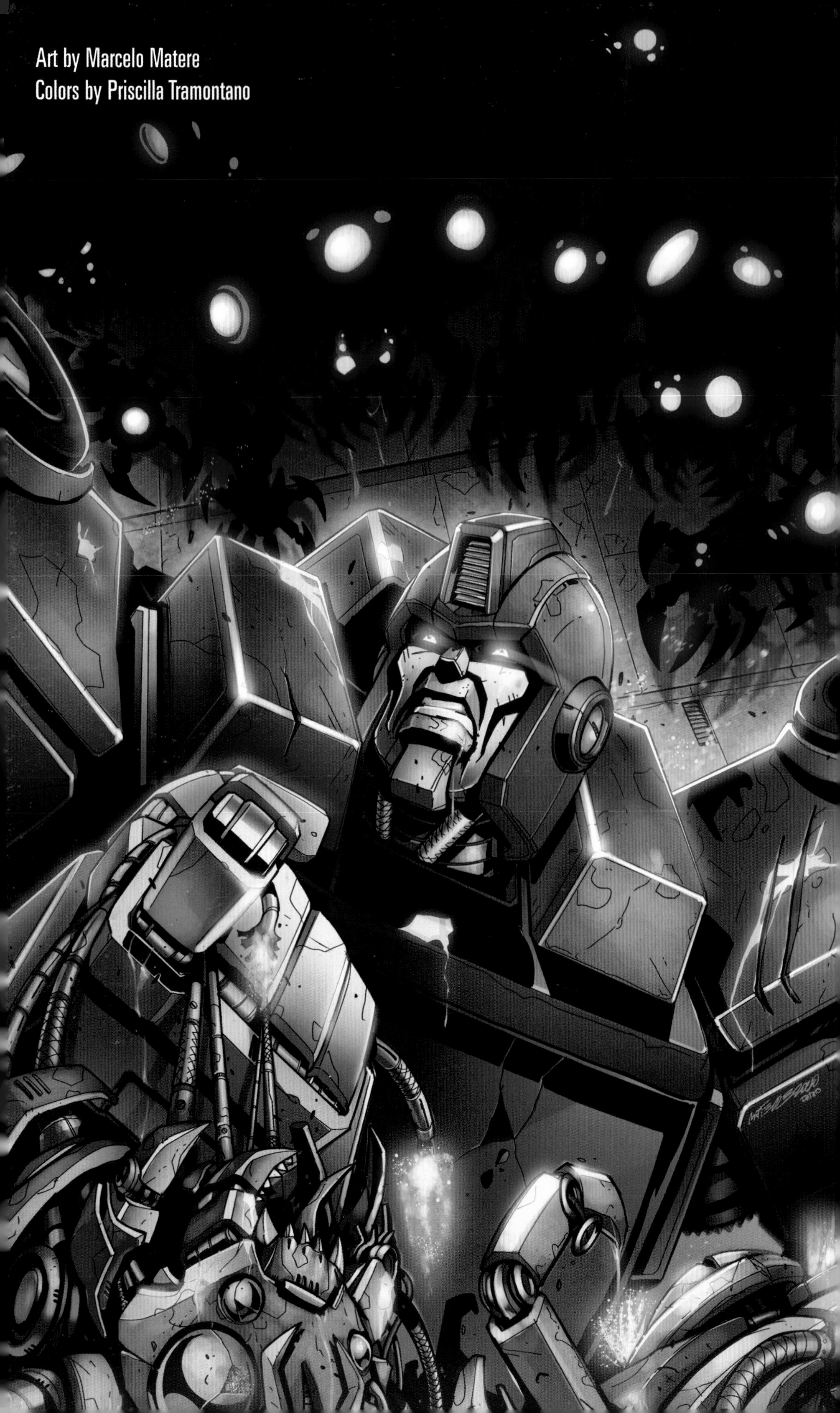

Art by Marcelo Matere
Colors by Priscilla Tramontano

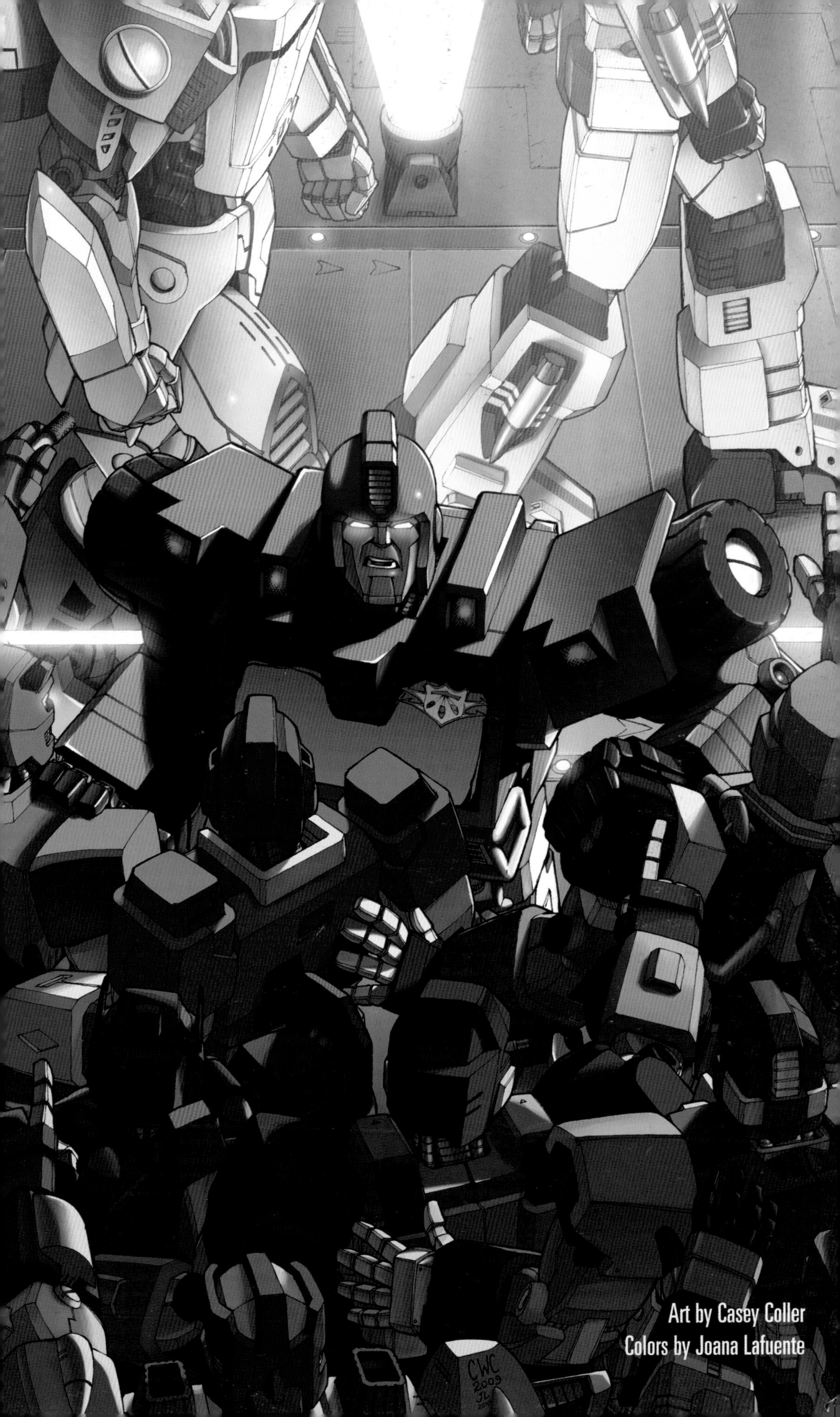

Art by Casey Coller
Colors by Joana Lafuente

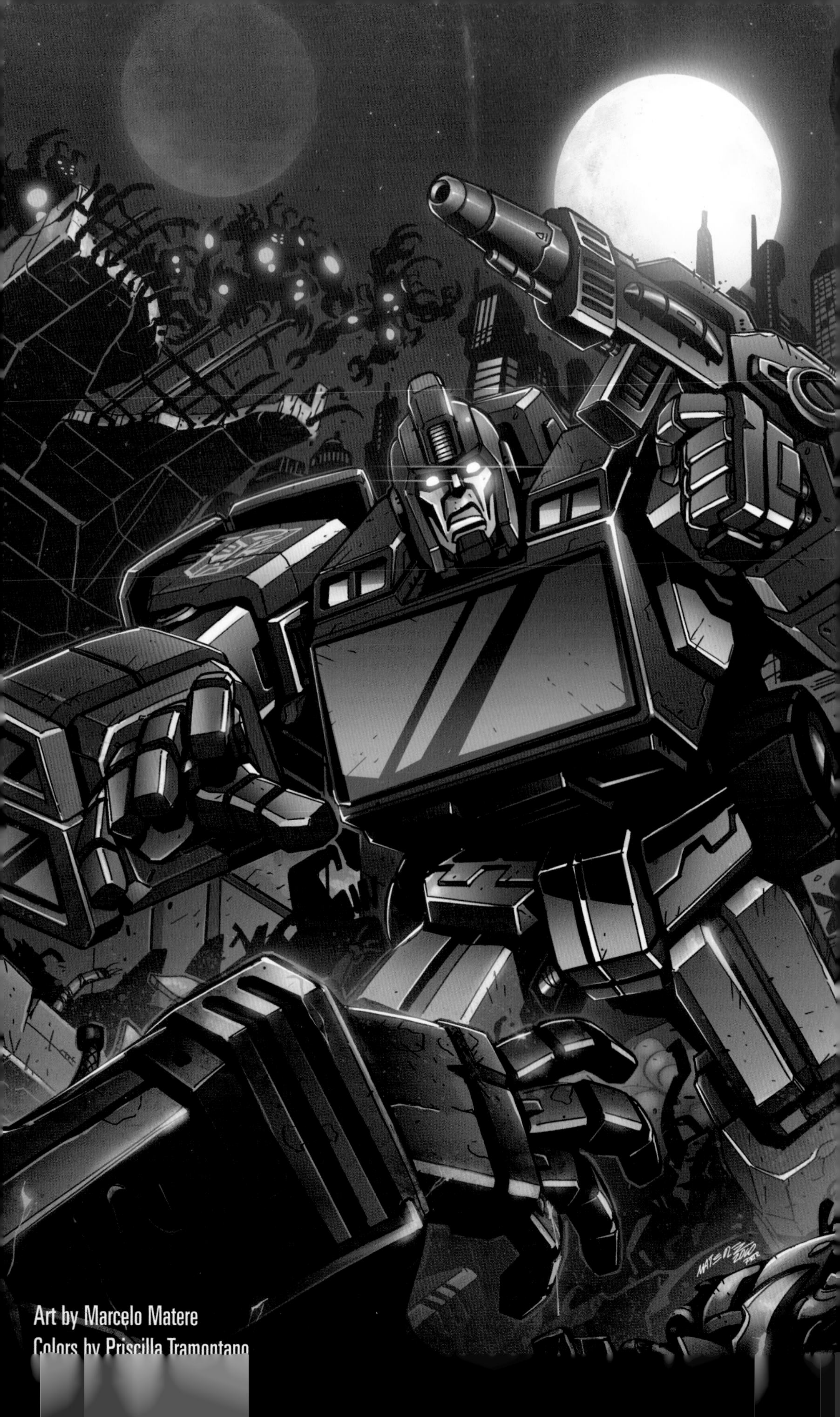
MATERE 2010

Art by Marcelo Matere
Colors by Priscilla Tramontano

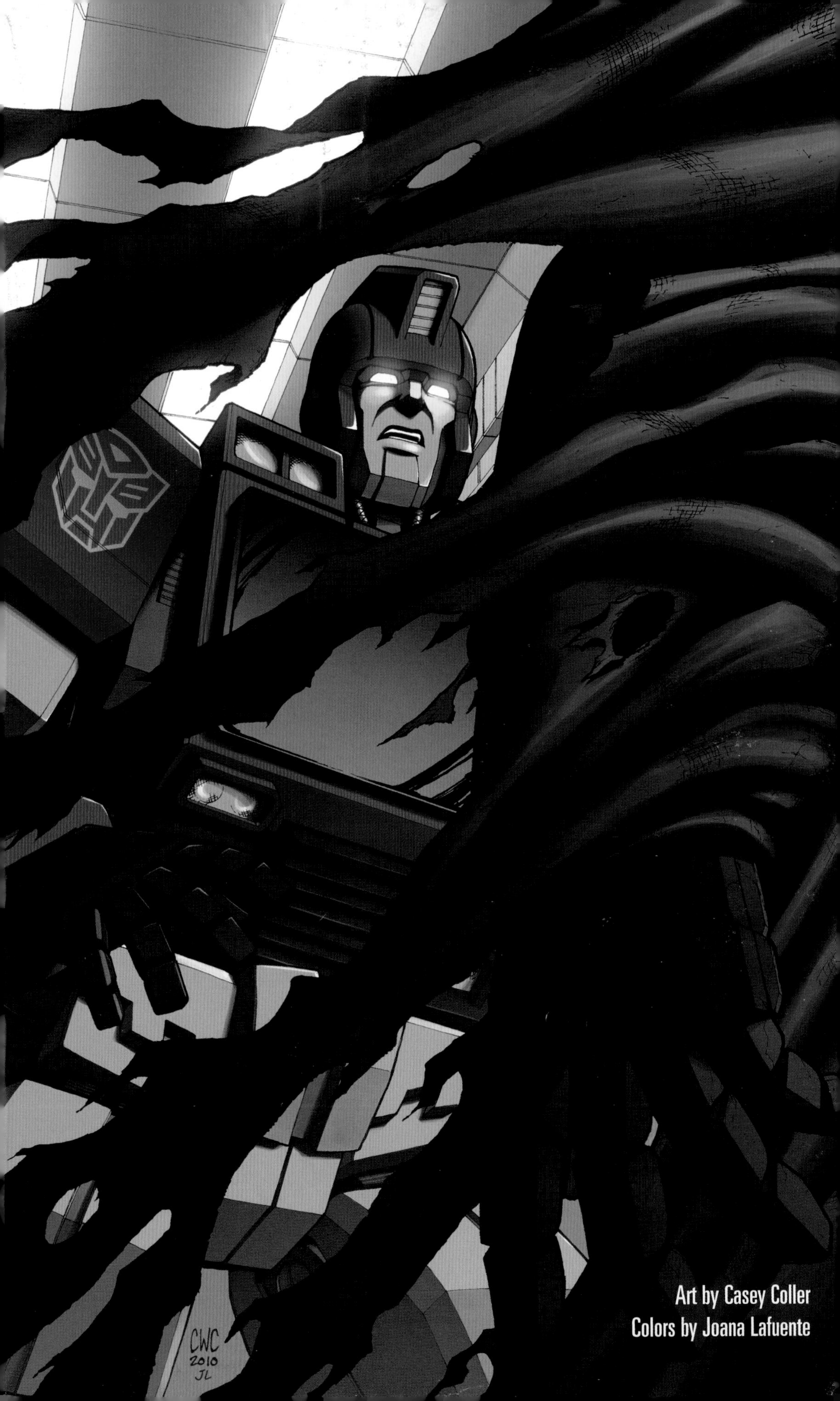
CWC
2010
JL

Art by Casey Coller
Colors by Joana Lafuente

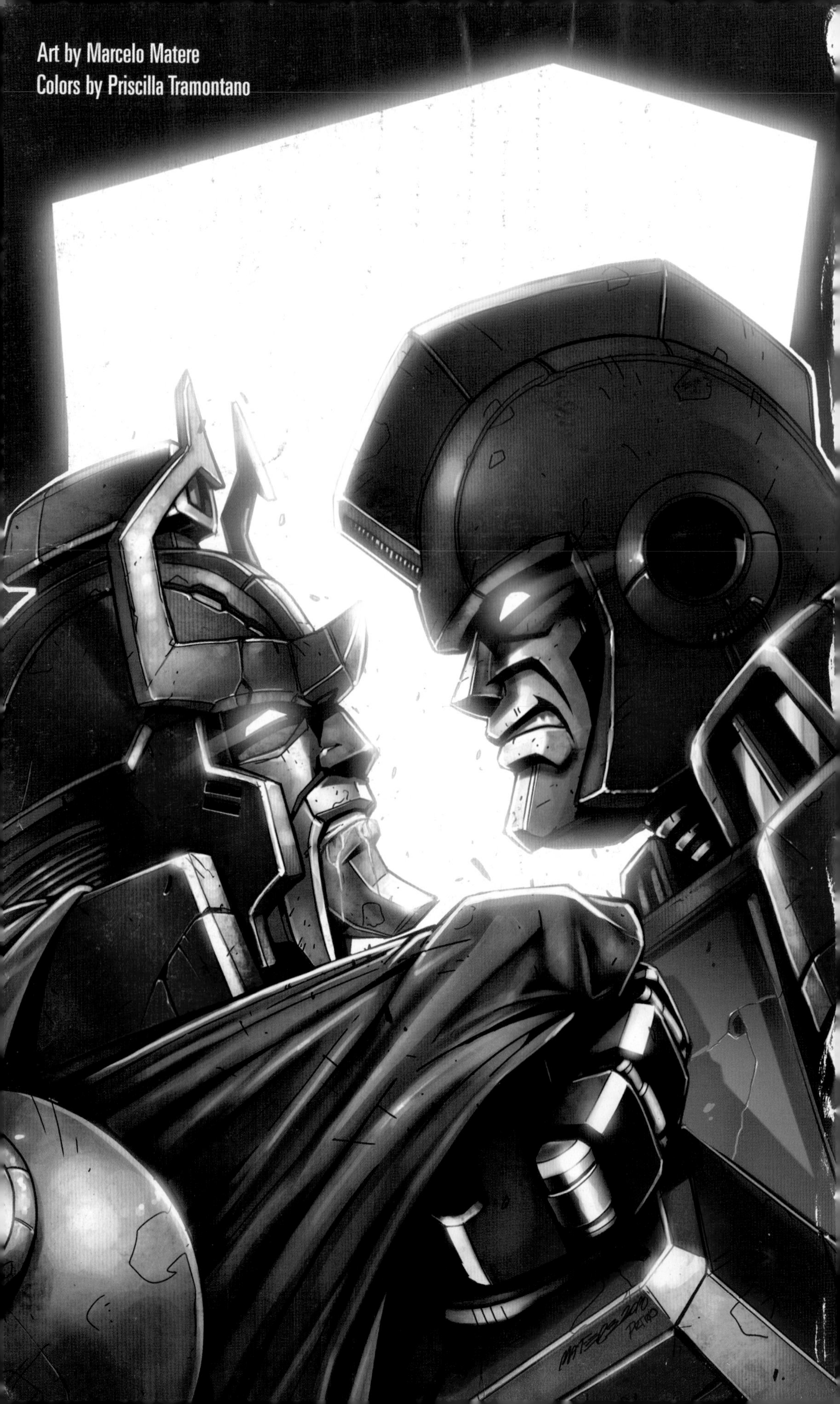

Art by Marcelo Matere
Colors by Priscilla Tramontano

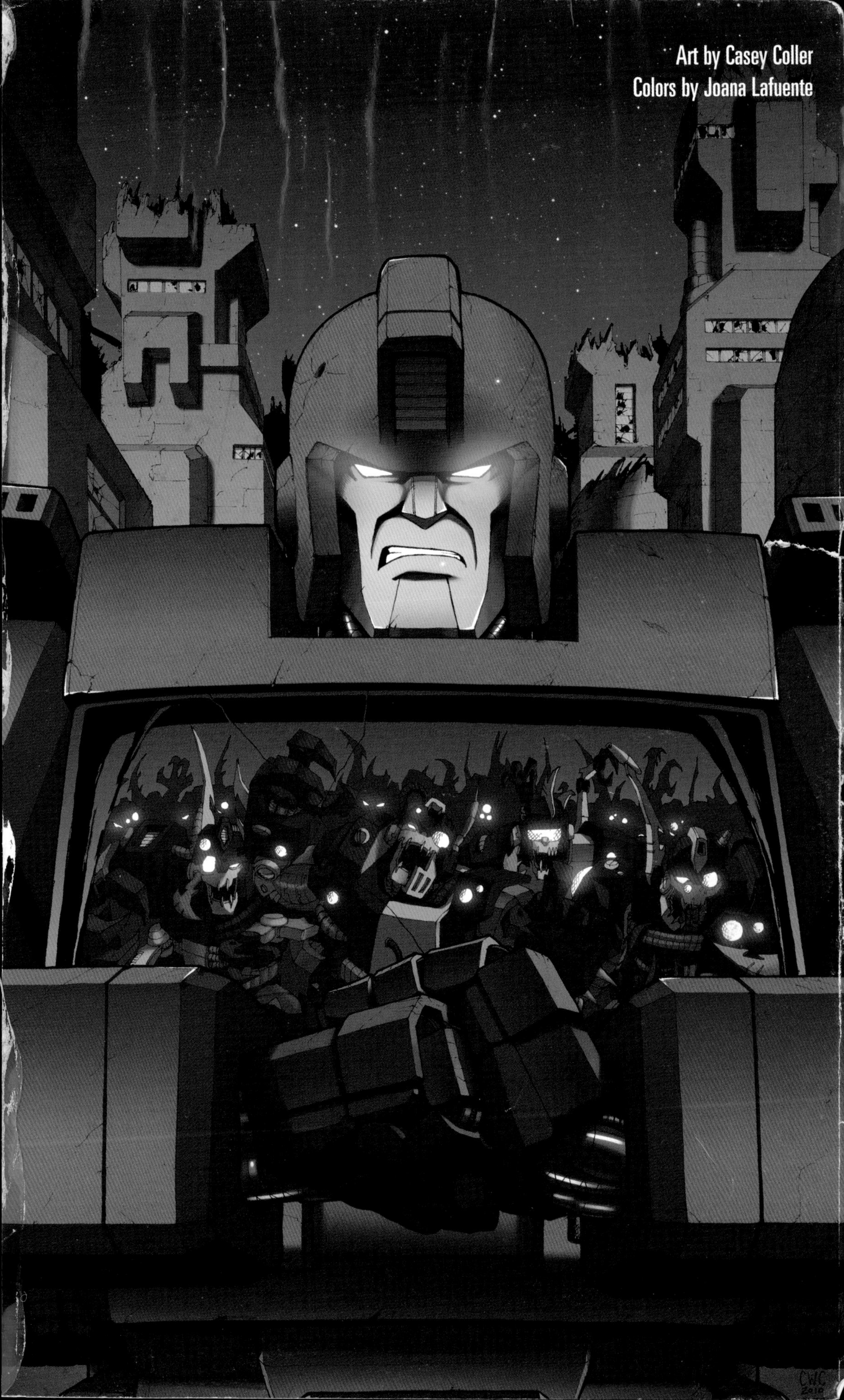
Art by Casey Coller
Colors by Joana Lafuente

THE EVOLUTION OF IRONHIDE

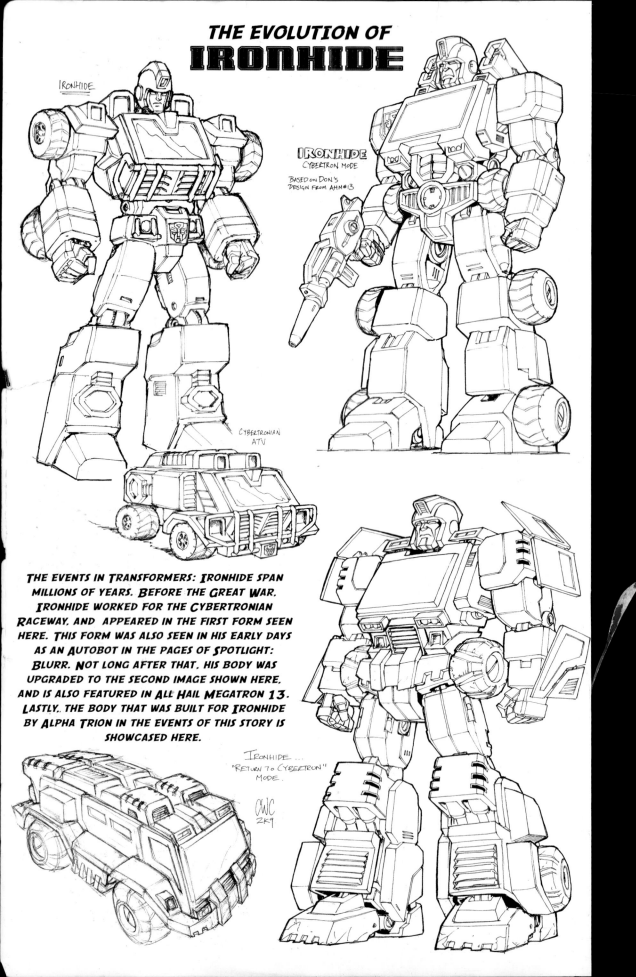

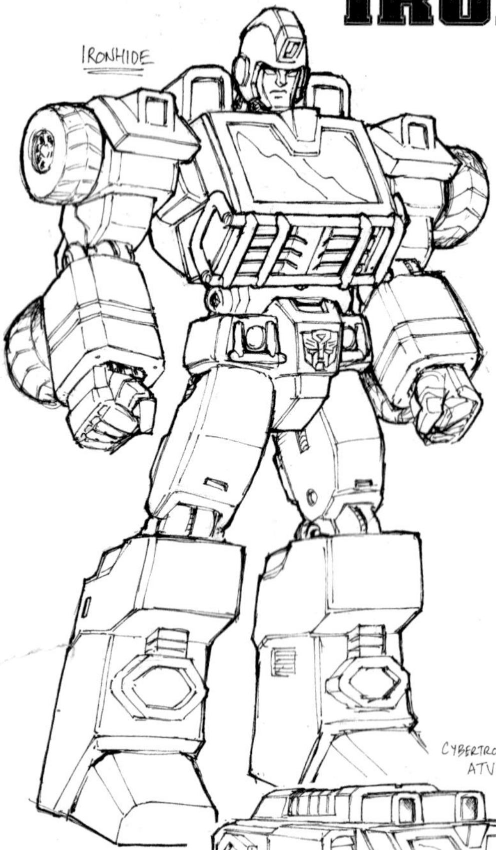
IRONHIDE

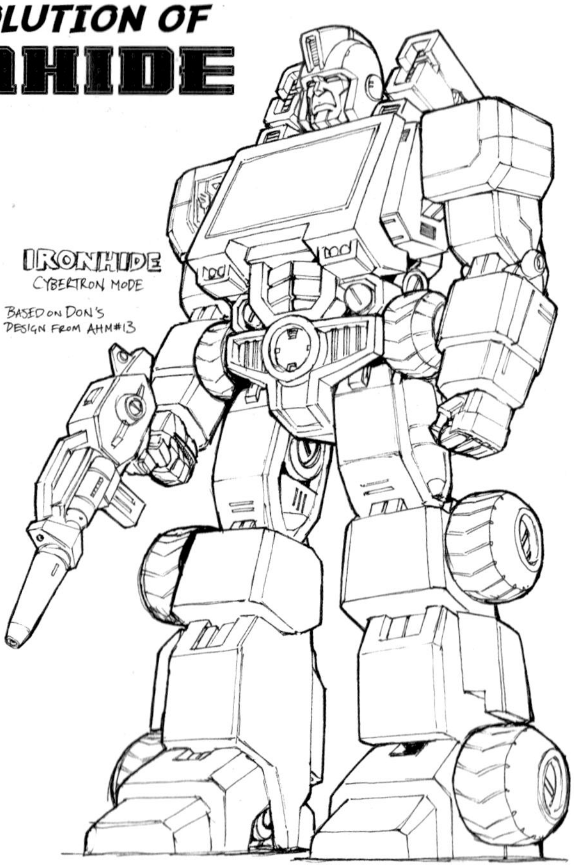
IRONHIDE
CYBERTRON MODE
BASED ON DON'S DESIGN FROM AHM#13

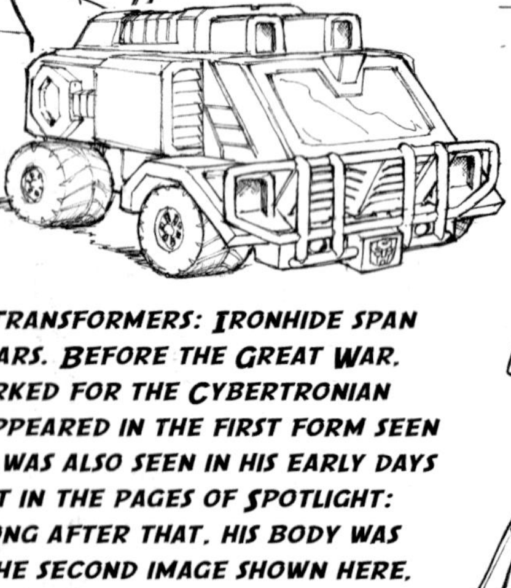
CYBERTRONIAN ATV

THE EVENTS IN TRANSFORMERS: IRONHIDE SPAN MILLIONS OF YEARS. BEFORE THE GREAT WAR, IRONHIDE WORKED FOR THE CYBERTRONIAN RACEWAY, AND APPEARED IN THE FIRST FORM SEEN HERE. THIS FORM WAS ALSO SEEN IN HIS EARLY DAYS AS AN AUTOBOT IN THE PAGES OF SPOTLIGHT: BLURR. NOT LONG AFTER THAT, HIS BODY WAS UPGRADED TO THE SECOND IMAGE SHOWN HERE, AND IS ALSO FEATURED IN ALL HAIL MEGATRON 13. LASTLY, THE BODY THAT WAS BUILT FOR IRONHIDE BY ALPHA TRION IN THE EVENTS OF THIS STORY IS SHOWCASED HERE.

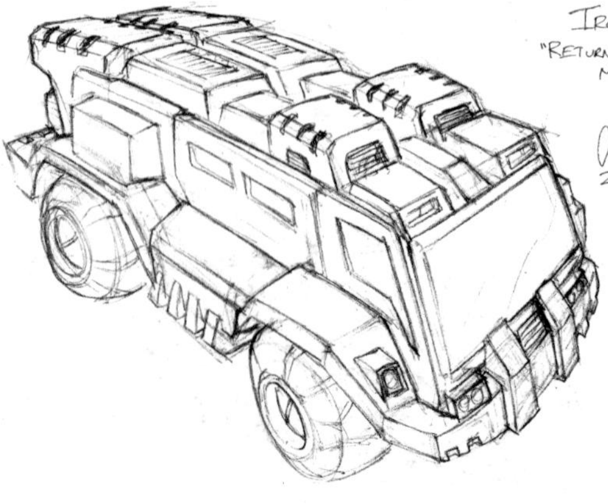

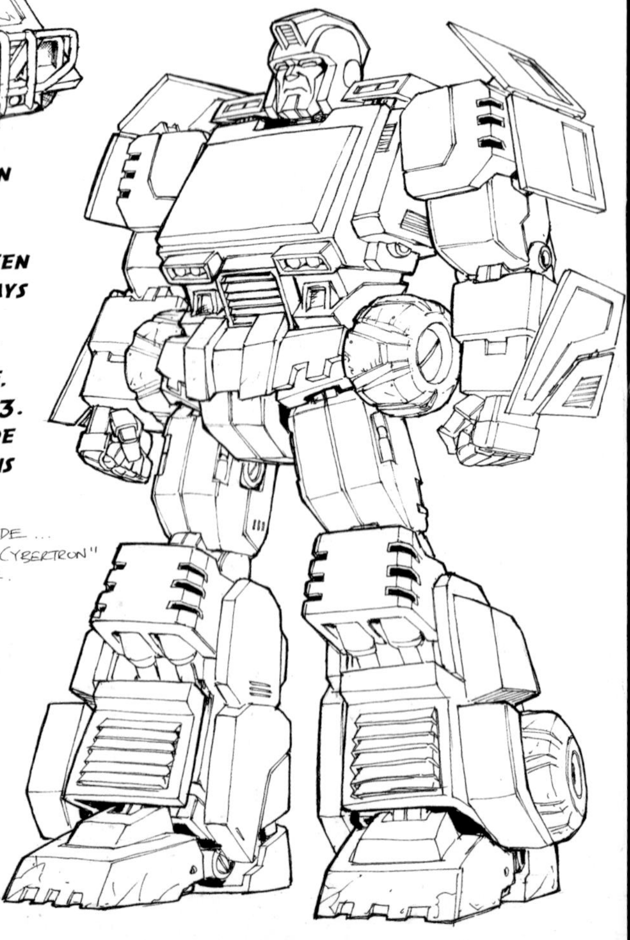
IRONHIDE...
"RETURN TO CYBERTRON" MODE.
CWC
2K9

CHARACTER SKETCHES

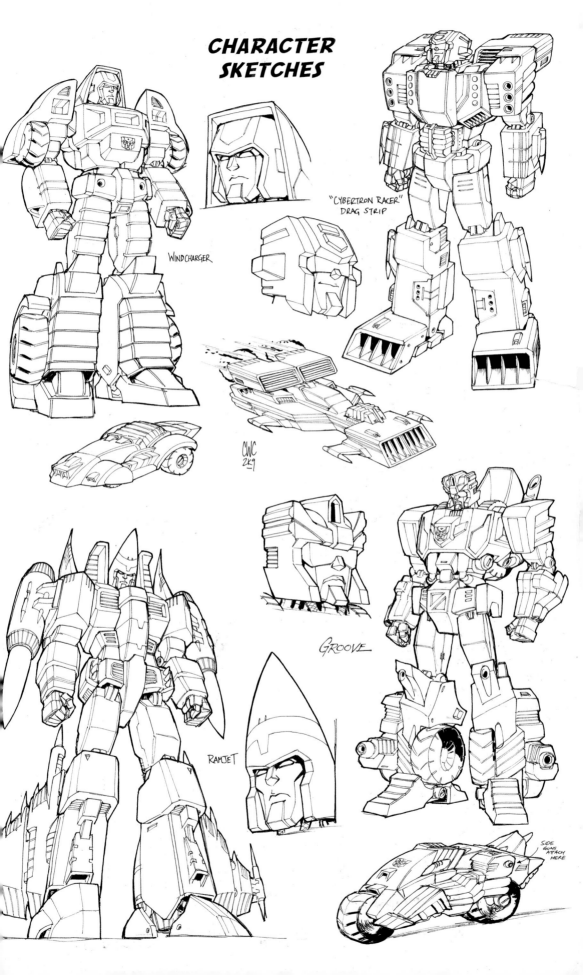

WINDCHARGER

"CYBERTRON RACER" DRAG STRIP

CWC 2K9

GROOVE

RAMJET

SIDE GUNS ATTACH HERE

CHARACTER SKETCHES

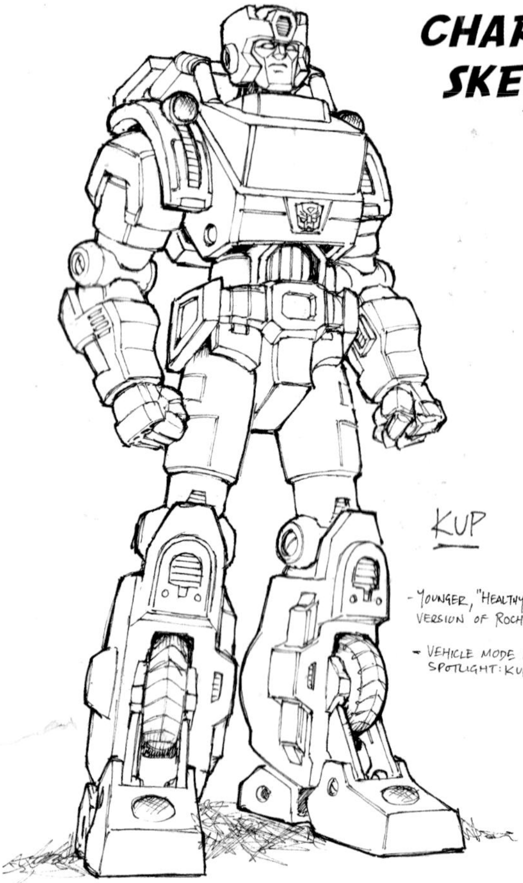

KUP

- YOUNGER, "HEALTHY" VERSION OF ROCHE'S KUP
- VEHICLE MODE REF. SPOTLIGHT: KUP

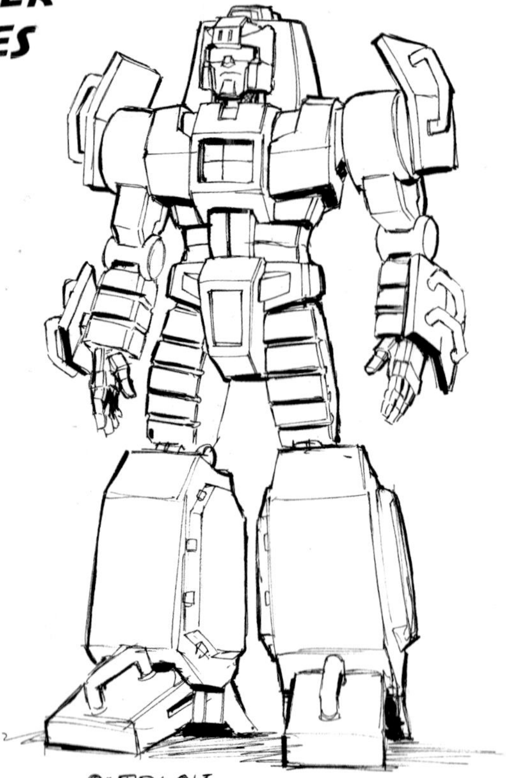

OUTBACK

AS SEEN IN SPOTLIGHT: KUP
(WHAT WAS LEFT OF HIM, ANYWAY.)

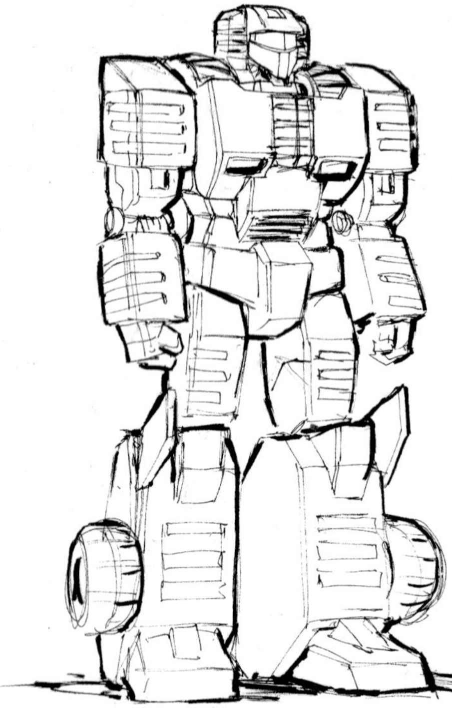

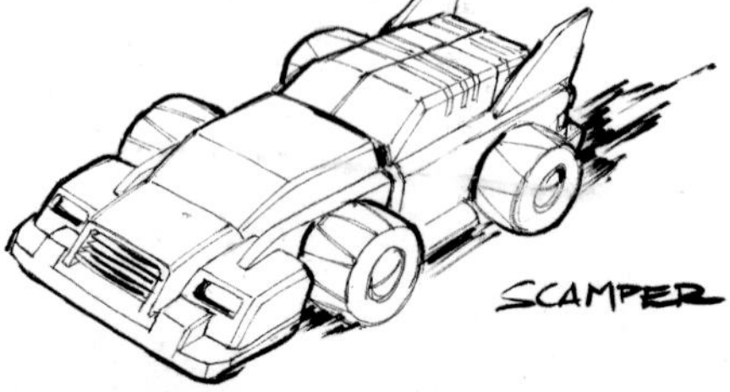

SCAMPER

RACE PROMOTER

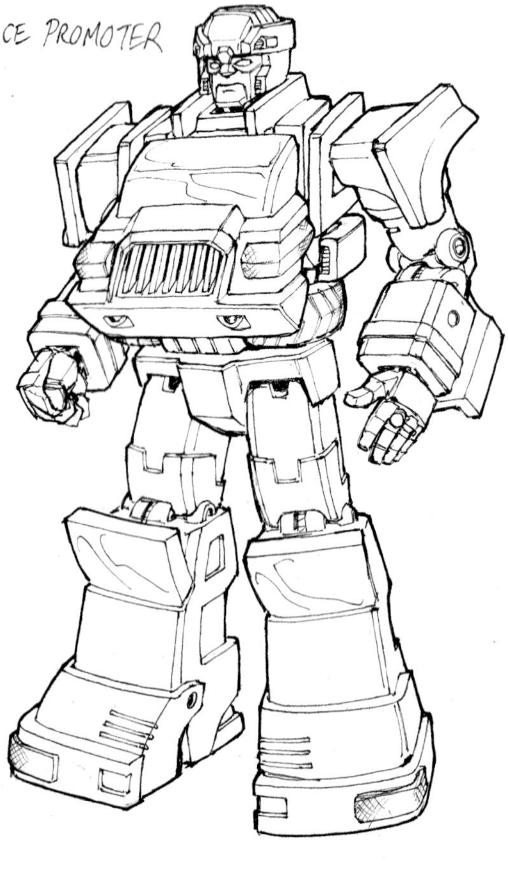

ALPHA TRION

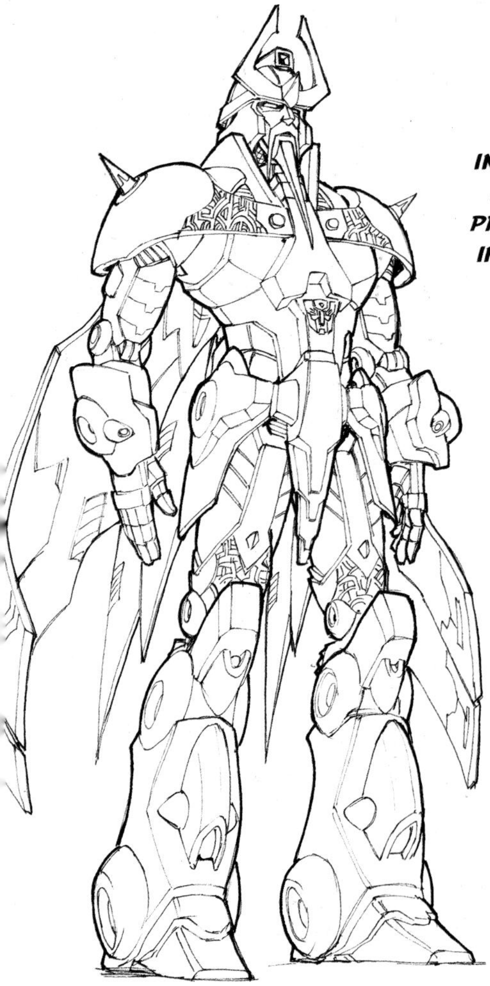

ALPHA TRION WAS INITIALLY DRAWN WITH HIS "BEARD" AS HE PREVIOUSLY APPEARED IN VARIOUS FORMS OF TRANSFORMERS FICTION.

WE THEN DECIDED TO GIVE A BIT OF A DIFFERENT TAKE ON HIS APPEARANCE BY REMOVING HIS BEARD AND ADDING A CLOAK AND A CLOTH COVERING HIS FACE. THE GOAL WAS TO GIVE HIM THE LOOK OF A "CRAZY OLD WIZARD."

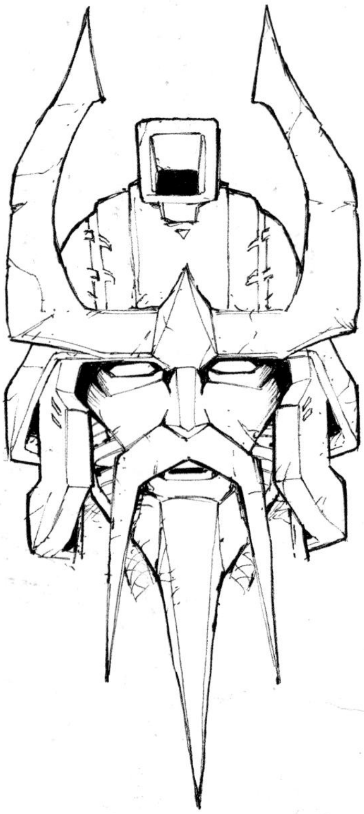

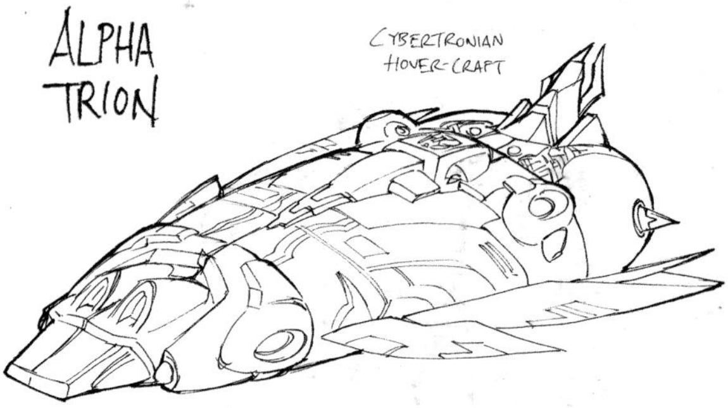
ALPHA TRION
CYBERTRONIAN HOVER-CRAFT

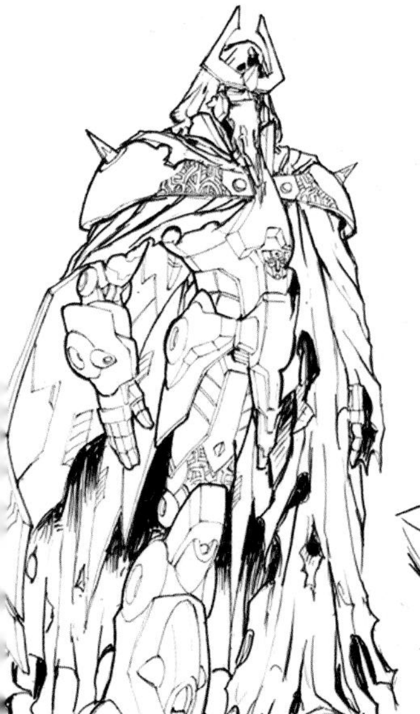

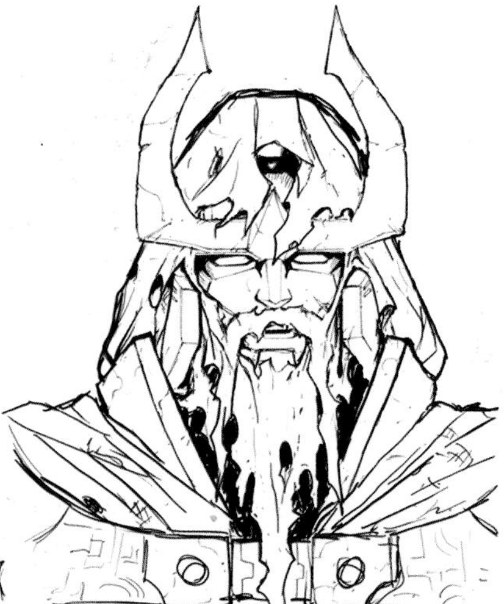

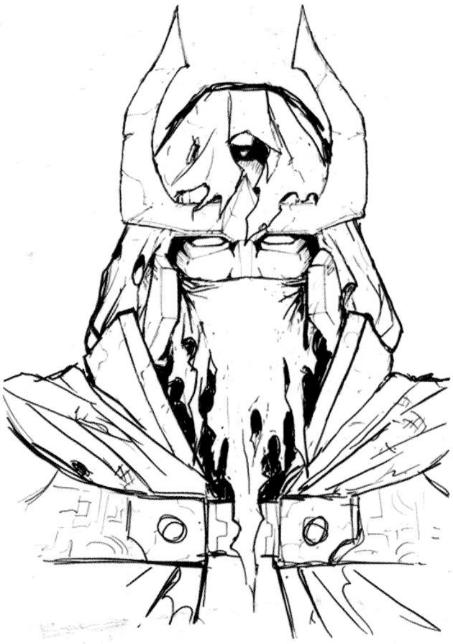

THE TRANSFORMERS
IRONHIDE

IDW™